# BORROWERS & LENDERS

RURAL FINANCIAL MARKETS AND INSTITUTIONS
IN DEVELOPING COUNTRIES

edited by JOHN HOWELL

Overseas Development Institute
10-11 Percy Street, London W1P OJB

OVERSEAS
DEVELOPMENT
INSTITUTE

The Overseas Development Institute (ODI) is an independent
non-government body aiming to promote wise action in the
field of overseas development. It was set up in 1960 and
is financed by donations from British business and by
grants from British and American foundations and other
sources. Its policies are determined by its Council.

The functions of the Institute are:

1  to provide a centre for research in development issues
   and problems and to conduct studies of its own;

2  to be a forum for the exchange of views and information
   among those, in Britain and abroad, who are directly
   concerned with overseas development in business, in
   government, and in other organisations;

3  to keep the urgency of development issues and problems
   before the public and the responsible authorities.

# CONTENTS

"Neither a borrower nor a lender be;
For loan oft loses both itself and friend,
And borrowing dulls the edge of husbandry."

*Hamlet*, I, iii

"It is one of the complexities of the subject
that debt may be as much an indication of
prosperity as of poverty. . . .

. . . in Faridpur, Major Jack found that nearly
half the debt had been incurred by cultivators
in comfortable circumstances and that 48 per
cent of the poorest class had no debt at all.
The villager's remark that he was too poor to
have a debt goes to the root of the matter.
No one but a fool or a philanthropist will
lend to a pauper."

Malcolm Lyall Darling, *The Punjab Peasant
in Prosperity and Debt*, Oxford, 1925

# INTRODUCTION

*John Howell and Dale W. Adams*

When it comes to encouraging production and raising incomes of small farmers, governments in develcping countries have not lacked policy advice. Measures widely advocated include reforms in land tenure, subsidies on producer prices, research on technologies appropriate to small farm resources, and improved extension and technical support. Yet in practice, such measures are often politically difficult to implement, and they frequently encounter professional indifference in agricultural ministries and in other government agencies. As a result of such political difficulties and professional indifference, those who offer policy advice are not often able to draw upon the evidence of widespread policy experience in making their recommendations. And, in consequence, it is difficult to establish the general validity of much of the received wisdom on the relationships between agricultural development and, for example, tenure reform, price policy, appropriate technology, and extension services.

The provision of cheap credit is another measure that has often been encouraged upon governments as a means of stimulating production, especially among the rural poor. Credit programmes have found considerable support in both political and professional circles, and there is no shortage of reports upon which to form judgements on the relationship between agricultural development and the workings of rural money markets.

The popularity of agricultural credit programmes
is due, in part, to the ease with which most of them can
be carried out. For the political leader it is easy to
announce a new lending policy, or to establish a new
credit agency, or to increase the amount of funds available
for lending in response to some pressing problems in rural
areas. Lending, particularly on concessionary terms,
allows governments to show an immediate concern for the
problems of small farmers.

There are other reasons for the popularity of credit
programmes. Informal credit markets are regarded as working
at best inefficiently, and are frequently cited as exploiting small borrowers. For many of those offering technical
advice to governments, small farmers are seen as in des-
perate need of additional loans, and the adoption of new
and profitable technologies is regarded as dependent upon
access to formal loans at concessionary interest rates.

All of these reasons have led to the widespread
adoption of cheap agricultural credit policies in developing
countries, and this has provided the opportunity of examining the results of such policies. But the results are not
encouraging.

In all too many countries rural money markets are
doing little to encourage savings and capital formation.
They are badly fragmented and doing a poor job of helping
the economy to allocate real resources efficiently and
equitably. The use of concessionary interest rates accompanied by rapid inflation, means that these markets are
also transferring very large income subsidies to those who
receive loans that are negatively priced in real terms.
High loan default rates, the lack of economies of scale in
lending, and generally high loan transaction costs are all
helping to undermine the financial integrity of many formal
financial institutions.

The examination of existing rural money markets and
institutions and the contribution of research to policy
issues in supplying credit to small farmers is the main
subject of this book.  It is based on papers originally
written for a conference on Rural Financial Markets and
Institutions held at Wye College in June 1979.*  Participants at this conference were invited from government
lending agencies, private commercial banks, research
institutions and universities, and international aid
agencies.  As a consequence, the papers presented covered
a wide range of topics and approaches, from comparative
analysis of the policy environment of agricultural
credit expansion in low-income countries as a whole, to
detailed research findings on farm-level credit use and
demand in project areas.  The papers can be grouped into
three main categories.  These categories are intended as
markers for those involved in rural credit policy and
research who wish to understand more clearly why financial
markets often fail to help the intended beneficiaries.
Within each category there are also attempts to identify
those changes that are required to improve the performance
of these markets.

The first category covers issues of national credit
policy and the effect of macro-policy upon the performance

* The co-sponsors of the conference were the Agricultural
Administration Unit of the Overseas Development Institute
and the Department of Agricultural Economics and Rural
Sociology of The Ohio State University.  The work of the
Agricultural Administration Unit is supported by the Over-
seas Development Administration with the United Kingdom's
Foreign and Commonwealth Office.  The work on rural
finance conducted by The Ohio State University is supported
by the Office of Rural Development and Development Admin-
istration in the US Agency for International Development.
The conference itself received financial support from the
following: Agency for International Development, Barclays
Bank International Development Fund, Standard Chartered
Bank, and the Commonwealth Foundation.

of rural financial markets and institutions. The second
category examines the ways that financial intermediaries
operate. These include government agencies, private
banks, informal moneylenders, traders, and farmers'
organisations. The third category discusses the rural
household and the role and impact of credit within the
small farm enterprise.


*Policy and the Performance of Financial Markets*

The first section of the book contains four papers
dealing with government credit policies, particularly
towards the smaller farmers, and the impact of such policies upon rural financial markets. Two of the papers look
at particular country experiences - Jamaica and India - and
two have a broad comparative perspective. The paper by
Dale Adams examines the main problems for rural financial
markets which have resulted from national policy and the
sorts of response to such problems: including nationalisation of banks, new specialist institutions, loan quotas,
lending guarantees, and differential interest rates. His
overview suggests that the poor performance of credit
programmes and the inadequacy of these sorts of responses
is due to incorrect assumptions about money markets and
the behaviour of both lenders and borrowers. He stresses
the counter-productive aspects of concessionary interest
rate policies and the failure to use formal rural financial
markets to mobilise savings.

The evidence from both India and Jamaica supports much
of this analysis. Despite the limited successes that
L. D'Mello claims for India in providing institutional
credit to small farmers it is evident that the emphasis
upon the supply aspects of credit has not been matched by

attention to aspects of demand. The unprofitable use of
cheap institutional credit is noted, together with the
continued preference on the part of the small farmer for
informal credit agencies. It is in this context that
D'Mello examines some of the policy responses to the
weaknesses of small farm credit programmes in India.

The Jamaican case, prepared by Compton Bourne and
Douglas Graham, is a vivid illustration of Dale Adams'
earlier contention that increasing the amount of concessionary priced loans is not a substitute for economic
policies that result in increased production and investment
returns at the farm level. A number of other countries
experience the same type of problems: for example, Turkey,
Guyana, Peru and Bangladesh. In these countries, as in
Jamaica, the financial infrastructure is reasonably well
developed, but the level of real economic activity and
economic stability in the country is such that it is very
difficult to maintain a healthy and viable financial system.
Countries like Jamaica that are experiencing negative real
economic growth rates present especially difficult problems
for those interested in rural finance. If farmers find
that their product prices are relatively low, that many of
the modern inputs they need are in short supply, that
marketing conditions are chaotic, and that little or no new
agricultural technology is available to them, they will
realise low returns to loan use in agriculture. This leads
to a fall in loan demand and/or severe loan repayment
problems. This in turn ties up a good deal of the lender's
managerial time and causes staff morale problems. Political
interventions are common in this environment as the government tries to expand the supply of loans as a means of
overcoming deficiencies in real economic activities.

The paper by J. D. von Pischke looks at a particularly
common policy response to such deficiencies: the establishment

of financial institutions specialising in agricultural
loans to small farmers.  He argues that the cost  of
providing loans to small producers is frequently under-
estimated; and the willingness of foreign aid agencies
and national treasuries to sustain the subsidies needed
to maintain financially viable formal institutions tends
to weaken considerably as the costs of the credit programme become more evident.  In the face of such reluctance,
it becomes increasingly difficult for specialised institutions to maintain or expand loanable funds or even to
cover operating costs, as interest charges and loan
repayment are insufficient to sustain the real value of
the loan portfolio.

*Financial Intermediaries and Institutions*

In this section there are five papers covering various
forms of rural financial intermediation.  Barbara Harriss
looks at informal lenders in South India and at the links
between lending activities and other aspects of marketing
of inputs and agricultural produce.  She argues that it
is difficult to understand credit transactions without
reference to the working of commodity markets as a whole.
Her particular concern is with the ways that rural commodities and markets operate to constrain the expansion of
peasant agriculture, but the evidence also illustrates
the importance of the informal financial system in providing services to small farmers which are not available
from the formal system.  She goes on to describe some of
the procedural aspects of informal lending that sustain
the effectiveness of the system.

The paper by Frank Wilson reviews some of the problems
faced by commercial banks as they try, or are forced, to

add more agricultural loans to their portfolio.  These
commercial banks face many of the same problems encountered
by the specialised banks.  They also have some advantages:
they are able to depend more on deposits for loanable
funds than is typical of specialised agricultural banks,
and they generally have a large part of their loans extended
to other sectors of the economy where the net rates of
return on loans are higher than on agricultural loans.
Commercial banks may be forced to lend to agriculture at
concessionary rates, and end up  losing money on these
operations, but such losses do not threaten the long-run
viability of the bank as is the case for many of the
specialised agricultural banks.  Commercial bank lending
is encouraged by a number of methods, including loan
quotas, loan guarantee programmes, special rediscount
facilities at central banks, and pressure on banks to
open branches in rural areas.  It is very difficult to
evaluate the results of these methods as money and loans
are fungible and divisible.  It is easy for the lenders
(as well as the borrowers) to appear to be responding
positively to government inducement and pressure, but
frequently they change the way they do business very little,
if they do not see such inducements as being in their
interests.  They may, for example, give multiple small
loans to a single wealthy borrower to effectively evade
loan size limit restrictions.

If informal money markets are not well funded and
are unable to provide effective financial services to
small farmers, and if commercial banks are unwilling to
extend substantially their services in rural areas, the
major responsibility for credit provision falls upon government agencies and government-promoted farmers' organisations.
The nature of such agencies and the relationship between

government agencies and various forms of local-level
organisation is the subject of the paper by Anthony
Bottrall and John Howell. They discuss some of the
other services that might be provided along with loan
and the kinds of changes in economic activities that
must be made in order to create an environment in which
additional financial intermediation is useful. Farmers
will not borrow and repay loans if they cannot get a
decent price most of the time for their products, if
modern inputs are not generally available at reasonable
prices, and if they cannot expect a good yield
from their farm enterprises under normal conditions. It
is often necessary to develop administrative capacity
to carry out a number of development activities before
or along with loans to ensure success of the credit
programmes.

Richard Roberts' paper on the management requirements
of such programmes reinforces this discussion by pointing
out that many credit agencies need staff training in order
to handle the difficult tasks of lending to agriculture
and also co-ordinate lending activities with other development efforts. He also argues for the development of
internal evaluation capacity that can provide management
with information needed for timely decision-making.

The quality of services provided by credit agencies
and the issue of reducing costs to lenders (and borrowers
for that matter) is another subject raised in the Bottrall
and Howell paper, among others. A number of countries are
experimenting with group loans as a way of reducing the
costs of serving small farmers. To date, the results of
these group loans appear to be mixed. One of the problems
associated with group lending is repayment. Many of the
group loans are made on the basis of joint liability. It
appears that when groups are formed solely for the purpose

of getting access to loans, that the joint liability is
not very effective in inducing repayment. If one member
does not repay, the other members may decide not to
repay. On the other hand, when a group is joined in
order to realise other group benefits beyond loans, it
appears that the groups tend to hang together better.

The final paper in this section, written by the late
Bert Youngjohns, shows that one of the most widely-
established of all forms of group activity - the co-
operative society - encounters many of the same problems
faced by specialised or commercial banks when they try to
provide financial services in rural areas. This paper
stresses the essential business component of co-operatives;
many people blame the collapse of a co-operative on corrupt
management or the lack of understanding of co-operative
principles by management and members. Too few people
explain co-operative failures on the basis of business
failure. Co-operatives often fail because they cannot
generate enough revenue to cover their costs of operation,
and/or their services are so poor that few members want to
do business with them. When co-operatives are used by
governments as conduits for channelling cheap credit into
rural areas, local elites inevitably attempt to capture
control of the co-operative in order to monopolise the
distribution of loans, and to exclude from borrowing those
less fortunate farmers. As a result, the intended beneficiaries of credit are excluded from cheap loans, and
where there is the additional benefit of unpunished default,
this is enjoyed mainly by those co-operative members least
in need of such largesse. There is no unique financial institution that can provide adequate financial services in
rural areas. Those interested in co-operatives often argue
that they are the proper vehicle; others argue that only
government agencies - development banks, commercial banks,
specialised small farmer development programmes, or supervised

credit agencies - can provide the proper services. In
most of these discussions the role of the informal lender
is ignored, or it is assumed that informal lenders do
not provide legitimate service, and that they should be
driven from the rural scene by expanding formal financial
services.

In fact, financial intermediation is a simple
process that involves an intermediary taking claims on
real resources from one individual or institution and
lending these claims to some individual or agency that
has too few resources for available opportunities. This
transfer of contracts that represents claims on real
resources can be done in a variety of ways. The critical
aspect of this transfer is not the institutional form of
the intermediary, whether the intermediary is formal or
informal, or whether it is privately owned or state-owned.
Rather, the vital issue is the cost of financial intermediation, the dependability of the lender, and whether the
intermediary is providing the appropriate range of financial service. More emphasis ought to be placed on
improving the process of financial intermediation rather
than just building new institutions. This involves more
investigation into why existing institutions, formal or
informal are not providing the kinds of financial services
that are necessary. Such investigation may explain why
new financial institutions soon begin to perform like the
old institutions they were designed to improve upon.

*Farm Households and Credit Use*

The third section of the book contains two papers
that discuss issues of research method and conceptual
analysis in examining credit use at the farm household

level; and two papers that describe particular research
on credit use in West Africa.

The paper by Cristina David and Richard Meyer is
partly concerned with a detailed review of the various
approaches to evaluating the impact of credit.  It also
focusses on the limitations of a great deal of research
in providing useful generalisation on the ways that rural
households make borrowing decisions.  The paper by
Michael Lipton similarly stresses the complexity of this
type of analysis and draws particular attention to
dimensions of time in understanding credit behaviour.
Both papers are concerned with eliminating the distinction
between the household and its consumption requirements and
the farm enterprise with its production requirements.
Loans to the "farm household", they argue, are fungible
between production and consumption uses, and all sources
of liquidity, not just formal loans, must be considered
in attempting to gain an overall view of credit needs and
use.  From a research perspective there is an interesting
difference between the two papers: David and Meyer advocate
a detailed case-study approach of farm families and the
decisions they make on liquidity use.  Lipton, on the other
hand, offers an outline of a simulated model of borrower
and lender decision-making during typical family life-
cycles, using different categories of farm household
within a single village.

The final two papers examine aspects of farm-level
credit use.  Adeniyi Osuntogun's paper deals with the
sources of credit available to co-operative farmers
in western Nigeria and various credit uses.  It is
clear from his evidence that many borrowers use agricultural loans to meet health and education costs  of
the family.  The paper by Thomas Stickley and Edouard
Tapsoba discusses various ways of measuring loan delinquency

in Upper Volta and explains some of the reasons for loan
repayment problems at the borrower level.  One conclusion
they draw is that lender shortcomings are often an important
factor in causing default and diversion of funds.

Relatively straightforward data collection on credit
use at the farm household level is fraught with difficulty,
as the papers in this section illustrate.  There is the
prospect, however, of high returns from research if policy-
makers are able to make more intelligent decisions about
credit programmes as a result of well-designed research.
In particular, it is clear that credit too often has been
viewed as an input in the production process and not as
part of the financial intermediation process.  The evidence
in papers in the book suggests that far too much attention
has been directed at providing cheap credit to farmers and
not enough attention paid to what low interest rates do to
savers, the performance of financial institutions, the
efficient allocation of resources, and the distribution of
incomes within rural societies.

*Part One:*

POLICY AND THE PERFORMANCE OF FINANCIAL MARKETS

## RECENT PERFORMANCE OF RURAL FINANCIAL MARKETS

*Dale W. Adams*
*Department of Agricultural Economics*
*and Rural Sociology*
*The Ohio State University*

### Introduction

During the past three decades financial services have expanded substantially in rural areas of many low income countries. This has included the funding of a large number of rural credit projects, major increases in volume of formal loans, building many new financial institutions, and some mobilisation of financial savings. The overt objectives of these activities have been to increase agricultural output, to ease rural poverty, or to offset the effects of disasters or public policies that damage rural interests. Despite the very substantial changes realised, the overall performance of rural financial markets (RFMs) is unsatisfactory.

Formal RFM activities in a majority of the low income countries are fraught with problems and they are contributing little to development.[1] In the following discussion I attempt to outline and clarify the main issues that must be addressed if the performance of RFMs is to be understood and also improved. This includes a brief review of historical views on financial markets, a critique of the assumptions that underlie many programmes in this area, and a summary of common problems and policies. The paper concludes with suggestions for policy changes.

*Evolution of Views on Financial Markets*

Views on the role of finance in economic development have changed substantially.  For centuries financial market activities were viewed with hostility, and usury was widely condemned.  Both the *Bible* and the *Koran* forbid the taking of interest.[2]  These negative attitudes toward financial markets were carried to the Americas as well as Africa.  Similar anti-lender, class-struggle views are also prominent in many socialists' works.

During the past 100 years much of the animosity toward banks and lenders in general has disappeared,[3] at least in most Christian countries.  Initially, this was replaced by a feeling that financial markets played largely a neutral or passive role in development.  Some have argued that these financial services emerge automatically as the demand for financial intermediation is created by growth in real economic activities:[4] it is argued that loans are merely "lubricants" for real production processes.  The introduction of a high yielding wheat variety, for example, may stimulate farmer demand for purchased inputs.  Farm-households lacking sufficient liquidity to buy optimum amounts of these inputs seek loans to satisfy their additional needs for liquidity.

In the past 20 years it has become common in many countries to attempt to use financial markets to force the pace of economic development - a "supply led" strategy.  Policy makers have concluded that rapid expansion in the supply of financial services combined with concessionary interest rates and non-market loan rationing, can be used to accelerate economic development.  A few observers recently have focussed criticism on the distortions in financial markets caused by this strategy.  They have

concentrated particularly upon interest rate policies with
critics claiming that low and fixed interest rates on
financial instruments retard savings and capital formation,
fragment financial markets, cause inefficient allocation
of resources, and also cause further distortions in income
distribution and asset ownership.  They go on to argue that
policy makers should adopt flexible interest rates that
adjust with general price changes, and that this would
cause financial markets to play a positive role in the
development process.[5]

Concerns about the effects of a supply led strategy
are particularly relevant in low income countries, where
RFMs are heavily distorted.  In most cases, RFMs are force-
fed large amounts of funds by central banks, and interest
rates are set below other rates allowed on non-agricultural
loans.  It is also common for the policy makers to fix
interest rates still lower on loans for the rural poor.
Usually, RFMs are more heavily administered, regulated,
and distorted than any other set of markets in a country.
Unfortunately, many of the policies that strongly affect
the performance of RFMs are built on assumptions which have
not been verified.


*Common Assumptions*

A casual observer is often impressed with the unique-
ness of RFMs in each country.  In part, this is due to the
diversity found among financial institutions servicing rural
needs.  More careful analysis, however, reveals a large
number of similar assumptions supporting most rural credit-
savings programmes.  To understand the current maladies in
RFMs, it is necessary to expose and evaluate these assumptions.

At the farm-household level it is often assumed that the rural poor face credit shortages, that they pay exorbitant amounts for the use of informal loans, and that they need careful supervision in order to use loans wisely. It is further assumed that most farmers need additional loans in order to adopt profitable new technology, and that concessionary interest rates are needed on formal loans to induce farmers to borrow. It is also assumed that interest charges make up the bulk of the borrowing costs for most farmers, and that the loan demand among most farmers, especially small farmers, is very interest rate elastic. Typically, rural households are also stereotyped as having little or no voluntary savings capacities.

Several strongly held assumptions relate to lender behaviour. These include the feeling that informal lenders provide the majority of the loanable funds in most low income countries, and that formal lenders are tradition-bound and do not make loans in a socially desirable manner. It is also assumed that formal lenders can effectively ration funds by granting loans only for production or by making loans in-kind. Policy makers also feel that formal credit should not be extended for consumption purposes.

Important assumptions about informal lenders are also prominent. These include the ubiquitous feeling that money lenders regularly extract large monopoly profits, charge exorbitant interest rates, take advantage of the economically weak, and fail to provide legitimate economic services. As a consequence, it is widely felt that they ought to be closely regulated or eliminated.[6]

There are also a number of widely-held assumptions about the overall performance of RFMs in low income countries. One of the most common is that RFMs can be closely regulated and their performance controlled by administrative fiat. Governments often feel a need to be visibly active in rural areas, and it is common for new agricultural loan programmes to be established that include loan supply increases as well as concessionary terms. They may also include refinancing or forgiveness of formal debts. A number of governments also try to offset product pricing policies, or exchange rate policies, that are adverse to farmers, by introducing concessionary interest rates in RFMs. Foreign aid agencies eagerly jump into this process because it is generally easy for them to prepare and implement agricultural credit projects.

*Common Problems*

Because many countries base their RFM policies on very similar assumptions, it should not be surprising that their policies are much alike. This includes low and inflexible contractual interest rates on agricultural credit and deposits, major infusions of loanable funds into RFMs via central banks, and formation of new specialized institutions to provide financial services to specific segments of the rural population. It is also common for governments to attempt to alter the performance of RFMs by some combination of policies.

Two sets of problems tend to be associated with these activities. The first set includes relatively tractable, and widely recognized problems that are often associated with any new business: management and training difficulties. There is almost always a shortage of adequately trained people to fill positions in financial institutions. As a consequence, there is often slowness in making loan decisions, high cost lending operations, data processing problems, poorly designed loan repayment procedures, and lack of coordination

between credit programmes and other development efforts.
As financial markets develop, most of these problems are
eased.

The second set of problems is much less widely recognized, although probably more important.  These problems
might be labelled "unsatisfactory performance of RFMs".
At least ten features of this unsatisfactory performance
are present in a large number of low income countries.
In many countries these problems have intensified during
the past few years.  They include the following:

- with significant amounts of inflation, it is
  often difficult for some governments to increase or
  even maintain the purchasing power of the formal
  agricultural credit portfolio.  Capital erosion
  caused by fixed interest rates and substantial
  inflation is often a major contributing factor;

- serious loan repayment problems further reduce the
  vitality of some loan portfolios.  In many cases
  these loan repayment problems emerge in all loan
  size groups;

- it is often the case that financial markets resist
  lending to the agricultural sector.  In some cases
  changes in the economic environment may cause
  financial markets to retract from agricultural
  lending;

- closely associated with this, it is very difficult
  to induce RFMs to service the rural poor.  Under some
  conditions RFMs may resist lending to small farmers
  even more strongly than they resist lending to
  agriculture in general;

- in almost all cases, RFMs do not provide a significant amount of medium and long-term loans. The average term structure of the formal loan portfolio is typically quite short, and much of the agricultural credit is granted for only a single cropping season;

- in most countries the RFMs are ineffective in mobilizing voluntary rural savings. With only a few exceptions, formal RFMs largely depend on central banks to supply a large part of their loanable funds. Many agricultural banks do not provide savings deposit facilities. In the few cases where rural institutions do mobilize financial savings, they are often siphoned out of rural areas for use in urban centres;

- it is also common for formal lenders to burden at least part of their actual or potential borrowers with relatively large loan transaction costs. Part of these costs is transferred from the lender to the borrower indirectly by lender procedures;

- typically, RFMs are badly fragmented. Each lender tends to service a narrow slice of the rural population. There is also relatively little competition between formal and informal lenders. As a result, a wide range of interest rates and borrowing costs can be found across RFMs and intermediation by RFMs does not result in efficient allocation of resources. Some individuals are forced to consume their "surpluses" or invest them in very low return activities, while others must skip profitable investment opportunities because they lack additional liquidity;

- in many countries, activities in RFMs adversely
  affect income distribution and asset ownership.
  In large part, this is due to the concentration of
  most formal loans in the hands of relatively few
  borrowers. These fortunate borrowers may realize
  an income transfer due to negative real rates of
  interest on the credit. They may add to this by
  turning a profit through the productive use of
  credit. In addition, borrowers may be able to bid
  away productive resources from less fortunate non-
  borrowers. As a result, non-borrowers are forced
  to pay higher prices for resources, or to do
  without. Small savers are almost always denied
  decent rates of return on their financial savings
  deposits;

- many current RFM policies make it very difficult
  to introduce successful innovations into rural
  financial markets. Typically, a promising RFM
  innovation is tried on a pilot project basis, but
  ultimately fails because it cannot reduce cost
  enough to overcome the effects on lender revenues
  of suppressed interest rates. As a result, many
  innovations in rural financial markets are aimed
  at circumventing regulations. These kinds of
  innovations typically increase rather than decrease
  costs.

Governments use several general strategies in attempts
to alter the performance of RFMs. One strategy includes
creating *new specialized financial institutions* to service
the needs of a specific target group in rural areas.
Another strategy concentrates on inducing a *major part* of
the financial system to provide more financial services
in rural areas. This latter strategy may include large
increases in the supply of formal loans, nationalization

of all or part of the financial system, use of loan size
limits, and adoption of lending quotas.  It may also include
policies like loan guarantees or crop insurance, differential rediscounting spreads, government purchases of equity
in financial institutions, and differential interest rates
for various ultimate borrowers.  A brief critique of
these strategies and techniques follows.

*New Institutions*

Governments often attempt to achieve certain goals
by focussing on one segment of the rural population.  In
many cases  target groups in rural areas, such as small
farmers or livestock producers, are thought to have unique
needs that require a new financial institution.  A supervised credit programme, new agricultural banks, co-operatives,
or commodity banks are often established to service these
needs.

In some cases, especially in Africa, new financial
facilities clearly are needed to extend financial coverage.
There are a number of instances, however, where more
bricks and mortar in financial facilities are not needed.
Ample financial facilities exist in many Latin American
and Asian countries; the main problem is that the overall
performance of RFMs is unsatisfactory.

Frustration over this poor performance often results
in new financial facilities being built.  Many governments
feel that the new facility will be more flexible, enlightened, and more co-operative in helping governments to
achieve public goals.  Typically, however, the new institution is staffed with individuals hired from existing
financial institutions.  Also, the new institution usually
is required to live within rules laid down for other lenders.

Governments or foreign agencies typically provide special
short-term subsidies to start the institution. The new
lender initiates its activities with a flourish fortified
by a number of radio announcements and newspaper head-
lines about how, for the first time, a certain group
in rural areas is finally receiving formal loans. A
small farmer credit agency, for example, will quickly
fill its loan portfolio with loans extended to operators
of small farms. In some cases, many of these "new"
borrowers are former borrowers of other financial institutions who have been encouraged to seek credit from the
new agency. Everyone is happy with the new arrangement:
old lenders get rid of the least profitable part of their
loan portfolio, the new agency extends money to the
desired target group, borrowers often receive less hassle
and larger loans from the new agency, governments feel
good about reaching the target group, and foreign agencies
feel that terms of their loans or technical assistance
agreements have been met.

Over the next several years things proceed relatively
smoothly. Some of the farmers who received credit the
first year or two have problems repaying loans, but are
refinanced. As the agency starts to question the refinancing of short-term loans, a number of medium-term loans come
due, and it slows the expansion in volume of loans, loan
repayment problems become much more visible. At about the
same time, foreign agencies or local governments begin to
insist that the lender do without external subsidies. The
lender often is given a double blow: default problems
escalate at about the same time that subsidies are withdrawn.

The very existence of the lender is threatened unless
these two problems can be resolved. Typically, lenders do

this by rotating their loan portfolios toward those
borrowers with better repayment records, those cheaper to
supervise, those with ample loan collateral, and those whose
loans result in relatively low marginal costs to lenders.
The lender goes through a metamorphosis. Like a chameleon
the lender takes on the same spots and shades as other
financial institutions and performs in much the same
manner as its financial cousins. Country after country
has gone through the frustrating experience of seeing
credit agencies set up to service rural poor, but later
rotate their activities away from the original target
group.

*Supply Increases*

The basic notion behind using the technique of supply
increase is that if sufficient loanable funds are poured
into RFMs, eventually some of these funds will filter down
to the desired target groups. Results from the recent
Brazilian experience, however, strongly suggest that large
supply increases, when combined with concessionary interest
rates, may not reach a large majority of the rural residents.
Adams and Tommy report that very little of the three-fold
real increase in formal credit in Brazil over the 1965-1969
period filtered down to small or new borrowers in one area
of Southern Brazil. Out of a total of 338 representative
farmers surveyed, they report that 11 of the largest farmers
received over two-thirds of the increase in volume of formal
loans made to all 338 farmers over the 1965-1969 period.
Because of the negative real rates of interest in Brazil,
borrowers who have access to the "sweet money" want very
large amounts. Lenders, at the same time, have strong
incentives to concentrate loans in the hands of borrowers
who have substantial wealth, experience with the lender,
secure collateral, and who will take large loans.[7] The net

result is that very little of the increased supply of cheap
loans filters down to small and new borrowers, despite
major increases in credit supply.

### Nationalization

Several countries including India, Bangladesh, Costa Rica,
Sri Lanka and Afghanistan have nationalized part or all of
their formal rural financial markets in an attempt to influence their performance more directly.  Fragmentary evidence,
especially from Bangladesh, Costa Rica and India, suggests
that nationalization may have a weaker effect on lender
behaviour than many policy makers had hoped.[8]  It is
relatively easy to draw up regulations for a financial
system, but difficult to enforce these regulations where
decision-makers affected by these regulations are widely
dispersed.  In market economies it appears to make little
difference whether lenders are private, mixed, or publicly
owned; managers are judged by the amount of economic surplus
they generate.

### Loan Size Limits

A few countries have used loan size limits in an attempt
to force lenders to alter the make-up of their loan portfolios.  These limits often specify a maximum size loan.
The policy maker assumes that these limits will force lenders
to direct part of their lending to new, more socially desirable activities.  Unfortunately, loan size limits are often
ineffective in forcing lenders to alter loan portfolios.
If lenders reduce the number of large loans in their portfolios while adding more small loans, they will often
experience a substantial increase in lending costs.  To avoid
this, lenders may meet the letter of the loan size regulation,

but evade the spirit, by making multiple small loans
to former borrowers of large amounts.


*Lending Quotas*

   Most low-income countries use some form of lending
quota as a way of allocating loanable funds among sectors
of the economy, among lenders, and among ultimate borrowers.
At a sectoral level, governments may impose certain minimum
percentages or amounts that institutions must lend to
certain sectors.  For example, currently in Thailand
all commercial banks are required to lend a minimum of
11 per cent of their loan portfolio for agricultural
purposes.  In Colombia, banks must lend a minimum of
15 per cent of all their loans to agriculture.

   At the lender level, regulations may state that a
certain part of the loan portfolio must go to a specific
target group.  In the Philippines, for example, banks
at one time were required to lend a minimum of 10 per cent
of their new loans to agrarian reform participants.  At
the borrower level it is common for lenders to allocate
credit on the basis of so many units of money for each
unit of land in a given crop.

   There are at least three major drawbacks to these
loan quotas.  The first is that lenders may simply redefine
loans to meet new loan quota regulations or lenders may
ignore the credit plan altogether.  Lenders may be able to
re-define a sufficient number of their loans and meet quota
requirements without changing the real pattern of their
lending.  The second disadvantage emerges when quotas are
in fact effective in changing real portfolio make-up.  Some
specialized lenders may find it difficult to effectively
place and administer loans outside their areas of special-

ization. A third disadvantage results from fixed loan
quotas for individual farmers. Some farmers may have
profitable investment opportunities that are much larger
than their loan quota. Other borrowers may find their
loan quotas far exceed their additional liquidity needs.

## Loan Guarantees

A number of countries, including Mexico, Peru, the
Philippines and Sri Lanka, have used loan guarantees or
crop insurance to alter lender and borrower behaviour.
Loan guarantees transfer part of the risks and uncertain-
ties of lending from one agency to another agency. The
most serious disadvantage of these guarantees is the
administrative difficulties of assessing, in a timely
manner, the legitimacy of claims. Agricultural disasters
may affect large numbers of producers in very short periods
of time. It is very difficult, for example, to correctly
assess massive and widespread crop damage from hurricanes
or typhoons within several weeks after they happen. Loan
guarantee programmes, as a result, are costly and cumbersome
to administer.

## Rediscount Spreads

One of the most widely used techniques for altering
lender behaviour is preferential rediscount spreads. A
major part of foreign capital assistance for RFMs in low
income countries flows through these mechanisms.
Operationally the technique is very simple. A central
bank may offer to rediscount loans made for selected
purposes at rates much lower than normal rediscount rates.
This provides lenders with a wider spread between rates paid
for loanable funds and rates that can be charged to the

ultimate borrower.  If the spreads are wide enough, this technique can be very powerful in inducing lenders to rediscount certain kinds of loans with central banks.

This technique has several serious weaknesses, however.  The first is that rediscounting certain types of loans with central banks may not result in much additional lending in the desired direction.  Because of fungibility, for example, a lender may rediscount most of its small farmer loans and use the additional loanable funds to expand lending to large borrowers.

The second and more serious weakness in this technique is that it may sharply reduce the incentives for lenders to mobilize part of their loanable funds through savings deposits.  In all too many cases lenders get funds from central banks through rediscount mechanisms at lower rates than they must pay for voluntary household deposits.

## Differential Interest Rates

Many countries apply interest rates to agricultural loans that are lower than regular commercial rates.  As mentioned earlier, it is also common for policy makers to assign interest rate limits on small farmer loans, or loans for special development projects that are lower than regular agricultural loans.  Other things being equal, these lower interest rates discourage lenders from servicing the very target group or sector stressed by the policy maker.  Why should a lender be excited about lending to small farmers at 8% when they can lend to wealthier borrowers at higher rates?  Typically, the concessionary priced loan is aimed at a target group which has been difficult for lenders to service and which often involves higher costs of servicing than for other borrowers.  The low interest

rates, combined with higher costs, give lenders double
disincentives to service the intended target group.

*Policy Suggestions*

Not all observers are convinced that RFMs are performing
poorly. Researchers still have a good deal of work to do
in carefully documenting and explaining the recent performance of RFMs. Further, there is an argument that RFMs *are*
very effective in doing what policy makers covertly want,
which is to buy and maintain political support from powerful people in the society. It is for this reason, arguably,
that the benefits from current RFM policies flow to elites.
As Lipton has pointed out, this may result from a conver-
gence of interests on the part of beneficiaries and policy
makers rather than from outright conspiracy.[9] Cheap
credit and lax loan recovery procedures are part of a
system to buy support. The case of expanding loan portfolios and manipulating interest rates makes RFMs a very
attractive political tool. If this cynical view is correct,
neo-classical economists have little useful to say about
recent events in RFMs; Marxian tools of analysis may be
more appropriate.

I have yet to be persuaded into joining the "cynical"
camp, but after working on RFM issues in more than a
dozen countries, I am convinced that most RFMs are not
helping these countries to realize publicly stated
objectives. The adverse effects of rapidly expanding
RFM activities on income distribution, resource allocation
and capital formation are too serious to be ignored or
excused. It is also clear to me that this poor performance
is the result of faulty policies based on incorrect assumptions. And I continue to hope that these faulty policies
will be changed if policy makers are clearly shown the

inconsistencies between current policies and overt public
objectives.

Policy makers and researchers need to re-assess the
role that RFMs should play in the development process.
I feel that major changes in how RFMs are used are long-
overdue. Some of these changes include the following:

- policies and programmes which stress mobilization
  of voluntary financial savings in rural areas should
  be initiated. These policies should include strong
  incentives for households to save in financial forms,
  as well as providing convenient and inexpensive ways
  for households to hold their savings. Initially,
  savings mobilization and not credit allocation should
  be the top priority for RFMs;

- flexible, nominal interest rate policies should be
  adopted that allow RFMs to charge and pay positive
  real rates of interest on agricultural loans and
  savings deposits;

- interest rate policies plus other incentives should
  be used to induce a major portion of the financial
  market in a country to service rural financial needs;

- much less emphasis should be placed on allocating
  loanable funds among sectors, lenders, and borrowers
  by administrative fiats. Market forces and realistic
  prices in RFMs should be the main way of forcing
  lenders, borrowers, and savers to act in ways
  consistent with efficiency, equity, and development
  goals in market economies;

- much less attention should be focused on concessionary interest rates as a way of inducing small

farmers to use formal credit. Instead, attention
should focus on reducing borrowers' loan transaction
costs. Concessionary interest rates have a strong
adverse impact on the willingness of lenders to
service agriculture in general and small farmers
in particular. Higher rates would help to overcome
this problem and would have little effect on loan
demand among small and new borrowers.

- if monopoly profits exist in informal RFMs, concessionary interest rates on formal credit, even with
large credit supply increases, will not cure this
problem. Higher interest rates on formal credit
would induce formal lenders to compete away part
or all of these monopoly profits.

Critics might argue that these policy suggestions
ignore political realities, and that concessionary priced
credit is needed to buy widespread political support in
rural areas. It seems to me that this view overlooks a
very important point: low interest rates on credit force
governments and lenders to set even lower rates on
financial deposits. In most societies, enlightened policies
could result in a larger number of people holding savings
deposits than the number receiving credit. As a result
higher interest rates on savings deposits may elicit more
widespread political support than is lost by higher rates
on credit. Higher interest rates on credit may result in
expanded opportunities for small farmers to get formal
loans at lower total borrowing costs. If the above holds,
the net political effect of flexible and generally higher
interest rates on formal financial activities in rural areas
may be to influence positively *more*, rather than less,
support for governments.

These changes in RFM policies are not a panacea for

the problems of low income countries:  technological change,
improvements in water control, land reform, investments in
infrastructure, and appropriate pricing policies are more
central to the success of most rural development programmes.
At best, RFMs play only a supporting role in these activities.
It is an important role nonetheless, and I am concerned that
too many of the current RFM policies and received wisdom on
this topic are medieval in character, and I feel that it is
time to drag rural financial market policies into the
twentieth century.

1  For a review of these problems see the various papers
   prepared for the *A.I.D. Spring Review of Small Farmer
   Credit* sponsored by the Agency for International
   Development.  A summary of many of the points made
   in these papers can be found in Gordon Donald,
   *Credit for Small Farmers in Developing Countries*,
   Westview Press, Boulder, Colorado, 1976.

2  See Benjamin N. Nelson, *The Idea of Usury:  From Tribal
   Brotherhood to Universal Otherhood*, Princeton University
   Press, New Jersey, 1949.

3  The recent reversion to strict Islamic Laws on interest
   payments in several Islamic countries, and the blowing
   up of the Central Bank in Kampuchea suggests that a good
   deal of latent animosity still lingers.

4  See, Hugh T. Patrick, "Financial Development and Economic
   Growth in Underdeveloped Countries", *Economic Development
   and Cultural Change*, Vol. 14, No. 2, January 1966.

5 See for example, Edward S. Shaw, *Financial Deepening in Economic Development*, Oxford University Press, New York, 1973; Ronald I. McKinnon, *Money and Capital in Economic Development*, The Brookings Institution, 1973.

6 These views are especially prominent in literature which treats Pakistan, India or Bangladesh.

7 D. W. Adams and J. L. Tommy, "Financing Small Farms: The Brazilian Experience 1965-69", *Agricultural Finance Review*, Vol. 35, October 1974, pp. 36-41.

8 See, for example, A. M. A. Rahim, "The Performance of the Banking System, 1971-77", *Journal of the Institute of Bankers Bangladesh*, Vol. 6, December 1977; S. L. Shetty, "Performance of Commercial Banks since Nationalisation of Major Bank: Promise and Reality", *Economic and Political Weekly*, Vol. 13, Nos. 31-33, 1978; and C. Gonzalez-Vega, "Small Farmer Credit in Costa Rica; The Juntas Rurales", *AID Spring Review of Small Farmer Credit*, Vol. 2, 1973.

9 Michael Lipton, *Why Poor People Stay Poor*, Harvard University Press, Mass., 1977, p. 19.

# LENDING TO SMALL FARMERS: THE INDIAN CASE

*L. D'Mello*
*Chief Economic Adviser*
*State Bank of India*[*]

## Introduction

A notable feature of the agrarian scene in India is
the predominance of small holdings.  Small farmers, defined
as those with land holdings up to 5 acres, constitute
69.6 per cent of the total number of farmers in the country,
though the area commanded by them is only about 21 per cent
of the total area.[1]  Along with tenants, farmers and
sharecroppers, small farmers account for a very large
proportion of the "weaker sections" in rural areas.

In view of these facts, improvement of the productive
capabilities of the "weaker sections" is an important
objective of economic policy in India.  Provision of
adequate and timely credit has received a good deal of
attention in this connection.  This paper deals with the
problems of providing satisfactory institutional credit
to the farmers in India.  The institutions established or
reoriented for the specific purpose of increasing the
availability of credit to small farmers will be discussed
in section 1.  In section 2, the policy framework within

which credit institutions operate will be discussed. In
section 3, the quantitative growth of credit supply to
agriculture in general and small farmers in particular
will be briefly described. The problems which institutions
face in lending to small farmers will be highlighted in
section 4 of the paper. The final section will deal with
some issues of an appropriate institutional framework
for effective provision of credit to small farmers.

## 1. *Institutional Development*

*(a) Co-operatives.* Co-operative institutions were introduced in India over half a century ago to provide credit,
especially to the small farmers. In the fifties and early
sixties, vigorous efforts were made to strengthen the
co-operative credit institutions through measures such as
State participation in the share capital, and representation
of Government nominees on boards of directors.

By 1976-77, the primary agricultural co-operative
societies (PACS) covered 90 per cent of all the villages
in the country and had a membership of 44.8 million while
the membership of central and primary land development
banks was 7.8 million. The total working capital of all the
co-operative credit institutions amounted to *Rs.*91,670 million. During 1976-77, the PACS had advanced loans of the
order of *Rs.*12,110 million for short-term and medium-term
purposes; long-term loans given by central and primary
land development banks during the year totalled
*Rs.*4,410 million.[2]

*(b) Commercial Banks.* Despite the impressive growth in the
number of co-operative institutions and their coverage it
was decided in the late sixties to press the newly nationalised and other commercial banks into service to meet the

expanding credit needs of an agricultural sector which
had begun adopting new technology on a large scale. Rural
offices of commercial banks increased from 2,233 as at
the end of December 1969 to 12,806 in December 1978. The
percentage share of rural offices in the total went up
markedly from 25.3 in 1969 to 43.4 in 1978. During the
year ended June 1977, scheduled commercial banks issued
directly to farmers *Rs*.3,150 million of short-term credit
and *Rs*.2,500 million of long-term credit. The biggest
public sector bank of the country, the State Bank of India
and its seven associate banks, have made a pioneering
contribution in the form of opening  Agricultural
Development Branches (ADBs) which cater exclusively to the
needs of the farmers and extend to them a measure of
extension support so as to enable the farmers to make gain-
ful use of credit.

An important element of commercial banks' assistance
to the agricultural sector is in the form of what has come
to be called "indirect finance". This involves loans
given to institutions or enterprises for relending or for
the distribution of inputs to the farmers and provision of
various types of facilities. At the end of December 1976,
the outstanding amount of indirect finance was *Rs*.3,320 million.[3]

*(c)  Farmers' Service Societies.* Based on its view that
small farmers needed various services along with credit,
the National Commission on Agriculture recommended the
setting up of Farmers' Service Societies (FSS) - one
for each block. The FSS are expected to provide to small
farmers and rural artisans not only finance but also inputs,
technical advice and services such as storage, transportation,
processing and marketing. The FSS are also expected to assist
small farmers to diversify their operations by adopting
supplementary activities especially in the field of animal

husbandry. The crucial difference between the usual
co-operative societies and the FSS is that the control of
the latter rests with the weaker sections since two-thirds
of the elected members of the Board of Directors are
required to be small farmers.

*(d)   Regional Rural Banks.* Mainly due to the realisation
that public sector commercial banks had shortcomings in
financing weaker sections of the rural population, a
policy decision to establish State-sponsored regionally
based and rural-oriented commercial banks was taken in
1975.   It is expected that the new institutions (Regional
Rural Banks) will "combine the local feel and familiarity
with rural problems which co-operatives possess and the
degree of business organisation, ability to mobilise deposits,
access to central money markets and a modernised outlook
which the commercial banks have".[4]   In a negative sense,
RRBs are expected to be free from the managerial inefficiency of co-operatives and high operational cost of the
commercial banks.

A distinguishing feature of the RRBs is that they are
required to lend "directly only ... ... to the small and
marginal farmers, agricultural labourers, rural artisans,
small entrepreneurs and persons of small means, engaged
in any productive activity and also (indirectly) to all
types of co-operative societies and the FSS operating
within its area of operation".[5]

*(e)   Agricultural Refinance and Development Corporation.*
An important measure for ensuring the flow of adequate investment funds for agricultural development was the establishment
of the Agricultural Refinance Corporation (later renamed
as Agricultural Refinance and Development Corporation - ARDC)
in July 1963.   The ARDC provides refinance facilities to
central land development banks and commercial banks to

enable them to provide finance for agricultural development
projects. By June 1978, ARDC had sanctioned 6,221 schemes
of co-operative and commercial banks for which refinance
of the order of *Rs*.17,704 million had been sanctioned.
There are specific built-in measures in ARDC lending
policies to bring about a deliberate small farmer bias in
the lendings of institutional agencies. These measures
include a lower rate of down-payment, longer repayment
period and facility of 100 per cent refinance for schemes
in districts in which Small Farmers' Development Agencies
(SFDA) have been set up. The ARDC has stipulated that at
least 50 per cent of the lendings of institutions should
go for the benefit of small farmers.

*(f) Credit Guarantee Corporation.* The Credit Guarantee
Corporation of India established in 1971 provides guarantees
in respect of small loans to borrowers from commercial
banks in the priority and neglected sectors (including
agriculture). The Corporation generally reimburses
seventy-five per cent of the total amount of loss of
individual loans subject to a maximum ranging from
*Rs*.2,500 to *Rs*.37,500 depending on the nature and purpose
of the facility granted, term of the loans and repayment
programmes. Thus most of the loans granted to small and
marginal farmers by commercial banks are covered by the
Credit Guarantee Corporation of India.

*2. The Policy Framework*

The operations of credit institutions pertaining to
financing small farmers are carried on within the framework of policy of the Government and the Reserve Bank of
India. As for the Government, the major emphasis is in
sponsoring special programmes for the benefit of weaker
sections in rural areas. In regard to the commercial

banking system, the Reserve Bank of India has introduced
credit planning, the chief ingredients of which are the forward budgeting of banking operations, regulation of the
refinance mechanism, and the penalties and relaxations
in the enforcement of monetary policy.

*Credit Planning.* The Reserve Bank of India has purpose-
fully used its control mechanism to enlarge credit supply
to small producers both in the agricultural and industrial
sectors. As a part of credit planning exercise, considerable attention has been given in recent years to the
reduction in regional imbalances in the matter of credit
deployment. Banks were advised that by March 1979, their
credit-deposit ratios in rural and semi-urban areas
should be at least 60 per cent. Further, banks have also
been asked to lend 33.33  per cent of their advances to
priority sectors consisting of agriculture, small scale
industries and small business. These targets have been
nearly achieved. Taken together, they have contributed
to a more liberal availability of credit in rural areas.

*Differential Interest Rates Scheme.* The Differential Rate
of Interest Scheme introduced in 1972 may be regarded as
an aspect of credit planning specially attuned to the
deployment of banks' funds in favour of weaker sections.
Under the Scheme, the banks are expected to lend a minimum of one per cent of the aggregate advances at the
concessional rate of 4 per cent to individuals whose
annual income does not exceed *Rs.*2,000 - in rural areas
and *Rs.*3,000 - in semi-urban and urban areas. Farmers
whose land-holdings are of less than one acre in irrigated
areas or 2.5 acres in unirrigated areas are eligible for
the concessionary finance under the Scheme.

*Programmes of the Government.* The implementation of various
agricultural strategies in the sixties (such as the Intensive

Agricultural District Programme and the High Yielding
Varieties Programme) led to an aggravation of disparities
between different regions on the one hand and between
farmers and agricultural labourers and between small and
large farmers on the other. This resulted from the very
nature of the strategies which favoured regions and farmers
endowed with irrigation and other resources. It was
realised that small farmers and agricultural labourers
would need special assistance if they were to share in
development in an equitable manner. Accordingly, the
Small Farmers' Development Agency and the Marginal Farmers'
and Agricultural Labourers' Development Agency (subsequently
integrated into a single agency called Small Farmers' and
Agricultural Labourers' Development Agency (SFAL) were
set up in a few districts in 1970-71 on a pilot basis.

By the end of 1976-77, the SFAL programmes covered
239 districts out of 360. The Agency provides assistance
to co-operative credit institutions by way of outright
grants related to the amount of loans extended by them
to small farmers; the grants are intended to cover risks
and provide an incentive to the credit agencies. Subsidies
are also provided to these agencies to underwrite the
cost of extra staff that may have to be employed by them
for this work. Subsidies are given to marginal farmers
and small farmers at the rate of 33.33 per cent and
25 per cent respectively of the cost of projects for
which loans are taken from banks and co-operatives. The
subsidy constitutes the down-payment of the borrowers from
the lenders' point of view. As a result of the facilities
and incentives, the share of small farmers in total loans
advanced by co-operative institutions and commercial banks
operating in the districts covered by the special programmes
is  expected to increase appreciably.

In addition to the introduction of credit planning,
the Reserve Bank of India has taken a variety of other
measures to encourage the credit institutions to lend
to farmers in general and small and marginal farmers
in particular. The most important of these measures
include the following:

- in order that the limited loanable funds of
  co-operatives are not cornered by large farmers,
  the Reserve Bank of India has directed co-operative
  banks to fix ceilings on individual crop loans
  between $Rs.$5,000 and $Rs.$10,000 in the predominantly
  unirrigated areas and at $Rs.$20,000 in irrigated
  areas;

- small farmers, who are generally unable to make the
  required down-payment of 10-15 per cent of proposed
  capital expenditure, generally have their payment
  fixed at 5 per cent which can also be contributed
  in the form of labour;

- in order to prevent small farmers from having to
  make distress sales of produce when the prices are
  unremunerative, the banks are permitted to extend
  the period of crop loans up to 3 months for
  sensitive commodities and longer periods for other
  commodities;

- commercial banks are provided re-finance by the
  Reserve Bank of India against loans granted through
  Farmers' Service Societies for approved purposes,
  at a concessional rate of 5 per cent;

- the Regional Rural Banks are being treated as
  scheduled banks eligible for refinance facilities
  from the Reserve Bank. Under the Refinance Scheme

for RRBs introduced in 1976, the total refinance
limit for each RRB is fixed on the basis of a
prescribed formula at 15 : 50 : 35 indicating the
proportions of RRB deposits, RBI refinance and
the sponsor bank's advances respectively, in the
aggregate lending programme of each RRB.

*Programmes of the Commercial Banks.* Initially, on their
entry into the rural finance field in 1969, commercial
banks financed agriculture as a walk-in business. Farmers
from the area of operation of a branch of the bank
would approach the bank for finance and their proposals
would be entertained. The usual terms and procedures
of lending were applied in their dealings with farmers.
This resulted in scattered lending and rendered supervision, guidance and extension work both difficult and
expensive.

In view of these shortcomings, banks evolved an "area
approach" for financing agriculture and a group guarantee
system of securing the advances granted to farmers without
mortgageable assets. The pioneers in this regard were the
State Bank of India and its Associates. The "area approach"
involves the selection of an area comprising a cluster of
villages and the extension of credit to all viable and
potentially viable farmers in that area. While making the
credit available, banks endeavour to ensure that along
with credit, other important prerequisites for development
and increases in productivity are also made available. The
Agricultural Development Branches of the State Bank Group
are equipped to prepare integrated area development projects
and to provide technical guidance and extension services
to farmers for implementing them.

A variant of the "area approach" is the Village
Adoption Scheme of the banks. Under this scheme, branches

of the banks select villages in consultation with the
concerned Government departments or agencies, after
conducting a detailed survey of the potential for development. The selected villages come under intensive financing
and end-use of credit is continuously supervised.

The practice followed by commercial banks of
sanctioning loans on the basis of tangible collateral
was a severe constraint on the flow of credit to the small
farmers. To overcome this, the State Bank Group resorted
to the Group Guarantee Scheme. Under this scheme, loans
are advanced to individuals forming a group of 3 to 5
persons with the loan of each person guaranteed by all the
other loanees of the group.

Judging from the experience of the State Bank of India,
the Group Guarantee Scheme is of tremendous help in providing credit to the small and marginal farmers and rural
artisans. Apart from making it possible to loan to persons
who do not have any security to offer, it also reduces the
cost of lending as the loanee is saved the cost of stamp
duty, etc., that would have to be incurred if mortgages
were insisted upon. One of the weaknesses of this scheme
has been that all the members of the group could be
unfairly penalised by any one member defaulting on repayment.
To overcome this, loan conditions have been modified.

Along with the above efforts to provide farm finance
on a progressively expanding scale and to achieve integrated
development of selected areas, the banks have been endeavour-
ing to co-ordinate their efforts with those of other concerned
agencies in the areas so that the needed material inputs,
technical support and services such as marketing and
processing are adequately available to the farmers. Indeed,
banks are keenly aware that tie-up arrangements for provision
of inputs and services are crucial to the success of their

agricultural financing schemes especially in relation
to small farmers.


3.  *The Quantitative Growth of Credit Assistance*

The vigorous efforts made in the last two-and-a-half
decades to make available institutional finance to agriculture have achieved notable results.  Taking the most recent
data, short-term loans issued to those engaged in agriculture
increased from *Rs*.11,375 million in 1972 to *Rs*.25,064 million
in 1978, or by 120.3 per cent.  During the same period,
medium-term and long-term finance registered an increase
of nearly 100 per cent from *Rs*.5,313 million in 1972 to
*Rs*.10,318 million in 1978.

In terms of the relative shares of different institutions,
in 1974 co-operatives accounted for 84.8 per cent of total
short-term finance provided by various institutions whereas
the share of commercial banks was only 8.2 per cent.  In
the subsequent four years, however, commercial banks increased
their short-term advances substantially.  In 1978, the
relative shares of co-operatives and commercial banks in
total short-term credit were 77.8 and 15.6 per cent respectively.

As important as the absolute growth of institutional
finance over time is its share in total borrowings of
cultivators.  The relative share of institutional agencies
in total cash debt owned by cultivators' households has
evidently increased.  The data collected for the All-India
Rural Credit Survey (AIRCS) and the All-India Debt and
Investment Survey conducted in 1951-52, and 1971-72
respectively, indicate that the share of credit provided
by institutional agencies in total cash-debt owned by
cultivator households increased from 7.3 per cent in

1951-52 to 31.7 per cent in 1971-72.

Institutional finance for agriculture has succeeded, to a significant degree, in replacing exploitative non-institutional finance. In the context of the powerful socio-economic forces which operate in the rural areas of India, the fact of institutional agencies being able to satisfy a growing proportion of the credit needs of cultivators is quite gratifying.

In the examination of credit provided to small farmers it is important also to assess the validity of the view-point that a large chunk of the institutional credit is pre-empted by the large farmers with the result that the small and marginal farmers are deprived of their due share. Data to assess the position are not available in the required details for a long period, but the Reserve Bank of India's *Statistical Statements Relating to the Co-operative Movement* gives the loans and advances of Primary Agricultural Credit Societies and Land Development Banks according to size of ownership holdings in three years (1970-71, 1975-76 and 1976-77). These clearly show that in respect of short-term credit, the share of small farmers has been steadily increasing over the years. From 26.7 per cent in 1970-71, the share of co-operative short-term credit disbursed to small farmers increased to 34.8 per cent in 1976-77. Share of small farmers in term loans has remained around one-third of the total. Their share in total advances made by Land Development Banks during 1976-77 worked out to 37.8 per cent.

As regards the share of small farmers in the credit disbursed by commercial banks, published data for 1975-76 show that of farm loans disbursed the percentage share of small farmers was 56 in respect of short-term credit and 21.3 in respect of medium and long-term credit.[6]

It would, therefore, appear that complaints about small farmers not getting their due share of institutional credit is not well-founded, although institutional agencies have not been able to take adequate care of the credit needs of small farmers. This inadequacy becomes a more severe constraint on production and investment than in the case of larger farmers because of the limited owned resources and surplus generating capacity of small farmers.

New agricultural crop technologies despite their supposedly size-neutral character, tend to favour farmers possessing or using assets like irrigation, tractors, etc. In view of this, the inadequacy of credit supply in general and the relatively small share of small farmers in the term credit in particular places them at a considerable disadvantage in availing of benefits of the technology. Institutional agencies, therefore, need to devise ways of enlarging the share of small farmers in the credit which they dispense.

## 4. *Problems of Financing Small Farmers*

While the share of small farmers in institutional farm finance does not appear to be disproportionately low, it ought to be noted that finance provided by institutional credit agencies forms only a small proportion of the total credit taken by small farmers from all sources. According to the *All-India Debt and Investment Survey, 1971-72,* small farmers (defined as the cultivators holding assets worth *Rs.*5,000 and below) reported having borrowed only between 6.2 and 14.5 per cent of their total borrowings from institutional agencies. Similar evidence is available from other sample surveys.[7] Admittedly, in the total debt of small farmers, a large proportion consists of unproductive debt incurred for meeting household expenses, expenditure

on litigation, repayment of debt, etc.  Even so, the
continued reliance of small farmers on non-institutional
credit agencies for satisfaction of their credit needs is
indicative of difficulties involved in making available
to them adequate institutional finance.  These difficulties
and problems exist both on the demand as well as on the
supply side.

On the supply side, an important factor which impedes
adequate flow of credit to small farmers is their small
coverage by co-operative institutions.  The available
data on this aspect, though not extensive, clearly show
that enrolment of small farmers as members of co-operative
institutions is quite small in relation to their total
number.  A Reserve Bank of India Study of small farmers in
12 districts of the country also revealed that: "In all
the districts, the proportion of large farmers reporting
co-operative membership was higher than that of small
farmers.  The disparity between these two groups in this
respect was marked in 11 districts. ... Even within the
group of small farmers, a direct relationship between the
size of gross farm income and co-operative membership
is discernible in most of the districts.  Thus, the
extent of co-operative membership showed a general trend
to increase with an increase in the size of gross farm
income."[8]  Among the reasons for non-membership in
co-operatives, were "lack of owned land", "unwillingness
to borrow","cumbersomeness of procedure for getting loans
and inputs", "lack of awareness of facilities" and "lack
of expected benefits".

Operational weaknesses in co-operative institutions
are also responsible for their limited capability to extend
adequate credit support to the small farm sector.  The most
serious weakness  is their inability to effect recoveries
of loans advanced.  Overdues as a percentage of outstanding

loans of primary societies have been continuously on the
increase; from 32 per cent in 1967-68, they rose to 44 per
cent in 1971-72 and were only slightly lower at 43 per cent
in 1975-76 and 1976-77.  Due to the high default rate,
both the loanable funds available to the credit institutions
and the proportion of members who can avail of credit
assistance from the institutions have diminished.  The
proportion of borrowing members in total membership of
PACS declined from 51 per cent in 1961-62 to 41.8 per
cent in 1965-66 and further to 39.3 per cent in 1969-70.
In 1976-77, this proportion remained almost unchanged at
39.9 per cent.[9]

The Study Team of the Reserve Bank of India which
examined the problem of overdues of co-operative credit
institutions concluded that "lack of will and discipline
among cultivators to repay were the principal factors
responsible for the prevalence of overdues of co-operatives".
Among other contributory factors to the problem, the
committee included "defective lending policies pursued by
the co-operatives".  Apart from such deficiencies as
fixation of unrealistic due dates and financing of
defaulters, the committee drew attention to low scales
of finance, delays in sanction and disbursement and
arbitrary cuts in sanctions which had acted as deterrents
to maximising production.  Lack of supervision over the
end-use of credit was another notable reason for the overdues.  The committee observed that either the workload
of the supervisory staff of District Central Co-operative
Banks was very heavy or the staff appointed was incompetent
or negligent.  Further, hardly one-third of the total
number of PACS in the country had full-time paid secretaries
with the result that full and proper attention to the factors
essential to good lending was not given either at the DCCB
level or at the level of PACS.

50

*Estimation of Credit Demand.* In order that supply of
credit matches demand precise estimation is essential.
The procedures followed by credit institutions in
estimating the demand are not satisfactory.  By and large,
demand for credit for different schemes is over-estimated.
In the case of small farmers and other weaker sections,
correct understanding of the constraints faced by them in
improving their economic lot is clearly helpful in
assessing their absorption capacity.  Properly conducted
surveys of the development potential of target areas and
target groups would enable credit institutions to gain
these insights and estimate demand for credit for specific
schemes more accurately.  However, such detailed surveys
are rarely carried out.  For example, schemes have been
prepared for supply of heavy duty pneumatic bullock carts
to small farmers in areas in which bullocks are weak,
disease-prone and suffer from high mortality rates; or
for supply of cross-bred dairy animals to small farmers and
landless labourers most of whom had no previous experience
of dairying; or for creation of minor irrigation facilities
and modernisation of farming in an area in which farmers
are highly traditional in outlook and too poor to afford
risk of crop failure.

*Formulation of Credit Schemes.* Another important aspect
which influences credit flow through institutions is the
estimation of incremental incomes for a credit scheme.
These estimates are not always based on realistic assumptions.  In minor irrigation schemes, for example, if the
crucial assumptions with respect to crop pattern and cropping intensity, per acre use of complementary inputs, per
acre yield, prices of crops, etc., are not realistically
made, they may jeopardise the viability of the schemes.
In a study of a minor irrigation scheme implemented by
a nationalised bank, it was found that assumptions with
respect to the major parameters which affect income from
the use of irrigation were unrealistic, the irrigation

capacity created through credit assistance was considerably
under-utilised, use levels of complementary, yield-raising
inputs was much below the expectation and incremental incomes
were also very small.  Consequently, there were defaults
in repayment and an accumulation of large overdues.

An expert group, appointed by the Reserve Bank of
India, to examine the agricultural credit schemes of
commercial banks summed up the position ".....the organisational arrangements for scheme formulation and procedures
which are followed in carrying out this task in most of
the banks are quite inadequate to take into account
area-specific realities".  The Committee further added
"This limitation is serious because at present there are
no micro-level operational plans of development activities
from which credit schemes could be readily derived."[10]

The schemes formulated by credit institutions often
necessitate collaborative arrangements with other developmental agencies functioning in the selected areas.  Thus,
success of tractorization schemes would depend upon easy
availability of tractors, fuel and lubricant oil, spares,
servicing facilities, other farm inputs such as fertilizers,
pesticides and satisfactory arrangements for marketing
of larger production that would result from the use of
tractors and modern farm inputs and practices.  In schemes
which are prepared mainly for small farmers and other
weaker sections in rural areas, provision of technical
guidance is a critical aspect, especially when sophisticated
technology is sought to be popularised through the schemes.
Experience has shown that this aspect has not received the
attention it deserves either at the hands of the institutions
which prepare and implement the credit schemes or of the
government departments which are expected to help the
credit institutions in putting through the schemes successfully.  For example, in a dairy development scheme implemented

by a nationalised bank mainly for the benefit of small
farmers and landless labourers, cross-bred cows were
supplied to the borrowers (who were largely inexperienced
in dairying) but arrangements for providing technical
guidance to them in maintaining and breeding the animals
proved so inadequate and ineffective that the borrowers
found  the animals unprofitable and also lost a sizeable
number of them through death.

*Provision of Comprehensive Credit*  The idea of providing
comprehensive credit (which would not only cover investment
and working capital credit but consumption credit as well)
to small farmers and weaker sections has received general
acceptance in principle, but with the exception of the
newly established Regional Rural Banks, credit institutions
have not yet evolved concrete policies to integrate consumption credit with production credit.  Unless this is done
the problem of substantial overdues and diversion of loans
will persist and the objective of replacement of informal
credit agencies by institutions will remain difficult to
accomplish.  It is significant that in the Reserve Bank's
study of small farmers' preference in borrowing, it was
the group "private credit agencies" consisting of landlords,
professional moneylenders, agriculturist moneylenders,
traders, relatives, etc., which emerged as the most popular
credit agency for small farmers in 11 districts.  In almost
all the cases, the availability of loans at all times
emerged as a major reason for the preference shown for
private credit agencies.

It was expected that the Farmers' Service Societies
would provide comprehensive credit together with inputs
and other services so as to enable small farmers to make
productive use of credit.  The brief experience of
working of the FSS is not encouraging.  In the study of
166 FSS undertaken by the Agricultural Credit Department

of the Reserve Bank of India,[11] it was found that:

- about one-third of the societies had not been provided
  with any technical staff or assistance;

- nearly 45 per cent of the societies had not issued
  any medium term loans for agricultural purposes;

- more than 90 per cent of the societies had not
  issued consumption loans;

- 46 per cent of the societies were not supplying
  even agricultural inputs and such of them as
  were giving this service  had done meagre business;

- as many as 80 per cent of the societies had not undertaken marketing of agricultural produce of the
  members.


## 5. *Appropriate Institutions*

The discussions in the preceding sections have highlighted the fact that despite the efforts made so far to
set up a suitable framework of credit institutions and
policy, success in providing institutional credit to small
farmers has been achieved only to a limited extent.  This
may be attributed to problems on both the demand and the
supply sides.  In the past emphasis has been laid, perhaps
for valid reasons, on the solution of problems on the supply
side.  It would appear that now problems of credit absorption capacity, identification of worthwhile projects for
financing, profitable use of credit and similar problems
on the demand side have become far more important than
those on the supply side.  A number of institutions exist
to lend credit support to improve the resource base and

productive capabilities of the enterprises of small farmers
but the effective demand for the credit offered to them
is still not large.  On the other hand, small farmers
seem to satisfy a large part of their total credit needs
from informal agencies and prefer them to the formal
institutions.  This suggests that there is also a problem
of the mis-matching of the credit supplied and the credit
demanded.

Solutions to these two problems of lack of credit
absorption capacity and mis-matching of supply of and
demand for credit seem to lie in integrated supply of
credit, inputs, marketing and extension facilities as a
package.  Credit support itself should include a minimum
of consumption requirements and should be given on suitable
terms, especially in regard to repayment schedule.  In
these respects, the credit operations of informal agencies
should be marked by comprehensiveness and flexibility which
are virtually absent in the case of formal institutions.
The major advantage of informal agencies is that they
operate simultaneously in credit input and product markets.
Formal institutions may have to reorient their policies
and procedures if they are to successfully replace informal
agencies in the financing of small farmers.

Three critical elements in the required reorientation
are:

- integration of production and consumption credit
  with a view to ensuring intended end-use and recovery
  of loans;

- making savings mobilisation an integral part of loan
  programmes to mop up surplus incremental incomes of
  farmers;

- integration of working capital programmes with term
loans to ensure full utilisation of assets created
from term loans.

Further, the operations of credit institutions should not
be confined to provision of credit alone; there is need for
the institutions to perform a multi-functional role by way
of assisting small farmers in the adoption of new technology,
new activities and in the provision of marketing, processing
and storage facilities.

It is conceded that even if a reorientation of the
above nature is possible in the policies and operations of
commercial banks, they would hardly prove to be appropriate
institutions to serve small farmers.  The real cost of
(a) providing relatively small loans to the vast numbers
of small farmers, (b) ensuring functional linkages
between the activity financed and other activities which
have a bearing on the economic viability of the loans,
and (c) supervising the end-use of credit and recovery of
loans, would be prohibitively high.  Also, the operational
area of a commercial bank branch cannot be extended much
beyond the present limit of 16 kms  and this puts most
farmers outside the scope of direct financing by banks.

The recommendations of a recent Working Group appointed
by the Reserve Bank of India is that rural credit should
be the primary responsibility of co-operative institutions.
Commercial banks and Regional Rural Banks are expected to
route funds through them and supplement their efforts by
direct lending when necessary.[12] Co-operative institutions,
being grass-root level organisations, have a distinct
advantage in reorienting their functions and policies on
the lines indicated above.  They can effectively link
credit with marketing.  The linkage will be more effective
if it is forged from the marketing side rather than the credit

side.  Successful experience of this method is evident in
the functioning of cotton co-operatives and sugar
co-operatives in the western parts of the country.  Similarly, the Amul Dairy at Anand, and the other dairies in
Gujarat State patterned after it, have been successful in
integrating veterinary and other services, milk production
and processing.

Farmer Service Societies (FSS) as conceived by the
National Agricultural Commission, qualify to perform the
role outlined above.  As local level institutions, they
can plan area development, supervise credit use and
recover the loans at low cost without the legal and managerial overheads incurred by commercial banks.  They have
adequately large areas of operation to develop sufficient
business to achieve viability, they are expected to
provide a package of inputs and services in addition to
credit, and supply essential items of consumption.  Since
two-thirds of the members of boards of directors are to be
from small farmers and other weaker sections, the pre-
emption of the benefits of the societies by large farmers
would hopefully be eliminated.  Thus, organisationally,
FSS are best suited to achieve integration of functions
as envisaged above.  At the same time, it should be
granted that FSS would succeed in achieving integration only
if they are provided with adequate support in terms of
finance and qualified personnel.

The working of FSS has so far revealed some serious
weaknesses.  These should not be ignored or glossed over.
Operational reforms and adaptations must be urgently
undertaken.  But the basic framework of a grass-roots
level organisation, catering to the credit and other complementary needs of small farmers, who have considerable say
in its affairs, is crystallised in FSS.  It would not be
unreasonable to hope that FSS could be developed, over a

period of time, into institutions which might become the answer to India's complex small farmer credit problem.

* The views expressed in this paper are the personal views of the author and do not necessarily represent the views of the State Bank of India.

  The author acknowledges the assistance received from his colleague Mr. Mahendra D. Desai, Senior Agricultural Economist, in preparing this paper.

1 *All-India Report on Agricultural Census 1970-71*, Government of India, Ministry of Agriculture and Irrigation, New Delhi, 1975.

2 *Statistical Statements Relating to Co-operative Movement in India 1976-77*, Reserve Bank of India, Bombay, 1979.

3 *Regional Rural Banks: Report of the Review Committee*, Reserve Bank of India, Bombay, 1978.

4 *Ibid*, para 2.4.

5 *Ibid*, para 2.8.

6 See, *Agricultural Credit Schemes of Commercial Banks: Report of the Expert Group*, Reserve Bank of India, Bombay, 1978.

7 For example, *The Small Farmers (1967-69) - A Field Study*, Reserve Bank of India, Bombay, 1975.

8 *Ibid*, p. 59.

58

9  *Report of the Study Team on Overdues of Co-operative Credit Institutions,* Reserve Bank of India, Bombay, 1974; *Statistical Statements relating to the Co-operative Movement in India, 1976-77.*

10 See, *Agricultural Credit Schemes of Commercial Banks - Report of the Expert Group.*

11 The findings of the study have been summarised in the *Report of the Reserve Bank of India Review Committee,* para 3.28 and 3.29.

12 See *Multi Agency Approach in Agricultural Finance, Report of the Working Group,* Reserve Bank of India, 1978, p. 22.

# AGRICULTURAL CREDIT AND RURAL PROGRESS IN JAMAICA

*Douglas H. Graham & Compton Bourne*
*Department of Agricultural Economics and Rural Sociology*
*The Ohio State University*

## Introduction

The agricultural credit system in Jamaica has experienced substantial growth, institutional changes and financial difficulties in the past decade. In many ways the experience of the system as a whole and the diverse institutional strategies to deal with the problems of credit supply, illustrate the classic dilemmas of agricultural finance in developing countries. This experience takes on special poignancy in the light of the island's economic difficulties in the post 1974 global recession and the hopes, inspired in the early 1970s, that a new democratic political order with a socialist programme would guide Jamaica's future. A political mandate for increased public sector activity and redistributive policies coincided with a shift in world economic conditions that severely compromised the island's growth potential. This should be kept in mind as the context within which changes in rural credit institutions and strategies occurred.

The Jamaican economy in the late sixties and early
seventies registered respectable rates of growth in
output, investment and savings for the economy as a whole,
although the agricultural sector registered an average
annual rate of decline of 4.3% between 1965 and 1972. The
mid-seventies, however, saw a sharp decline to stagnant
or negative rates of growth overall and for many major
sectors in the economy. This decline in the rate of
growth is understandably matched by sharp declines in
savings and investment. The net result of this process
was a negative aggregate and per capita growth of GDP
between the early 1970s and the present. A growing
deficit in the balance of payments has been a crucial
negative influence on the economy which forced the Manley
Administration to adopt an IMF stabilisation package from
late 1977 onwards. Deterioration in the net reserve
position had placed Jamaica on the verge of international
bankruptcy by 1976-77, largely due to a sharp decline in
export earnings (bananas, sugar, tourist revenues and
bauxite) combined with a failure to reduce imports sufficiently. Domestic inflation also rose during this period,
in large part growing out of the growing deficit in the
government accounts as public sector activity increased
markedly. In 1978 inflation had grown to an annual rate
of 35% due to the impact of massive devaluations on the
domestic price level.

The impact of this "stagflation" has been felt particularly on the financial sector and structure of interest
rates. Government notes have increased substantially as
a proportion of commercial bank assets - in part, because
the decline in aggregate demand has affected the demand for
bank loans. The depressed state of the economy has also
caused a decline in real savings while inflation has contributed to negative real rates of interest. Savers are
subsidising borrowers in that they are receiving a negative

rate of return in real terms on their savings deposits in
commercial banks. This hidden tax on savings had grown
even larger in 1978 with the rapid rise in inflation.

In summary the Jamaican economy has experienced a
long period of economic decline and stagnation since 1971-72.
Exports have declined, balance of payments deficits grown,
inflation risen to unaccustomed levels contributing to a
situation of negative real rates of interest in which
savings are penalised and borrowing subsidised. Within
this setting the agricultural sector has been the one area
experiencing some degree of positive growth and the role
of agricultural credit has been substantial in magnitude
but controversial in result.

*Expansion of Agricultural Credit*

There have been five major formal sources of agricultural
credit in Jamaica throughout the 1970s: (i) the commercial
banks; (ii) the Agricultural Credit Board (ACB); (iii) the
Jamaica Development Bank (JDB); (iv) the Self-Supporting
Farmers Development Program (SSFDP); and (v) the Crop Lien
Program.

Commercial banks are the largest single source of credit
to the agricultural sector. This credit is largely short-
term and goes to medium-sized and larger farmers with good
credit ratings and limited risks. In more recent years the
commercial bank network has extended loans to large government agricultural co-operatives such as the sugar co-operatives
which bought out the foreign-owned sugar estates. There are
eight commercial banks on the island, two of which have been
nationalised. The remaining six banks are either wholly
or partly-owned foreign banks. Within this essentially
oligopolistic market structure two banks alone comprise

close to half of the total loans made in the system: the
Bank of Nova Scotia and the National Commercial Bank (NCB),
a nationalised bank that formerly belonged to Barclays.

The remainder of the agricultural credit sources are
public sector institutions or programmes. The oldest of
these public institutions is the Agricultural Credit Board
(ACB), created in 1960. This institution has two portfolios:
one serving larger farmers through direct loans; the other
aimed at small farmers and channelled through the national
network of small people's co-operative banks (P.C. Banks)
scattered throughout the island. The loan purpose in both
cases is largely short-term and seasonal and, in the case
of the P.C. Banks including small loans as well.

The Jamaica Development Bank (JDB) began making large,
medium-to-long term, "development" loans from the early 1970s
onwards. The Self-Supporting Farmer Development Program
(SSFDP) was also launched at the same time as the JDB. Its
focus is also on medium-to-long term loans but to much
smaller farmers than those serviced by the JDB. Limitations
on farm acreage, gross sales and assets have created a
clientele for the SSFDP that can be characterised as the
medium-sized farmer. Finally there is the Crop Lien Program
launched by the Government in 1977 and administered by the
Ministry of Agriculture through their extension agents working with the co-operation of the P.C. Banks as retail outlets
for these loans. Here the loans are strictly small, short-
term and seasonal, limited to domestic foodstuff producers
and focused on small farmers with little or no previous loan
experience.

Table 1 summarises the growth of formal agricultural
credit through these five major sources. In nominal terms
loans outstanding grew almost seven-fold in seven years
(1970-77) but this increase was only 2.6 times in real terms,

Table 1

Total Agricultural Loans Outstanding in Current Values and
1970 Dollars (End of Year Balances) 1970-78

| Year | Current Values (J $000) | In 1970 Dollars (J $000) |
|------|------|------|
| 1970 | 25,320 | 25,320 |
| 1971 | 30,557 | 28,558 |
| 1972 | 35,162 | 32,141 |
| 1973 | 49,005 | 37,041 |
| 1974 | 60,060 | 34,817 |
| 1975 | 112,743 | 55,731 |
| 1976 | 136,715 | 61,088 |
| 1977 | 166,821 | 65,207 |
| 1978 | 167,821 | 51,605 |

Table 2

Growth in Total Agricultural Loans Outstanding from
1970 to 1977 in 1970 Dollars by Institutional Source

| Source | 1970 (J $000) | 1977 |
|------|------|------|
| Commercial banks | $10,093 | $35,606 |
| Agricultural Credit Board | | |
| (i)   Total | 13,038 | 8,144 |
| (ii)  Direct borrowers | 1,008 | 1,090 |
| (iii) Peoples Co-op. banks | 12,030 | 6,235 |
| Jamaica Development Bank (JDB) | 55 | 9,637 |
| Self-Supporting Farmers Development Program (SSFDP) | 2,133 | 8,337 |
| Crop Lien Program | -- | 3,731 |
| Total | $25,320 | $65,455 |

Source: *Statistical Digest* (Bank of Jamaica), various years;
*Monetary Statistics* (Department of Statistics), various
years; Annual Reports of the JDB, SSFDP and Ministry
of Agriculture.

Note: The implicit GDP deflator was used to correct for
inflation.

reflecting the inflationary erosion of the capital base for
agricultural lending.  In 1978 there was practically no change
in the amount of credit in nominal terms and a pronounced contraction in real terms.  Table 2 shows that of the net increase
in real loans for agriculture, commercial banks accounted for
the largest contributions followed by the JDB large farmer
development loan facility and the SSFDP programme.  The older
line ACB loan source actually experienced a net decline in
loan activity (in real terms) with all of this net decline
associated with the small farmer P.C. Bank line of credit
within the ACB portfolio.[1]

*Institutional Change*

Table 3 shows the changing roles of the several institutions
and programmes comprising the agricultural credit supply network
during the 1970s.  The sources are classified into the farm
size categories that most typically reflect the majority of
their portfolio.  From this profile it can be seen that large
farmers benefited handsomely from the agricultural credit
initiatives in Jamaica during the 1970s.[2]  Commercial banks
and the large farmer JDB development loan portfolio have
increased their relative portfolio substantially while, at the
other end of the spectrum, the small farmer oriented ACB-P.C.
Bank programme lost ground markedly.  Only in 1977 was there
an improvement in the credit status of small farmers with the
launching of the Crop Lien Program.  This programme alone accounted for almost one-third of the incremental increase in net
loans outstanding from 1 January through 31 December 1977.  It
was the largest source of credit increase during that year, even
eclipsing the customarily dominant role of commercial banks within the total portfolio.  No doubt the substantial erosion of
the older small farmer credit line through the ACB had
accumulated sufficient concern and grievances that a new
initiative and programme was felt necessary to redress

this imbalance.  Unfortunately this initiative led to
substantial problems of default, which we discuss shortly.

In addition to the large versus small farmer profile
set forth in Table 3, there is an interesting foreign
versus domestic resource division that merits discussion.
A large majority of the resources loaned out in the JDB
and SSFDP programmes come from foreign sources (ie the
World Bank and Caribbean Development Bank in the former
case and the Inter-American Development Bank in the latter
case).  Domestic sources are almost exclusively geared to
short-term seasonal loans(through commercial banks, the ACB
and Crop Lien Program),  while foreign resources are
designed to service medium to long-term developmental loans
(the JDB and SSFDP).

Prior to the 1970s there were only two sources of
agricultural credit in Jamaica.  Both were exclusively
domestic sources (the commercial banks and the ACB lines
of credit) and both were largely short-term in focus with
the commercial banks servicing large farmers and the ACB
small farmers.  By the mid-1970s this had changed to include
the new, internationally financed developmental institutions
(the JDB and SSFDP).  These institutions were the most
rapidly growing sources of funding for agricultural credit
in the country.  Whereas in 1969 they played no role what-
soever, by 1971 they accounted for roughly 48% of the net
increase in loans outstanding for that year.  This rose to
53% in 1974, declined slightly to 47% in 1976 and further
to 35% in 1977 when the domestically financed short-term
Crop Lien Program was launched.  By any measure the role of
international resources was crucial to the expansion of
total credit supply during the 1970s, and more importantly,
indispensable towards lengthening the term structure to
include developmental financing.

Table 3

Percentage Distribution of Total Agricultural Loans Outstanding at End of Year by Farm Size Categories and Sources for Selected Years in Jamaica

| Farm Size and Sources | 1971 | 1974 | 1976 | 1977 | 1978 |
|---|---|---|---|---|---|
| *Large Farmers and Co-operatives* | 45.8 | 60.8 | 77.4 | 72.0 | 68.2 |
| Commercial banks | 39.1 | 44.2 | 60.2 | 54.4 | 48.8 |
| ACB - Direct loans to farmers | 4.7 | 4.2 | 3.0 | 2.9 | 3.4 |
| Jamaica Dev. Bank (JDB) | 2.0 | 12.4 | 14.2 | 14.7 | 16.0 |
| *Medium-Sized Farmers* | 13.2 | 16.2 | 11.5 | 12.7 | 14.9 |
| Self-Supporting Farmer Development Program (SSFDP) | 13.2 | 16.2 | 11.5 | 12.7 | 14.9 |
| *Small Farmers* | 40.9 | 22.9 | 11.0 | 15.2 | 16.9 |
| ACB - Peoples Co-op. Banks loans | 40.9 | 22.9 | 11.0 | 9.5 | 9.9 |
| Crop Lien Program (Min. Agric.) | -- | -- | -- | 5.7 | 7.0 |
| TOTAL (J $000) | 30,556 | 60,060 | 136,715 | 166,821 | 167,821 |

A problem for the future is the prospective decline of these foreign source funds within the rural financial markets of Jamaica as can be seen in the contractions in the increase of credit in these foreign financed programmes in 1978. The growing problems of delinquency, on the one hand, and declining foreign exchange earnings on the other hand, raise serious questions as to whether Jamaica will be able to secure new international financing for these activities or, for that matter, even service the current debt obligations incurred on past loans with the international agencies. This is discussed further in a later section.

*Overall Performance*

Before evaluating the performance of each institution within the credit network, it is useful to look at the performance of the system as a whole through the various credit ratios in Table 4. This underlines the fact that total credit has been rising substantially as a percentage of GDP since the early 1970s. This reflects the growing rate of inflationary financing in the economy through substantial increases in the money supply to service the rapid increase in the demand for credit. From 1975 to 1977 agricultural credit grew more rapidly than the rapid increase in total credit, although the sharp jump in all credit ratios between 1974 and 1975 primarily reflects the "broader" definition of agricultural credit in the commercial banks loan reporting procedures to the Bank of Jamaica from 1975 onwards (see footnotes 1 and 2). Only in 1978 was there a decline registered in the agricultural credit / agricultural GDP ratio.

The rise in agricultural credit/agricultural GDP ratio in recent years can be explained by the "deadwood syndrome". In short, many of the loans outstanding are in permanent default (as far as the credit institution is concerned) on the one hand, and very likely permanently diverted to non-agricultural uses on the other hand. The high and rising

Table 4

Credit Ratios for the Jamaican Agricultural Credit System

| Year | Agricultural Credit/Total Credit | Total Credit/ Total GDP | Agricultural Credit/Agri- cultural GDP |
|------|------|------|------|
| 1970 | 7.8 | 27.2 | 32.3 |
| 1971 | 7.6 | 30.8 | 30.7 |
| 1972 | 6.4 | 31.5 | 33.0 |
| 1973 | 6.8 | 41.2 | 38.2 |
| 1974 | 6.5 | 41.2 | 36.9 |
| 1975 | 9.1 | 46.7 | 55.9 |
| 1976 | 8.9 | 55.3 | 60.1 |
| 1977 | 9.9 | 61.1 | 62.6 |
| 1978 | 7.8 | 62.1 | 53.2 |

Table 5

Estimates of Real Rate of Interest for Agricultural Credit
and Implicit Credit Subsidy as Percentage of Agricultural GDP

| Year | Rate of Inflation | Avg. Nominal Interest Rate Agric. Loans | Real Rate of Interest | Agr. Credit/ Agr. GDP | Credit Subsidy as % of Agric. GDP[1] |
|------|------|------|------|------|------|
| 1975 | 15.7 | 10.0 | -5.7 | 55.8 | 3.2 |
| 1976 | 8.2 | 10.0 | +1.8 | 60.1 | 0 |
| 1977 | 14.0 | 10.0 | -4.0 | 62.6 | 2.5 |
| 1978 | 27.9 | 10.0 | -17.9 | 53.2 | 9.3 |

Note: (1) Subsidy as a percentage of Agricultural GDP is estimated
by taking the proportion of total outstanding agricultural credit to total agricultural products (column
4) and multiplying this by the negative rate of interest
(column 3). This is equivalent to estimating the amount
of subsidy by taking the negative rate of interest and
multiplying it by the amount of agricultural credit outstanding and then discovering what proportion this is
to agricultural GDP.

credit/GDP ratio when combined with high and rising
delinquency strongly suggest that agricultural credit is
either not being applied to the agricultural sector or,
if it is, it is being applied inefficiently when compared
to earlier years. Given the growing stagnation in the
economy as a whole it is possible that much of this credit
may be leaking out of the economy as capital flight as
well as into real estate, land and other inflationary
hedges.

Another issue warranting discussion is the implicit
subsidy built into the current credit strategies. Table 5
presents estimates of the real rate of interest for agricultural credit. When inflation is taken into account,
it is clear that the average interest rate charged for
agricultural credit is clearly below the average rate of
inflation. The net result is a negative real rate of
interest which in recent years has been rising dramatically.
Furthermore if the real rate of interest is multiplied by
the agricultural credit/agricultural GDP ratio the implicit
credit subsidy can be estimated as a percentage of agricultural GDP. In 1978 this reached 9%  a high level by
any standard.

Thus we not only have a situation within which credit
appears to be increasingly used in an inappropriate (ie non-
agricultural) or inefficient fashion, but also a situation
where the beneficiaries or borrowers are enjoying an unusual
subsidy. In short, the social costs of this credit strategy
could be substantial if relatively large borrowers form an
important part of the credit portfolio and, as pointed out
earlier in this section, this would clearly appear to be
the case.

*Large Farm Arrears*

Table 6 summarises data on the arrears record for all
the institutions and programmes in Jamaica.  The commercial
banks register respectable recovery rates; however, all the
public sector programmes record alarmingly high arrears
rates.  This raises a serious question as to whether any
of these programmes are financially viable.  To place this
issue in context it is helpful to discuss the large farmer
and small farmer arrears separately even though the arrears
are high in both areas.

The JDB arrears issue is the classic large farmer
delinquency problem.  The JDB was originally set up in the
early 1970s to service the medium to long term developmental
needs of fairly large capital intensive activities.  These
investments represented a substantial part of the net increase
in annual loans to agriculture in the mid-1970s; therefore
any serious problem in delinquency in this programme
affects both an important component of the total credit
portfolio and  the strategy behind the modernisation drive
in Jamaican agriculture.

Table 6 offers additional insight into this problem
in the JDB with the wide discrepancy between the arrears on
amounts due and arrears on loans outstanding.  The rapidly
rising arrears on total loans outstanding from 1974 to 1978
reflects the aging of the portfolio as more of the longer
term debt falls due.  This is not a useful measure of
delinquency.  It hides the seriousness of the problem,
namely a high arrears on the amounts due.  Associated with
this problem is the aging of the arrears itself as more of
the outstanding debt falls due.  In 1976 only 38% of the
total arrears was overdue for 90 days or more.  By 1977
this had risen to 82%.

Table 6

Arrears Ratios for Selected Agricultural Credit
Institutions and Programmes in Jamaica

|  | Arrears on Amounts Due | Arrears to Total Loans Outstanding |
|---|---|---|
| *Commercial Banks* | | |
| 1978 | 4.4[1] | 4.4[1] |
| *Public Sector Agricultural Credit Programmes* | | |
| a. Jamaica Development Bank (Commercial Window) | | |
| 1974 | na | 2.2 |
| 1976 | 81.2 | 8.2 |
| 1978 | 82.6 | 19.6 |
| b. Self-Supporting Farmer Development Program (SSFDP) | | |
| 1978 | 38.0 | 18.0 |
| c. Agricultural Credit Board (People's Co-operative Banks) | | |
| 1978 | na | 39.0 |
| d. Crop Lien Program (Ministry of Agriculture) | | |
| 1978 | 94.6 | 94.6 |

Note: [1] Commercial banks classify a debt as in danger or "arrears" due to a variety of factors in the subjective judgement of a loan officer. The loan does not have to be formally "due" to be classified and, conversely, a loan may be beyond the due date but not be in danger of non-payment and hence not classified.

Curiously the JDB did not design its accounts in such
a way as to detect the arrears on the amounts due until
pressed to do so by its international creditors.  If the
institution had established effective arrears accounting
early on (say, 1973 or 1974) it would very likely have
found a high arrears on what would have been the small
amount due at that time.  This could have alerted the
authorities to the potential seriousness of the problem
if nothing were done to arrest this trend as the portfolio
matured.  In retrospect it is clear that insufficient
attention was paid to designing appropriate arrears rates
and setting up the machinery to implement effective and
timely collections.  It is quite possible that if the early
borrowers had been made forcefully aware of the presence
of a rigorous collection procedure (instead of receiving
due bills six months late), greater compliance could have
been secured.  Given the limited number of the portfolio
(several hundred) selective visits by an appropriate
official could have reinforced this repayment behaviour
early in the life of the loan.  Now that the numbers and
amounts have increased substantially, there is less possibility of turning this situation around.

At the same time there was clearly a deficiency in
loan appraisals, despite the early emphasis to staff this
division at the expense of the collection division. Arbitrary
interference with established loan review procedures became
common under the former Director of the Bank and, in retrospect, the institution has paid dearly for this behaviour
with rising arrears rates and low staff morale.[3]

A comment is in order on the policy of the international
agencies.  One cannot help but conclude that these sources
(primarily the World Bank) were too eager to push more loan
funds into the JDB than they were in a position to manage.
The JDB, on the other hand, found it difficult to exercise

any self-discipline in this situation and was largely
ignorant of the pitfalls of accepting more than could be
managed effectively.  In the end this places more responsibility on the international lender if only to protect
his potential loan recovery.  In this case it would appear
that this responsibility was too lightly regarded.

    In summary the vulnerability of the JDB has increased
markedly with the growing rate of arrears in its total loan
portfolio.  There is serious question about its financial
viability with no further capital inflows from international
sources and the mere trickle coming back on its outstanding
obligations.  In retrospect the institution would have been
less vulnerable if more of a banking mentality had prevailed
in its original design.  This perspective could have
emphasised a more balanced portfolio of assets including
shorter term and more commercial loans, while on the other
hand drawing upon deposits for shorter term lending as well
as international agency funds for longer term development
loans.  An extensive branch banking network would also
have helped rather than centralising all operations in one
establishment in Kingston.

    A different type of development bank may be necessary,
perhaps a merger with the successful, nationalised National
Commercial Bank.  In this case more rigorous banking practices
could prevail with a shorter term and more secure portfolio
and a deposit function to offer a broader array of financial
services in the market.  When this is combined with a
scaled-down development portfolio supported in part from
international sources, there could be a much more balanced
and less vulnerable financial institution that combines the
virtues and discipline of commercial banking with the visions
and long-run commitment of development banking.

*Small Farm Arrears*

Table 6 shows that the arrears performance of the
smaller farmer credit programmes, with one exception, is
no better than that for the large farmer JDB programme.
There is a wholesale delinquency issue that affects all
public sector programmes.  The old line ACB-PC Bank programme
records about a 40% arrears in relation to loans outstanding.
Not surprisingly these accounts are not designed to create
an arrears measure on accounts due.  No doubt this measure
is considerably higher since there are medium term loans
withinthis portfolio.

Through time the relative importance of the ACB-PC programme has declined.  Its reputation has suffered as a
result of its long-standing arrears problem.  Reports are
intermittent, accounting and managerial practices deficient,
and loan appraisal and collection procedures perfunctory.
The SSFDP programme, originally established within the ACB
in 1969, was transferred into the JDB in 1974.  Government
budgetary support to cover the ACB overheads, deficits and
new loan capital has diminished in the face of competing
demands by newer programmes in the public sector.  As a
result there was a decline in the real resources available
for loans in this programme during the 1970s.  Finally when
the Crop Lien Program was established in 1977, it was housed
in the Ministry of Agriculture instead of the ACB.  At
present the institution is engaged in a holding action on
a diminishing base of real resources.

The Crop Lien Program is the most recent initiative
to reach the small farmer.  Launched in 1977 in an effort
to stimulate seasonal food  production and save on foreign
exchange for food imports, the programme was widely publicised and reached a large number of farmers.  Roughly nine

and a half million dollars were dispersed to some 30,000
farmers.  Farmers with commercial, JDB or SSFDP loans were
supposed to be ineligible.  Ministry of Agriculture
extension agents engaged in the loan appraisals which were
rather casual and retailed through local P.C. Banks.
Repayments were expected to be voluntary with little
inducement needed.

By financial standards, the programme was a complete
failure with only a 6% recovery rate after one and a half
years of operation.  Clearly a "grants" mentality was
operating with no serious sanctions for default, and  no
serious consequences for the public officials responsible
for designing the programme with its built-in failure for
effective loan recovery.

The SSFDP programme is currently the only public
sector credit programme with a modicum of success.  The
arrears rate in this programme is only 38% for the amounts
due and 18% for loans outstanding.  In comparison to the
JDB, ACB or Crop Lien Program, this is a very respectable
performance.  Moreover, this programme has the additional
challenge of promoting longer term developmental loans to
small and medium sized farmers.  However, this success
comes with a price, namely, a high supervisory overhead
that is largely absent in the other programmes.  A highly
decentralised system of field officers with separate staffs
for loan appraisal, technical assistance and loan collection
guarantee a close monitoring of loans.

The SSFDP strategy has had relative success because
of its expensive supervisory credit programme that monitors
(or pressures) the farmer so frequently that it prevents
arrears from getting out of hand.  At the same time the
farmer may also value the technical assistance he receives

from this loan source highly enough  that he does not want
to risk being cut off from further assistance with high
arrears.  In any event the overhead supervisory costs in
this programme appear to offset the otherwise high arrears
that would invariably emerge without it.  In the end a
highly subsidised supervised credit programme like the SSFDP
which at least inculcates more responsible repayment behaviour
and effectively implements on-farm investments is preferable
to an equally subsidised non-supervisory programme (like
the ACB and Crop Lien) that saves on supervisory costs but
generates high delinquency, poor credit attitudes and
probably a diversion of resources to non-farm uses.


*Conclusions*


We conclude this paper by reviewing the Jamaican
experience over four broad areas: (i) the planning versus
the banking perspective; (ii) the dilemma of development
banking; (iii) the issue of credit delivery to small farmers;
and finally  (iv) the pathology of economic stagnation and
constraints on financial reforms.

Jamaica, in the 1970s, has shifted between a planners'
and a bankers' perspective on agricultural credit strategies.
This struggle is still not resolved.  The planners and the
plan-oriented Ministry of Agriculture have always viewed
credit from the credit use approach.  In short, after the
production targets have been established, all policy
instruments are directed to that end, including credit.
Arbitrary guidelines are established to determine how much
credit input is needed to produce so much agricultural
output.  Credit programmes are then launched to service
these production programmes.  The most recent example is
the Crop Lien Program.  The fact that practically none of

the loans were repaid in this programme was considered of
lesser importance than the fact that domestic foodstuff
production increased substantially.  There is an implicit
assumption that the opportunity cost of public funds is
low.  The planners'approach invariably transforms credit
programmes into income transfers and rationalises their
results after the fact.

The bankers' perspective is less concerned with
production *per se* and more concerned with institutional
viability.  Within this scenario bankers are more concerned
with the proper evaluation and administration of loans,
concerned aboutcharging a sufficient rate of interest to
cover costs, determined to protect their cash flow through
low arrears (emphasising collateral and foreclosure) and
pessimistic about the possibilities of servicing the credit
needs of small farmers without extensive monitoring, supervisory and collection machinery.  The JDB and SSFDP credit
strategies reflect this thinking, but in the case of the
former particularly, poor performance has not only damaged
the institution but compromised the credit strategy as well.
At present the current impasse between the planners' and
bankers' approach is at a stand-off with no firm political
direction being offered by the Government to resolve this
dilemma.

The development bank dilemma grows out of this impasse.
The poor performance of the JDB has seriously compromised
its financial viability and the institutional credibility
it once enjoyed.  The period of growth and expansion is
over.  The institution now faces a painful period of re-
trenchment and slow recovery.  More effort has to be spent
in recovering loans, foreclosing on properties and resched-
uling loans for salvageable projects.  The "grants"
mentality, favouritism and the image of lax loan administration
must be changed before the institution can function again

effectively and draw on outside funding. The possibility
of diversifying its loan portfolio to include more short
term liabilities and assets is an interesting possibility
but one which must follow rather than precede the retrench-
ment and recovery strategies.

Public sector credit delivery to small farmers has
proven difficult in most countries and Jamaica is no
exception. The possibility of achieving this goal and
maintaining the financial viability of the institution
offering this service is slim. Quick and widespread dis-
semination of credit invariably leads to an *ad hoc* income
transfer programme. On the other hand, careful, expensive
supervising of small farmer loans may reduce arrears but
the high operating costs limit the scope of the programme,
which may not be much more cost-effective than a low-cost
unsupervised programme anyway, unless the loan recovery
rate is high.

More helpful would be a package of agricultural policies
that distributed inputs in kind at subsidised cost and pro-
moted minimum price programmes and marketing arrangements
that would reduce the risk of income variance. Minimum
prices affect all farmers equally whereas subsidised credit
programmes are invariably rationed and, in the end, only
favour those who have access to the credit institutions.
In the light of this, the social return to the use of public
sector resources would be higher if applied in a combination
of policy initiatives to reach small farmers rather than
drained off into an ineffectively and inequitably administered
credit programme with high default rates.

Finally the pathology of economic stagnation is currently
constraining the prospects for financial reforms in Jamaica
today. Under other circumstances the growing pattern of

distortions in the financial sector which create a negative
real rate of interest and inequitable credit subsidies
could be dealt with through interest rate reforms to promote
a positive real rate of interest. But the constraint  in
this strategy is the lack of demand for loans in the economy
in the face of a severe economic recession. The high level
of excess liquidity in the commercial banking network
suggests that banks would be unable to find customers for
higher cost loans until overall inflation is effectively
controlled and economic recovery underway.

One common way to deal with this state of affairs is
to institute a rigorous stabilisation programme which
promotes an expansion of exports, sharp devaluation, wage
controls, budgetary constraints, indexing for inflation and
drastic financial decompression. This usually takes several
years and often requires authoritarian regimes to implement
the measures effectively and repress the inevitable popular
reaction against the short term consequences. The examples
of South Korea, Taiwan and post-1973 Chile come to mind.
This is hardly the political model that would conform to
Jamaica's more democratic traditions.

Thus the prospects for eliminating the inequitable and
inefficient credit subsidies currently built into the negative
real rate of interest are slim. This structure of interest
rates is bound to remain until inflation is reduced or some
indexing formula adopted. This implies that savings will
continue to be penalised and various forms of non-price
rationing utilised to allocate public sector credit. The
growth in the supply of agricultural credit will be much
slower than in the early and mid-1970s with a much smaller
number of farmers serviced. Only a significant reduction
in inflation and a modest economic recovery can create the
conditions that could modify this pessimistic scenario,

creating the room for manoeuvre that would permit the
financial reforms that are necessary in Jamaica.

1   The large rise in loans outstanding between 1974 and
    1975 and the relatively large role of commercial banks
    in the net increase in real credit from 1970 to 1977
    is partially due to a change in the Bank of Jamaica's
    classification of agricultural loans reported by
    commercial banks in 1975. Loans which had previously
    been reported under distributed trades and other sectors
    were hereafter listed as agriculture. It is estimated
    that slightly less than half of the net increase in
    loans outstanding from 1974 and 1975 was due to this
    change in classification.

2   Again allowance must be made here for the large relative
    increase in commercial bank loans from 1974 to 1976 in
    part due to the reclassification of agricultural loans
    in 1975 discussed in the previous footnote. Neverthe-
    less there was a large unambiguous rise from 1971 to
    1974.

3   See *Auditor-General's Report*, 1978, 1979.

THE POLITICAL ECONOMY OF SPECIALISED
FARM CREDIT INSTITUTIONS*

*J. D. Von Pischke*
*The World Bank*
*Washington D.C., USA*

*Introduction*

Specialised farm credit institutions (SFCI) primarily
engage in the provision of loans to farmers and others
undertaking agricultural production.  Their names, while
not invariably an accurate guide in terms of this strict
functional definition, include Agricultural Development
Bank, Agricultural Finance Corporation, Rural Development
Bank, Agricultural Credit Corporation, Supervised Credit
Agency, and Land Bank.  Their distinguishing features are
a loan portfolio consisting almost entirely of agricultural
loans and a narrow range of financial services offered.
For example, SFCI do not on any significant scale accept
deposits, provide money transfer services, store valuables
for safekeeping, or serve as fiduciaries, except as these
functions are required in the processing of loan applications
and in loan administration.

*   This paper is based on observations from a number of
countries and on research undertaken in Kenya while the
author was a research student in the Department of Political
Economy at the University of Glasgow.  The views and inter-
pretations in this paper are those of the author and should
not be attributed to the World Bank, where the author is
employed as an agricultural credit specialist, to affiliated
organisations or to any individual acting in their behalf.

SFCI may cater to specific agricultural subsectors of farm sizes or crops, and they may be linked with land tenure classifications or reforms. Their services may be directed towards beneficiaries of agricultural, settlement or rural development projects. These institutions are expected to provide an impetus to agricultural innovation and to promote certain social aspects of rural development policy, often in the small-farm subsector.

Development assistance agencies often play an important role in the design, establishment, financing and staffing of SFCI and in their reorganisation and rehabilitation. Cumulative World Bank lending for farm credit approximated the equivalent of US$ 2.1 billion by 1978. The combined commitments by OECD donors and regional development banks would probably be somewhat larger. Much of this assistance has been directed towards SFCI rather than towards enhancing the agricultural lending of diversified financial institutions such as commercial banks and deposit-taking co-operative banks.

SFCI in low-income countries have a checkered record as financial intermediaries. Their efforts to achieve institutional and financial viability and to expand their clientele encounter more complications that those of diversified lenders because of the vagaries of agricultural production and prices, and also because a certain portion of their activities have more in common with research and development activities than with commercial practice. However, losses appear to be larger than would be expected from *credit* institutions. These lenders often find it difficult to achieve loan recovery levels sufficient to break even financially before the allocation of administrative expenses.

Miracle estimated that approximately one third of the funds
loaned to farmers in the programmes described in the 20-
volume *Spring Review of Small Farmer Credit* were unrecover-
able.[1] Others have noted that SFCI provide services of low
quality.

*A Performance Pattern*

This paper attempts to explain why SFCI are created and
why they and their programmes frequently fail to become viable. This phenomenon of development finance may be explored and portrayed by a model, or a performance pattern,
incorporating financial logic and elements of political
economy. This pattern accepts technical aspects of agriculture as given. It demonstrates major causal links which,
in turn, produce typical forms of institutional response
(see Figure 1).

The presentation which follows outlines typical defects
in SFCI performance. While the analysis is undertaken at
the institutional level, it also applies to farm credit units
or components included in larger development projects or loan
portfolios. The basic statement of the pattern abstracts
through the consistent selection of sub-optimal alternatives.
The sub-optimality of any single decision in the sequence
may not be extreme or obvious. As each decision sets in motion
forces which lead to succeeding decisions, however, the cumulative result is the opposite of the stated objective towards which decision makers are initially oriented. That
objective is the creation of a viable farm credit system or
intermediary capable of providing an increasingly wider
array of services of an acceptable standard to an expanding
clientele of farmers. This performance pattern demonstrates
how situations tend to develop perversely unless checked by
departures from the sequence, and identifies the types of
costs encountered as the unfortunate progression unfolds.

Figure 1: A Performance Pattern of Specialised Farm Credit Institutions in Low-Income Countries

POLITICAL INFLUENCES                    FINANCIAL INFLUENCES

The Public Sector Farm Credit Complex
1. "Farmers are poor"
2. The farm credit need creed
3. Government should promote rural development
4. Supply-leading finance stimulates rural development
   ↓
   Cheap Farm Credit Policy ─────────────→ Low Interest Rates
                                              ↓
                                           Low or Negative Returns on Non-Prime Lending
                                              ↓
                                           Stringeint Credit Rationing by Commercial Criteria
                                              ↓
Establishment of a Specialised Farm Credit Institution ←───── Restricted Rural Access to Financial Services
                             (SFCI)                              ↓
                                                               Separation of Rural Saving from Rural Credit
                                                                 ↓
SFCI Dependence on Treasury and on External Support on ──→ Limited SFCI Access to Market Funds
                    Soft Terms                                   ↓
                                                               SFCI "Alienation"
                                                                 ↓
      Farm Credit Programme Design                             Stringent Credit Rationing by Political Criteria
                                                                 ↓                    ↓
                                                               Substitution of Debt    Inadequate Stimution
                                                               for Equity  →            → of Production
                                                                 ↓
                                                               Poor Loan Discipline
                                                                 ↓
Political Repercussions of Enforcing Loan Discipline ←─────── Delinquency Deceit Diversion
                                                                 ↓
                                                               Poor Loan Collection Performance
                                                                 ↓
                                                               Impaired SFCI Development

Note: Major linkages are shown by arrows and solid lines.
      Minor linkages and feedback relationships are not
      indicated because of space limitations.

The pattern incorporates two types of influences on
SFCI performance.  The first is political, which stems from
government's interest in rural development, in agricultural
production and in the use of political power to benefit or
to be seen to be benefiting various groups.  The second
type of influence is financial, comprising the inexorable
mathematics of the operation of financial markets and aspects of relationships forged in these markets.  Political
decisions affect financial market variables, while the performance of financial markets provides grist for the political mill.  Interaction of these influences largely determines the lagging performance of many SFCI.

The performance pattern begins with the assumptions
that the economy or a subsector in question is not served
by a specialised farm credit institution, and that most
rural families, or a target group in question, do not have
direct access to financial services provided by formal
sector institutions. It is assumed that the formal financial market, although not highly developed, is loss avoiding,
rational and workably competitive.  A third assumption is
that policy makers believe that supplying credit for agricultural purposes, or for the subsector, cultivators or
target group in question, would be advantageous.

This belief, "the public sector farm credit complex",
consists of four related assumptions on ways of viewing
rural people, the state of agriculture, the requisites of
rural development and the role of government.  The first is
that "farmers are poor".  Of all target group characteristics,
poverty is singled out as of primary interest.  The second,
"the farm credit need creed", holds that little agricultural
innovation or progress along desired lines can occur without access to credit.  The need creed is in harmony with
concern for the poverty of farmers.  The third is the axiom
that government should promote rural development or target

group welfare. The fourth is that supply-leading finance
can stimulate agricultural and rural development and contribute to target group productivity. Supply-leading finance
consists of providing funds in advance of demand in an
effort to stimulate enterprise - i.e. risk-taking by borrowers - in a socially useful manner. In agriculture it
is based on the assumption that credit tied to an innovation
such as improved inputs or a new crop, will accelerate the
adoption of the innovation by the target group of intended
borrowers.

The public sector farm credit complex defines the rural
development problem in terms of the poverty of farmers and
their lack of access to credit for specified purposes,
observes that the problem is one which ought to be solved
through public sector intervention, and specifies credit
as a medium through which political initiative may be ex-
ercised. Supply-leading finance responds to the perceived
poverty of farmers as well as to the belief that they
must have access to credit before an acceptable rate of
material progress will be achieved.[2]

*Interest Rates and Access*

The public sector farm credit complex produces advocacy
of cheap farm credit. Proponents note that credit should
be provided at a "reasonable" rate of interest for purposes
which are considered socially and economically imperative
and for target groups viewed as poor and having little
alternative but to use credit if they seek to progress.
Since informal sector interest rates, except on some kinship and friendship loans, are high compared to those found
in formal markets, the possibility of involving informal
lenders in the solution to the problem defined by the public
sector farm credit complex is not seriously considered and
would not be feasible within the low interest rate structure
proposed.

What constitutes a "reasonable" rate depends upon local circumstances, but proposals often advocate approximate parity with commercial bank loan rates to commerce and industry. Arguments raised against higher rates for agriculture often contend that it is objectionable to charge a high rate to disadvantaged elements in society. A similar position is that low rates of interest help to compensate farmers for losses of income from government price controls on produce. The usual result is agricultural interest rates below or roughly equal to the going rates on loans to other major sectors and to individuals not dependent upon agricultural incomes. The point of analytical interest is that potential agricultural borrowers currently without access to formal sector credit are to be accommodated under an interest rate structure not significantly different from that applied to present borrowers in other sectors.

Low formal sector interest rates on the types of loans most useful to rural people tend paradoxically to restrict their access to formal sector financial services. Rural customers at low levels of financial activity are a costly market to serve. They tend to deal in small transactions, which are relatively costly for a formal sector institution to process. They frequently are scattered geographically in areas with poor communications, making loan administration difficult. These factors preclude economies of scale because of the small size of the market around a rural office. Rural people may not be accustomed to modern commercial practice and not be so concerned about loan due dates as other customers, which raises the lender's costs of loan and liquidity portfolio management. For deposit-taking institutions, a clientele of small depositors which conducts business in cash rather than by some form of payment order requires that offices maintain relatively high levels of

cash. Cash kept to meet depositors' demands earns no
interest, adding to the costs of servicing these clients.

The rural economy is more variable than many other
types of financial activity. The marketed or cash-generating
portion of agricultural output is subject to even greater
uncertainty as a residual after relatively constant subsistence requirements are satisfied. Variability in income
tends to reduce lenders' evaluations of the debt capacity
of the target group which in effect is based on that portion
of expected future resources that would be available for
loan repayment in situations of reasonably expected adversity.
Such situations include poor harvests due to natural
factors, low prices and failures in the marketing system's
capacity to absorb produce. Lenders' rationale rests on
the requirement to meet the demands of their depositors
and other creditors. An unpredictable stream of collections
increases lenders' liquidity requirements, which raises
costs and reduces the supply of loanable funds.

Uncertainty concerning the amount of a borrower's future
cash flow available to service debt is viewed by the lender
as a credit risk. One determinant of willingness to bear
this risk is the interest and other income expected to be
realised from the class of transaction concerned. Loans involving substantial degrees of uncertainty tend to be avoided by lenders. When interest rates (used here to denote
all fees levied by lenders) are kept low, lenders are not
encouraged to expand their markets into activities which
incur higher costs, including the costs of greater uncertainty. Institutional factors inhibit lenders from raising
rates selectively to offset the costs of accommodating more
risky loan applicants. These include usury laws, the danger
of increased political exposure, the size of the increases
required, possible losses in economies of standardisation
of lending terms, and the costs of obtaining the information

and expertise necessary to contain the risks of marginal business. Low rates encourage lenders to perpetuate the *status quo*. Lenders stringently ration credit according to commercial criteria of credit-worthiness in low interest rate regimes, *ceteris paribus*.


## *SFCI as a Response to Credit Rationing*

Stringent credit rationing by lenders such as commercial banks results in severely restricted rural access to financial services. This is seen in the paucity of rural offices of banks, in loan security demands beyond the capacity of most households, in minimum transaction sizes and minimum deposit account balance requirements which are high relative to transactions and incomes normal for rural areas, and in other arrangements imposing transactions' costs on those seeking access to formal sector financial services. Adherents to the public sector farm credit complex perceive in this situation grounds for remedial intervention by establishing a specialised farm credit institution. This is intended to overcome alleged weaknesses in market performance and is therefore not designed to be dependent upon market resources. It is funded through the national treasury, frequently with support from external non-market sources such as aid agencies. (SFCI are good foreign exchange earners, opening new avenues of access to grants and loans from donors. This may help to explain their popularity in low-income countries.)

By definition, a SFCI is highly selective in the types of financial services it provides, operating on only one side of the rural financial market. Credit access is considered the primary problem, and deposit-taking and money transfer services are typically not developed. Rural savings capacities and liquid resources are usually thought to

be small.  Institutions already in place, such as post
office savings banks or commercial banks and co-operatives
may be thought to be providing adequate financial services
outside the credit sphere.  Policy makers may not see any
advantages in replicating facilities or stimulating competition for rural deposits or money transfers.  In addition, these services require managerial and accounting
performance of a higher order than those of loan disbursement, and there are merits in opting for simplicity initially.


*The Effects of One-Sided Intervention*

   Intervention solely on the side of the rural financial
market which issues loans has consequences which are frequently overlooked.  It tends further to fragment these
markets.  Credit channels are unrelated to savings channels
and make little direct contribution to stimulating rural
savings.  Such intervention may encourage the popular belief that formal sector credit is essential, or at least the
most feasible means of progress.  This may occur at the
expense of the tradition of self-help and self-finance, and
of the development of informal financial mechanisms such
as rotating savings and credit associations.

   Most importantly, dependence upon the national treasury
and external donors limits SFCI access to market funds and
information.  Lack of such access results in alienation of
the institution.  Alienation stems from inability to act
as a *rural* financial institution intermediating between
rural savers and borrowers rather than merely serving as a
link between the government and rural sectors.  Rural people
are not regarded by SFCI as a market to be developed but
rather as poor, exploited or economically incompetent elements requiring assistance.  Rural people, in turn, do not

view SFCI as something of their own but rather as a benevolent intrusion to be exploited. In these circumstances
a specialised farm credit institution does not have access
to information about rural financial flows, behaviour and
priorities which is available only to those who enjoy
sufficient confidence to operate on both sides of rural
financial markets as deposit takers, lenders and money
transfer agents. Denied such information and insight, and
divorced from the context required to view finance broadly
or creatively, SFCI management can develop only limited
decision-making expertise. SFCI are not in a position to
be stimulated by the discipline imposed and opportunities
offered by market forces.

Lacking essential information and limited by budgetary and operating constraints imposed by government sponsors,
SFCI generally are forced to ration credit stringently.
This stringency is different from that based on commercial
criteria applied by other formal sector intermediaries such
as commercial banks. It is based on considerations which
are fundamentally political. Political criteria, broadly
defined, are inherent in farm credit programmes designed
by governments and development assistance agencies seeking
to promote the welfare of target groups selected on extra-
market criteria.

*Credit Rationing by SFCI*

Credit rationing by SFCI tends to take two forms.
These depart from a financial optimum at which the borrower's level of indebtedness is matched with his repayment capacity in such a way that enterprise is stimulated.
These two forms may be termed intensive and extensive.
Intensive credit rationing involves identification of a relatively small target group and the provision to members of

that group of amounts of credit which are large in relation
to the existing scope of their operations. For example, a
small farmer planting local varieties and using only a
little organic fertiliser may be issued credit, possibly in
kind, to plant the entire holding with high-yielding varieties nourished by chemical fertilisers, or a farmer using
bullocks for draft power may be accorded a loan to purchase
a tractor.

Intensive credit rationing has features attractive to
aid agencies, and it is often found in externally funded
SFCI activities. The usual objective of intensive credit
rationing is to increase agricultural production and the
incomes of borrowers through technological innovation.
Because the size of the loan is such that borrowers could
not reasonably be expected to repay from their pre-loan
cash flow, loan repayment must come from the incremental
cash flow to be generated by the loan-supported investment.
Credit allocation under these circumstances tends to be
quite selective, and elaborate access mechanisms using farm
budgets are frequently employed by lenders.

An assumption underlying intensive credit rationing is
that lack of finance is a binding constraint to increased
production and augmented farm income. This implies that all
other elements essential to the realisation of these objectives, including the ability to accommodate the uncertain-
ties involved, are in place or can be provided as an adjunct
to credit and can be rendered operative by finance. Intensively rationed credit is supply-leading finance *par excel-
lence*.

Extensive credit rationing is motivated by considerations
of access as well as of production, and access mechanisms
are simple. Credit is rationed extensively to large numbers
of farmers in broad target groups. For example, all members

in good standing of a co-operative may have access to seed
and fertiliser loans. All commercial growers of wheat having land titles may be eligible for production loans.

Within SFCI budget or balance-sheet constraints, broad
access implies relatively small loans to numerous borrowers.
Loan limits under extensive rationing are frequently specified in terms of rules of thumb or standard amounts per
hectare of credit-supported enterprises, in contrast to the
more complicated derivation of loan limits from farm budgets used for intensive credit rationing. Extensive rationing
is most frequently found in seasonal input credit. Small
amounts are issued to each borrower, satisfying the prod-
uction-oriented bias of lenders and inspiring broad appeal
which is politically desirable. Programmes using extensive
rationing are usually funded by governments without support
from donors. Exceptions are found in donor-supported area
development projects, in certain aid for co-operatives and
in farm credit systems funded through centralised rediscounting agencies.

Each variety of stringent credit rationing under
political criteria contains the seeds of its own financial destruction. These seeds take root to the extent that
politics produces extremes in credit rationing which over-
whelm financial considerations. Programmes with highly intensive or extensive rationing self-destruct most rapidly,
assuming other things equal.

Intensively rationed credit attempts to perform the function of equity or ownership capital in absorbing the impact of uncertainty. The borrower's return consists of a
residual after permitting a steady flow of resources back
to the lender according to agreed loan terms. As a residual,
the return to equity is variable, reflecting the impact of
uncertainty on a borrower's overall financial situation.

Intensively rationed loans are large relative to the financial status of the borrower, impose relatively large debt service burdens, and change the on-farm factor mix significantly through the addition of higher levels of technology. Such loans may push the borrower's finances beyond his managerial and risk-bearing capabilities, especially during the critical initial period of adaptation to credit-supported change.[3] Adversity may be reasonably anticipated in agriculture and in the implementation of new technologies. In adversity, the new activity may not generate sufficient cash flow to repay the loan which permitted its adoption. Delinquency in repayment easily results. Borrowers may not regard transgression of SFCI loan contracts very seriously: they accept the public sector farm credit complex and view the lender as an alien institution with access to the tremendous resources of government.

Extensive credit rationing also tends to lead to financial problems. In promoting access, lenders offer credit to some borrowers who are not in a position to use it wisely or who have little intention of repaying, or who are so exposed to uncertainty or so close to subsistence that even small repayment obligations assume major proportions. In these cases, accumulation of arrears on the lenders' books is probable. For others who borrowed with the expectation that their agricultural incomes would be increased, small sums of extensively rationed credit may pose certain difficulties. Prescribed husbandry practices which lenders intend to support may be subject to indivisibilities far beyond the average loan size. For example, the loan may be small compared to the financial requirements of improved input packages, which may lead to incomplete adoption of the package. Incomplete adoption may produce disappointing results. Improved seeds without fertilisers, for example, may not perform much better than traditional varieties. Even if all inputs are provided in kind, the new grower may

not use them in prescribed proportions for reasons of risk
aversion or poor information. In these cases the borrower
may not produce incremental cash flow sufficient for loan
repayment. Access to extensively rationed credit does not
necessarily stimulate adoption, and loans may be trifling
and not engender any commitment to their productive use
or repayment.

Stringent rationing by political criteria easily
leads to poor loan discipline, defined to include delinquency, deceit and diversion. All constitute default
according to technical usage indicating any breach of a
loan contract.

Delinquency denotes the failure to pay on time, and
inability and unwillingness arise as credit rationing becomes increasingly intensive or extensive. Deceit arises
because borrowers have an incentive to circumvent the rules
of the game, especially rules made by a lender alien to them
and thought to have huge financial resources rationed according to political criteria. Incentives to build a good
credit rating are lacking, especially in the early years
of an institution when its permanency and efficiency have
yet to be demonstrated. One means of circumventing loan
limits per hectare under extensive rationing is to apply for
credit for a larger area than will be cultivated, or to
borrow simultaneously under different names. Another is
to borrow using a different name each season. If loan repayments are deducted at source from delivery proceeds, there
is an incentive to borrow and deliver under different names,
or to use others as delivery agents. These tactics are
often successful when loan supervision and records are not
finely tuned. Diversion occurs when the relatively large
size of intensively rationed loans tempts the borrower to
allocate a portion for purposes not envisaged by the lender,
especially if the borrower is not entirely comfortable with

the leap in risk and managerial demands which agreed loan
use involves. Loan-supported purchases or disbursements
in kind may be resold for immediate cash, or fictitious
invoices may be submitted by accommodating suppliers. Diversion is probably even more common under extensive rationing,
especially when loans are disbursed in cash.

While possibilities of abuse are found wherever credit
exists, stringent credit rationing under political criteria
creates incentives for abuse. Under the terms on which
credit is extended, rational behaviour and responsible
behaviour on the part of the borrower as specified in the
loan contract do not coincide.

*Repercussions of Poor Loan Discipline*

Poor loan discipline impairs SFCI development. Funds
which would have become available for relending, as outstanding loans mature, are locked up as arrears. As arrears
accumulate, SFCI resources fail to revolve full circle.
Potential new borrowers may find their access to credit delayed, restricted or denied because of the declining liquidity of the lender. Intensively rationed credit becomes
available to fewer new borrowers when funds available for
lending decline. Lenders may restrict access further by
increasing the average loan size for economy in loan administration, catering to an increasingly select group of
relatively low-risk, large borrowers. The lender of extensively rationed credit may maintain broad access by reducing average loan size. Causes of arrears are fortified
as extensively rationed loans become increasingly trivial,
especially in real terms as inflation raises the costs of
modern husbandry.

Arrears have an opportunity cost. Day-to-day collection

problems consume the lender's scarce managerial resources,
often at the expense of activities requiring a long time
horizon such as planning, staff training and designing
more effective services for rural people.  The accumulation
of arrears and associated poor financial performance may
demoralise staff having a financial or accounting outlook,
making it even more unlikely that the institution could
become financially efficient.

As damaging as these effects are within SFCI, they
may be small relative to external effects.  Rural access
to financial services provided  by lenders other than
specialised farm credit institutions may be retarded by
poor SFCI performance.  Dismantling the tradition of poor
loan discipline of government lenders has a cost, and
diversified loss-avoiding intermediaries outside the state
sector may be deterred from serving the poor because of
that cost.  They may be increasingly reluctant to extend
credit in experimental or innovative ways because of the
heightened political sensitivity surrounding the enforcement of rural loan contracts.

Achievement of development targets may be hindered by
poor loan discipline.  Defaulters, originally considered
as poor farmers deserving financial assistance, are placed
in an adversary position against their financial partner
in development.  The flow of communication between borrower
and lender is constricted.  A basis for distrust is created
between borrowers and rural development administrators,
extension agents and SFCI staff.  Distrust raises the costs
of promoting rural development by making consensus more
difficult to achieve, or by requiring the exercise of greater
force for the successful implementation of programmes involving rural participation.  One attempt to reduce these
costs is to accord SFCI extra-legal administrative recourse
against defaulters.  However, this power increases the

probability of arbitrary action against rural people.

Widespread default demonstrates to rural people that
government is not able or not willing to enforce contracts,
in this case the loan document to which an official institution is a party.  Cases taken to court by SFCI may strain
the ability of courts to dispense justice, especially if
defaulters are numerous.  The efficiency of legal administration may decline as the increased queue of litigants
makes it difficult for the courts to deal promptly with
routine cases, such as boundary disputes, inheritance and
cattle theft.  The legal force of contracts may be compromised by situations created by loan defaults.  Deterioration
in contract enforceability retards commercial advance and
the contribution which commerce and commercial practice make
to rural development.

Accumulation of arrears also makes SFCI more vulnerable
to political interference.  Those who formed the institution to assist the rural poor are seldom enthusiastic about
seeing their creation expropriate rural property or con-
struct a black list of defaulters to be denied further
credit.  Interference may be across the board, permitting
all defaulters to take a longer free ride, or selective,
favouring certain groups or individuals.  Default may also
be a source of conflict among rural people.  The selective
nature of credit access may be magnified by default and by
uneven efforts to enforce loan discipline.  Defaulters who
are not apprehended may incur the animosity or envy, or both,
of borrowers who repay and of defaulters who are caught.
To the extent that the pattern of default mirrors the rural
power structure, equity is violated by collection activities
manipulated by the power structure.  Thus, initial concern
for access, expressed through an inappropriate medium, ends
by violating the parallel concern for equity.

As the development of this performance pattern suggests, the public sector farm credit complex does not contain the basis for the correction of the many unfortunate direct and indirect consequences it so easily engenders. In addition, the tradition of poor loan discipline which it spawns tends to be self-perpetuating. Arrears remain on the books for a very long time, debilitating the lender. It may be argued that lagging SFCI performance requires much more time and effort to correct than the faltering or ineffective performance of an extension service or input supply or produce-marketing system. It may also be argued that the costs of lagging SFCI performance are higher, from almost any perspective except political expediency, than those associated with the poor performance of most development activities undertaken by government.

## Deviations from the Performance Pattern

The pattern describes the types of problems which to some degree affect most SFCI in low-income countries. In situations in which the basic statement appears not to offer a valid analytical approach, several factors may be at work. However, these factors vindicate the analytical framework it provides, (like the cobweb theorem, the pattern can yield cycles of expansion as well as of contraction, depending upon the assumptions used).

The most positive vindication in cases in which the pattern appears not to apply is found when policy or institutional design departs from the assumptions of the public sector farm credit complex. For example, rural people may be viewed as a largely untapped, potential market for formal sector financial services, and initiatives to tap this market may be oriented towards cost-effectiveness. Likewise, low interest rate policies may be abandoned in moves towards

financial liberalisation in efforts to enhance the quality
as well as the quantity of the financial sector's contribution to development.  In these cases reality may un-
fold in a manner consistent with the pattern outlined but
opposite to its basic statement.  The result is the growth
of strong, independent intermediaries and greatly expanded
rural access to financial services.

The pattern may also appear superficially not to apply
when government or donor assistance enables a specialised
farm credit institution to become larger and serve more
people in spite of its shortcomings.  Arrears may not im-
pede new lending while funds pour in as subsidies, debt
and equity capital.  In cases of poor SFCI performance
overwhelmed by access to new funds, the pattern is still
useful.  It provides a systematic basis for identifying
the costs of those policies and activities which require
outside support to keep the lender liquid.

But why would new funds continue to be provided?  A
weak loan recovery record may very well reinforce the public sector farm credit complex: not only are rural people
poor, they are too poor to repay their loans.  Disappointing
performance may increase the institution's ability to raise
funds in the short run and need not place it at any real
disadvantage in relation to its sponsors.  Assistance
agencies are often eager to shore up the operations of their
clients so that programme continuity is maintained and
country relationships solidified, and so that more farmers
may be helped.  Past losses or failures may be viewed as sunk
development costs contributing to expectations of greatly
improved performance in the future.

At some point, SFCI rehabilitation and reorganisation
may be necessary because of decapitalisation from bad loan
losses and lending rates which do not cover administrative

and other costs. This admission on the part of a government
provides the possibility for increasing donor leverage,
accompanied by substantial infusions of new funds. Skilful
governments may attempt to create competition among donors
to offset demands for increased controls, tighter performance commitments or more flexible interest rate policies.
In any event, support is usually forthcoming: more funds
enable more farmers to receive loans.

Lagging farm credit operations may also be used to raise
the institutional stakes in rural development. Poor performance can be attributed to any number of shortcomings
and conditions judged worthy of remedial intervention. Agricultural extension and farmer education are frequently
invoked palliatives, as are the formation of credit groups
or co-operatives. Some donors may be attracted by proposals
for the launching of ventures considered innovative or
experimental, such as loan insurance.

*The Future of the Public Sector Farm Credit Complex*

In view of the problems which plague specialised farm
credit institutions in low-income countries, what is their
future course? One certainty is that they will continue
to receive large amounts of funds from their sponsor
governments and donors because of their political appeal
and thirst for resources. Less certain is the survival of
the public sector farm credit complex, which faces four
major threats. First, the complex will be rendered irrel-
evant in some countries by measures going far beyond intervention in rural finance. Centralised control of agricultural production and of rural people and the transformation
of the formal financial sector into a set of accounts
for the planning authority eclipse the concerns raised by
a performance pattern based upon a mixed economy. Second,

rural development initiatives not involving supply-leading
finance will divert attention from the complex. One such
initiative has been the training and visit system popularised in India and elsewhere with World Bank support, which
has obtained substantial yield increases by effectively
packaging and marketing extension assistance to small
farmers.

The third and fourth threats come from the rural financial markets themselves. The complex will be eroded by
trends apparent for some time in rural financial market research. Assumptions which are increasingly challenged by
empirical data are that rural people are unable to save, that
rural financial liquidity is negligible, that the informal
credit market is characterised by "usurious" rates of interest and that specialised farm credit institutions and low
formal sector interest rates are relatively low-cost interventions serving the best interests of rural people. Finally,
the complex is undermined by the operations of farm credit
suppliers which operate effectively in financial terms on
bases which are at odds with the complex. These include
aggressive voluntary efforts to mobilise target group deposits and techniques of support which concentrate on building
viable financial institutions rather than on low interest
rates for target groups. In circumstances where research and
financial market performance constitute the main threats to
the public sector farm credit complex, the institutional
variable of greatest interest may be the length of the lag
between the realisation that present systems are often based
on inappropriate assumptions and the development of new responses by rural developers.

1   M. P. Miracle, "Notes on Developing Small Farmer Credit
    Institutions in Third World Countries" in <u>Small Farmer
    Credit Analytical Papers</u>, AID Spring Review of <u>Small
    Farmer Credit</u>, 19, 1973.

2   Supply-leading agricultural credit is frequently linked
    with other measures to stimulate rural development, such
    as extension.  These ancilliary factors are not crucial
    to the development of the relationships explored here.

3   F. J. A. Bouman suggests that the impersonal aspect of
    formal sector finance may increase the willingness to
    go into debt by removing from loan transactions the in-
    fluence of cultural norms, such as the obligation to
    reciprocate, which limit informal indebtedness.
    ("Indigenous Savings and Credit Societies in the Third
    World: A Message" in <u>Savings and Development</u> Vol. 1, No. 4,
    1977)

*Part Two:*

FINANCIAL INTERMEDIARIES AND INSTITUTIONS

# MONEY AND COMMODITIES,
# MONOPOLY AND COMPETITION

*Barbara Harriss*
*Overseas Development Institute*

## Introduction

In his analysis of the agrarian economy of Randam,
a village in North Arcot (a rice-growing district of southern India) John Harriss contends that a process of differ-
entiation is taking place and that a class of "capitalists"
is evolving in the countryside.[1] The process of different-
iation, which has been accelerated by the new agricultural
technology, is at the same time constrained by the fact that
capitalists cannot expand agricultural production further
without acquiring more land. On the one hand, marginal
petty commodity producers do not yield up their land to
capitalist farmers because the former are being reproduced,
albeit on unequal terms, by merchant and usurer's capital;
and on the other, their kinship systems maintain their land
"within a tight circle of kin". If this maintenance con-
tinues indefinitely then "capitalist production" will be
indefinitely constrained.

This paper is concerned with the nature of the rural
money market, particularly in North Arcot. It seeks to
explain the interests of both private and State administered
merchant and finance capital in maintaining, apparently in
a fairly stable manner, a sub-optimally efficient, marginalised

sector of the peasantry, which constrains overall agricultural expansion.  This involves a study of the private rural money market, using evidence from agricultural merchants and agricultural producers; the money markets organised indirectly and directly by the state: and the linkages between private and public finance and between the money market generally and the market for agricultural commodities.

The data come from field research on a random sample of 200 traders in agricultural commodities (paddy and rice), agricultural inputs (fertiliser and pesticides) and agricultural investment goods (pumpsets and accessories for lift irrigation); from random surveys of 20 village co-operatives and of 200 paddy producers in 12 villages of North Arcot District.[2]

*The Private Rural Money Market: Evidence from Agricultural Traders*

The unorganised money market is highly complex, (see Fig. 1) and involves the participation of a large number of producers.  There may be as many as 180,000 farmers in the rice-producing eastern *taluks* of North Arcot who market paddy to some 2,300 traders.  Traders lend money in cash or kind to about half of their customers.  In North Arcot the high and increasing demand for both production and consumption credit enables traders to discriminate between clients.  Private sector money is not necessarily a substitute for co-operative loans, it may be a complement ("If a man can't get a Government loan, he's likely not to be able to repay my loan").

A farmer's eligibility for short term loans is determined by traders in parallel fashion to the procedures of the State-

Figure 1
## Model of Circulation of Money around one Paddy Wholesaler

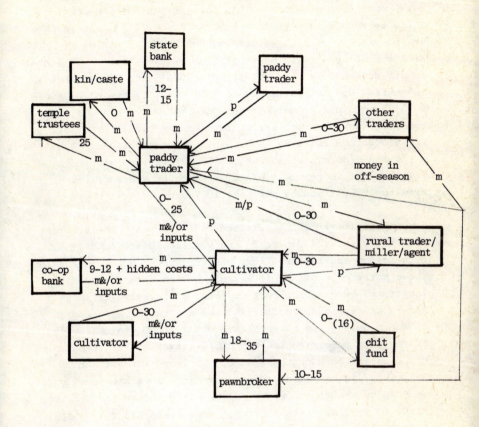

m    money
p    paddy
numbers are estimated annual interest rates

run co-operatives: traders assess landholding, crop size,
capital assets, and past repayment performance.  The private
money market is more accessible than is that of the State.
A trader's shop is open from 6.00 am to 10.00 pm, and loans
are obtainable with no perplexing paperwork requiring a
literacy not possessed by two-thirds of the sample.  Trader's
credit does not require formal collateral, and the request
is usually speedily attended to.  No security has to be given
by a farmer to a private trader, and borrowers can use the
money for any purpose, agricultural and social.  Data for
non-production loans in two of the twelve villages from
which the economic behaviour of 200 farmers was studied
reveals that 26 per cent of all such money was supplied by
traders in Duli and 50 per cent in Vengodu.

Agricultural loans obtained on the private money market
are rarely petty.  Minima to individuals in the paddy and
rice trades and in fertiliser dealing averaged Rs.200.  Below
those sorts of amounts, it may not be the risk attached to
lending so much as the cost of loans administration which
deters traders.  Agricultural loans are not large.  Maxima
to individuals were between Rs.2,000 - 3,000, which is also
the maximum permitted by the co-operatives.  Traders may
occasionally lend up to Rs.10,000 to large farmers and
relatives, but cultivators needing large sums are usually
advised by traders to apply to the nationalised banks or to
"private parties", the elusive, large scale and full-time
moneylenders operating from modest back streets of many
market towns.

The average annual interest rate attached to loans, at
the time of the survey, was remarkably consistent at 13-14
per cent, which was slightly above the legal ceiling of 12
per cent.  But the way in which interest is paid is varied.
Normally repayment is in kind after harvest, though loans
for pumpsets are allowed a longer repayment period.  In

some main collecting centres, no interest is charged (and
the prevailing market price is paid) to those who supply
the trader with more paddy than the repayment of their
debt necessitates. In Arcot an interest rate of 12 per
cent per annum was universal. In Arni and Tiruvannamalai
wholesalers subtracted as interest between Rs.0.5-2.0 per
75 kg bag of paddy from the ruling market price. This
amounts to a disguised interest rate of 4-10 per cent per
year (depending on the paddy variety and assuming a trader
lends three times a year).

In all towns interest rates start to climb if a farmer
repays more than a month after harvest. Data on default
rates are difficult to obtain because of the problems of
cross-checking and because of traders' interest in exagger-
ating. However, it would seem that about one-fifth of all
loans take longer than agreed upon to repay. Slow payers
are not always the smallest farmers; sometimes large
farmers, who have reloaned borrowed money, are tardy in
repayment. In cases of late repayment, interest rates vary
from 12 per cent to 25 per cent. The markets where funds
are least available - Cheyyar and Wandiwash - have highest
rates on overdue payments. Great social, moral - and
occasionally physical - pressure is exerted on slow payers,
unless there are obvious mitigating circumstances or
prominent ties of caste. Traders collude over information
on "bad risks", and according to traders, an average of
5 per cent of borrowers default completely. Every trader
attempts to retrieve this money, but they weigh the costs
of potential litigation against the size of the sum likely
to be lost.

Interest rates which are higher than the legal ceiling
are often attributed to a combination of inelastic and
rising demand, the costs of borrowing, and the costs and

risks of administering loans. It has also been contended
that high interest rates, blatant or disguised, have a
component of monopoly profit. This is obviously not the
case in our study area.

An interesting manifestation of the non-exploitative
nature of trade credit is the case of the trader as banker.
It is not uncommon for farmers, having made sales, to leave
cash with the trader as a safe deposit. The trader uses
this money in trade and will reciprocate the farmer's good
faith by giving small quantities of money (eg Rs.3-5 for
some medicines, a school exercise book) if needed, in lieu
of interest payments.

Credit and moneylending do not appear to be part of
an economically predatory relationship between trader and
farmer in North Arcot District. This is probably due to
the identity as both cultivators and traders of the two
main castes involved, and there exist strong ties of kinship as well as money between town and country, especially
among Mudaliars and Gounders, the castes accounting for
40 per cent of all agricultural traders.

Pawnbrokers also contribute to the private rural money
market in competition with the nationalised banks, which
also lend money on pledged jewels. The advantages of the
lending practices of pawnbrokers over those of banks are
ease of access,[3] speed of service, easier valuation procedures, and higher proportion of the value of the jewel
given. Of course, pawnbrokers also charge higher interest
rates than the banks and the traders, varying from 18-25 per
cent inversely with the size of the loan. Nevertheless,
pawnbrokers are becoming an important source of cash for
agricultural production, and the years since 1968 have seen
a massive increase in their number throughout North Arcot
District.

This recent increase in demand comes largely from
poorer farmers requiring small loans of Rs.50-100 to pay for
agricultural labour, bullock hire, fertiliser, or pumpset
repair. Demand is highly seasonal (January to May) so
that money may be idle at other times, and the interest
rate must partially reflect this. Paradoxically, pawnbrokers are held in social opprobrium by other lenders in
the market, but they are more acceptable to farmers than
the formal sector.

The evidence points to a relatively competitive money
market, and particular instances of the working of the money
market in Arni bear this out. Because of high default
rates and because of fears of State take-over of the grain
trade, the Arni Paddy and Rice Dealers Association of the
largest traders decided to act in collusion to reduce moneylending to farmers in the early 1970s. It was the only
*sangam* (society) in the District to take such action, and
by no means all traders complied, but flows of money from
the agricultural marketplace declined. Some traders,
anticipating drought, used their spare funds to stock
paddy to the legal limit and above (using other traders'
names). At the same time, credit from fertiliser dealers
also dropped in volume, firstly because fertiliser had
entered a phase of short supply and promotional credit was
unnecessary, and secondly because overdraft facilities for
fertiliser traders did not increase when the price of
fertiliser they sold more than doubled.

There was a marked result on the money market. Whereas
in 1965 there were 10 pawnbrokers (all North Indian *marwaris*),
in 1973 there were 72, and by 1974 there were 88. Most of
the new entrants to pawnbroking were South Indian castes -
Chettiars, Mudaliars, and Nainars. Within the pawnbroking
trade, demand for money for agricultural purposes trebled

in 1972/74 encouraging not merely a new intake of postulant pawnbrokers, but also the emergence of minor Government officials, teachers, and clerks, as moneylenders charging 18-25 per cent. However, while the interest rates charged were illegally high they were rarely equal to the net rate of return on capital from trade.

The lesson appears to be that the money market is structurally flexible. Private intermediaries (traders, pawnbrokers and jewellers) substitute for each other in catering for demand from different types of cultivator and traders' money substitutes for State loans of smaller farmers.

*Evidence from Agricultural Producers*

The sample survey of the debts of 200 farmers analysed by Chinnappa[4] shows that only a fifth of small peasant farmers (ie cultivating less than 0.4 ha) borrow money for cultivation expenses. But around a half of all other categories of farmer borrow. Among all farmers taking loans, borrowed money contributes just under a half of cultivation costs. Of the loans taken, private sources are less important with increasing farm size. Amongst the private sources, the farmer may choose between village moneylenders, pawnbrokers who charge interest rates, chit funds where a disguised interest rate is usually charged, and friends and relatives who may or may not charge interest.

The average size of loan is about Rs.180 per acre, and it is probable that many smaller farmers are more involved in borrowing from traders than from village moneylenders. Consumption loans may be obtained from traders, and it is possible, judging from the increase in

numbers of both agricultural traders and pawnbrokers, that
moneylending is being increasingly concentrated in urban
areas.

Demand for money in agricultural production has greatly
increased for two reasons connected with two rather different forms of production:

- Among the larger capitalist farmers, money is
  simultaneously lent and borrowed, juggling with
  interest rates and relative risks to ensure that
  a profit is made. This pattern is known as "rolling",
  and the English word is used. Harriss cites a
  case: ". . . in September 1973 Arcot Loganathan
  owed a total of over Rs.12,000 to traders and
  other farmers while he was himself owed Rs.10,000
  by others, and he explained that this was usually
  the case, with the balance varying one way or the
  other from time to time".[5] The same writer concludes: "even though oligopolistic moneylenders are
  now powerful within the village, and although
  moneylending profits have not notably constrained
  capitalist development in agriculture since the
  introduction of HYVs, usury remains an important
  factor in the agrarian economy. In Randam we see
  this in the continuing dependence of many farmers
  upon paddy or groundnut dealers or occasionally
  fertiliser dealers."[6] Debt in this case is not a
  sign of poverty, but of security and of relative
  prosperity.

- Among small and marginal farmers demand for cash
  has increased because of their compulsive involvement in markets. This is due to an increase in the
  need for cash to purchase the inputs of the modern

116

technology, including water; increased insecurity
because of the higher level of vulnerability (eg
the need to replace a team of draught animals, or
a coil, where they have a share in a pumpset); and
a high incidence of demand for consumption credit,
which puts farmers in debt to provision merchants.

*The Role of State Financial Institutions: Indirect Participation*

The involvement of national capital in rural money markets
originated in North Arcot District in 1967.  This coincided
firstly with the inauguration elsewhere of the High Yielding
Varieties Programme, and secondly with American pressure to
free the fertiliser distribution network from the "monopoly
stranglehold of the co-operatives".[7]  It coincided thirdly
with the point in the fertiliser cycle when production
exceeded demand and vigorous competitive tactics became
necessary to the marketing agencies.

The financing of agricultural production began in the
form of credit sales at no interest from a State-owned
inputs distribution company to private fertiliser dealers
or agents who repeated the procedure, with interest, to
farmers.  This innovation was followed in very quick
succession by the private companies.  At the height of this
credit boom, a trader's security bore no relation to the
loans which were extended, and by 1971 the distributing
companies themselves had very large quantities of outstanding debt.  Repayment was slow and laborious, and many
traders and agents went out of business.

By 1973, however, credit competition had stabilised,
largely due to skilful state intervention.  The source of
trader credit diversified out of company finance to involve

another type of financial agency altogether, namely the
large banks which had been nationalised in 1969. Evidence
is available on one of the fertiliser distributing companies
(E.I.D. Parry) to illustrate the terms of this involvement.[8]
A dealer in agro inputs was sanctioned credit purchases of
up to 80 per cent of the value on goods bought for purposes
of resale up to a specified absolute ceiling. A dealer
was also eligible for an equal quantity of 180-day crop
production credit, both for his own crops and for those of
farmers, with repayment after harvest.

The important organisational role of the private distributing companies in involving private agents in the
expansion of State credit was emphasised as follows by
Venkataramini who was the credit controller of Parry's:
"In the successful implementation of the scheme the manu-
facturers/suppliers have the most important role to play
. . . The suppliers have to initially screen every
applicant and fix a reasonable credit limit commensurate
with his assets." Dealers no longer had any privacy in
their financial transactions with companies and banks, a fact
which was acknowledged as follows: "It is also incumbent
on the part of suppliers to render such ancillary services
to the banks and dealers as are necessary to ensure that
their mutual obligations and interest are fulfilled."

Dealers were required to deposit 20 per cent of their
sanctioned limit with the banks. They had optionally to
yield up title deeds, hypothecated stocks, or promissory
notes. They had compulsorily to pay interest at $10\frac{1}{2}$ per cent.
Dealers were more strictly supervised, having to tender a
monthly stock statement and to submit to periodic inspection
of accounts by bank agents as well as "surprise stock
inspection" by the field representatives of the distributing
agencies.

In this situation of glut and severe competition, the
relative balance of power shifted to the nationalised banks.
Private companies     acted contradictorily: on the one hand
as promoters and on the other hand as regulators.  At one
and the same time they competed with other companies for
custom while the banks operated virtually identical schemes
through every company, and while much of the fertiliser
sold under three different brand names was identical and
produced by one manufacturing plant.  Meanwhile, belying
claims of "easy payment terms", the interest rates charged
to farmers were unsubsidised, and included a hike to cover
dealers' administrative costs, unlike co-operative credit.
And it must be remembered that all the private distributing
agencies also marketed fertilisers through the co-operatives
and competed with themselves there as well, while the co-
operative credit scheme was managed by a single co-operative
bank.  There is, in fact, indirect State control over the
financial behaviour of private input suppliers.

*Direct State Participation: the Nationalised Banks*

Private trade faces formidable competition by the State
in the areas of moneylending and credit in kind.  Private
moneylending activities are swamped by credit extended by
the nationalised banks and cannot meaningfully be disaggre-
gated from them.  The banks also offer 180-day production
credit directly to farmers with over two acres, at the rate
of Rs.250 per acre up to a ceiling of Rs.1,000-2,500 depending
on the bank.  These rates are lower than those of the
Panchayat Union and co-operatives, but the interest rates
are higher at 10-11.5 per cent per year.  The farmer has to
prove ownership and show all production receipts.  A bank
manager in North Arcot District explained that it was the
very large farmers who knew about this source of finance

and used it (often for relending).  They were often late
in repayment since long repayments were not penalised by
a rise in interest, and since the use to which the credit
was put was unpredictable.

As well as financing agriculture and trade directly
and indirectly, the banks also finance agriculture through
the Panchayat Union loans, though the subsidy on these
loans is borne by the Department of Agriculture.


*Co-operative Credit*

The major competitor with private trade remains the
network of co-operatives, financed by the Co-operative Bank,
which is also the recipient of a subsidy.  The Chinnappa
study shows that the 47 per cent of cultivators who took
loans among the sample of 200 North Arcot farmers got, on
average, 32 per cent of their production credit from co-
operatives.  The disbursement of co-operative credit was
disproportionately concentrated on larger farmers with the
share of co-operative loans in all production credit rising
with farm size from 10 per cent to 62 per cent.  In an
agricultural co-operative near Cheyyar, 80 per cent of
farmers had under 3 acres of land, but only 32 per cent of
the co-operative society production loan went to them.
Loans per person per season averaged Rs.800 for cultivators
with under 3 acres, but averaged Rs.2,300 for those possessing more than 3 acres.  Rs.2,300 is above the official
ceiling per individual on production credit.  The credit
is given on subsidised terms: interest rates vary between
8.7 per cent and 9.7 per cent per year on post-harvest
payments, rising to 12.6 per cent, the legal ceiling for
overdue payments.

Co-operatives also administer 5 year medium term loans of up to Rs.2,000 for well-digging, and up to Rs.2,500 for pumpsets, at an interest rate of 10.6 per cent. Farmers can also apply directly to the Land Development Bank for similar loans at a slightly lower interest rate, but credit, whether privately or State given, is not as important for these investment goods as for fertiliser.

Co-operatives are supposed to be a people's institution, but only in the case of a few large villages is the manager elected by the directors and paid independently from co-operative funds. In most cases the State finances agriculture in the guise of farmers, and the manager is appointed by, and paid by, the Department of Co-operation.

Co-operative loan statistics for all village societies were obtained from the Central Co-operative Bank, Vellore. To a remarkable degree, co-operative credit compensates where private credit is least abundant, that is in the rural *taluks* of Cheyyar and Wandiwash with small market centres and a long tradition of dispersed trade.

In the District as a whole, co-operative credit amounts to just under half the quantity supplied by private trade (Table 1). Further amounts - probably fairly substantial - are also supplied by farmers' families, friends, and by pawnbrokers for production.

In spite of the State sector's advantages in interest rates, other factors must reduce its competitiveness. The outright default rate on the production loans of 20 co-operative societies surveyed was 26 per cent, rendering the cultivators concerned ineligible for further production loans. Many of the defaulters are large farmers, the reason being that in 1972 farmers were promised that a vote

Table 1

Moneylending of Wholesalers, Millers and Co-operatives
in North Arcot District

| Town | Average money loaned out per trader (Rs) | Value of average turnover (Rs m) | % of traders lending | Estimate of total lent in 1972/73 (Rs m) | Co-op production credit lending/ taluk (Rs m) |
|---|---|---|---|---|---|
| Vellore | 80,000 | 85.0 | 90 | 23.4 | 1.2 |
| J. V. malai | 50,000 | 4.5 | 66 | 11.0 | 3.9 |
| Arcot | 30,000 | 7.8 | 75 | 8.4 | 2.5 |
| Arni | 24,000 | 5.3 | 50 | 2.1 | 1.6 |
| Polur | 26,000 | 14.6 | 70 | 4.3 | 3.6 |
| Cheyyar | 10,000 | 3.2 | 56 | 1.5 | 5.6 |
| Wandiwash | 16,000 | 3.7 | 17 | 0.5 | 3.7 |

Source: Field survey 1973; Village Co-operative Society
Accounts, Central Co-operative Bank, Vellore.

"correctly" cast in the election would write-off a loss.
As a result of their ineligibility for co-operative loans
and Panchayat Union loans, farmers are forced to seek
funds on the free market.  The ceiling of Rs.2,000 on
co-operative production loans also forces the relatively
few cultivators with land holdings in excess of 10 acres
to seek extra funds elsewhere if needed.  Further, the low
interest rate charged to the farmer by co-operatives con-
ceals high borrower costs.  These include the costs of
inefficient administration (lengthy application procedures,
untimely arrival of credit, inflexibility of repayment
procedures and necessity for proof of collateral) as well
as the cost of bribes (which effectively raises the cost
of loans virtually to a par with that of those from
private trade).

*State Lending to Commodity Traders*

    Finally, the State encourages nationalised banks to
extend distribution and production credit to fertiliser
dealers, but strongly discourages lending to paddy and rice
traders.  In practice this is unimplementable as often they
cannot be distinguished, and the financing of intra-season
paddy and rice stocks is a secure and profitable form of
investment for banks anyway.  As a result, wholesalers and
millers may obtain bank loans if they wish.  One much
publicised case in the Tamil press concerned a bank which
lent large sums of money to pawnbrokers and to professional
moneylenders in one of the towns in our study area.  In
this case, once this activity was discovered, it was
squashed, but there is no doubt that other such activities
continue.

The result of such intersectoral linkage and intersectoral competition is that the existence of cheap State
credit increases the availability of money for agricultural
production and exerts a restraining influence on private
sector interest rates.  As such it is progressive.  This
social benefit cannot be quantified but ought to be borne
in mind when assessing the social effects of the co-operative subsidy.  But internal competition within the State
financial apparatus mainly benefits large farmers.  As
such it is retrogressive.


*Conclusion: The Contradictory Roles of the Linked Finance
and Commodity Markets*


We are now in a position to reconsider the problem
posed at the beginning - the role of the complex money
market in constraining the very expansion of agricultural
production that it appears to facilitate.

Our answer to the central question takes a somewhat
similar form to John Harriss's analysis of the agricultural
economy.  Large numbers of small traders, some family firms
but many small capitalist firms are able to maintain themselves from trade and to compete with each other and big
traders.  One form which this competition takes is in
lending out money to farmers at rather low interest rates.
Thus the marginal trader allows the marginal farmer to
reproduce himself and survive.  This begs the further
question: why are there so many small traders?  This question
demands consideration of the linked commodity and money
markets.

There seems to be at least seven reasons why agricultural
commerce is relatively so crowded:

- Since commerce is more profitable on average than
  any other sector of this region's economy, it
  attracts entrants. Lenin's study of the evolution
  of the women lace traders in Moscow gubernia
  suggested that: "Such types develop from among the
  small producers themselves . . . There is no doubt
  that under commodity economy not only prosperous
  industrialists in general, but also and particularly
  representatives of merchants' capital, emerge from
  among the small producers",[9] and there is a con-
  tinuum of evolution from producer to independent
  trader. A similar pattern is found in North Arcot.

    Interestingly, entrants into trade may be drawn
  from the wage labour force, who accumulate the
  generally small quanta of starting capital slowly
  through years (generally about a decade) of wage
  labour during which period they also acquire the
  necessary skills and contacts. All this occurs
  despite debt bondage to the owner which suggests
  that, though debt bondage is frequent, it is not
  such as to characterise trading firms as feudal.

- Commerce may also be numerically crowded because of
  demographic expansion in this sector. Traders'
  families (average 7.5 members) are larger than those
  of the average peasant producer (5.9 members) and
  family members require employment. Joint family
  businesses become managerially unwieldy, and often
  split to provide each son, and occasionally each
  adult family member, with control over resources,
  particularly control over the ratio within "profits"
  between consumption expenditure and re-investment.

- The personal knowledge of clients necessary in moneylending also may set a limit to the number of clients
any mercantile firm can scrutinise and maintain,
and thus encourages the expansion by fission of
joint family firms.

- But commerce may be numerically crowded because
joint families split for another reason.  This is
that State tax legislation discriminates against
multiple-enterprise, joint family combines.  There
are powerful fiscal incentives for single-owner
businesses, and many traders have split firms for
that reason.  One split may of course create three
or four firms and does not necessarily, though it
does usually, involve splitting the social unit as
well as the economic one.

- The State encourages easy entry into commerce in
two other ways.  The State has a blatantly contradictory policy and legislation for paddy and rice
marketing (advocating both modern automatic mill
machinery and hand pounding: advocating both the
nationalisation of the grain trade and market
regulation which promotes private competition) and
it is therefore unstable in its control of commerce.
In North Arcot District the dominant form of intervention encourages competition through market
regulation in an effort to reduce distributive
margins at a minimum cost to public funds by
maximising numbers in trade.

- State intervention in money markets adds to the
crowding of trading intermediaries by institutional
fission, and forces an increase in money supply at
reduced rates from commodity speculators.

-   International pressure favouring private trade
    coupled with the Central Government's priority for
    expanding the fertiliser industry (both publicly
    and privately owned) in order to increase food
    production, has led to a spawning of small inputs
    dealers. The international fertiliser and pesticides
    distributing companies compete with an identical
    product through several separate networks of private
    dealers, through the co-operatives and even through
    the State's Department of Agriculture, though
    these systems suffer from organisational instability.
    However, the possibilities for private traders to
    concentrate capital through this kind of trade,
    given the control of allocations by the distributing
    companies and given the tight control over credit
    by the State's own financial institutions, are
    limited.

The expansion of commerce itself increases commodity
production and, via the marketed surplus, feeds back into
commerce again. But, competition among traders for commodities
takes the form of money lending at relatively low interest
rates. In this money market, the effect on interest rates
of subsidised co-operative credit has not been negligible.
The contradiction is that in allowing the marginal farm to
reproduce itself, this also constrains the expansion of
commodity production and the penetration of capitalism into
agriculture. Because commodity production is constrained,
commodity prices are sufficiently high at the retail end
for agricultural traders to exploit market imperfections,
which are in turn quite often the result of State interventions in marketing (such as rice levies and movement
restrictions) which ostensibly have the opposite objective.
Agricultural traders then reap the profits which fuel the
system. Crowding is usually associated with competitive

conditions which decrease profits and incomes, but under
these circumstances the reverse occurs.

Where there is a socially and technically determined
ceiling on the physical improvements a capitalist can make
to his land (and therefore a constraint on the expansion
of capitalist agriculture without the further acquisition
of land), the only alternative investment for the agri-
culturalist capitalist (as for the employee in trade or
the petty accumulator) is trade where he has to compete in
moneylending.  This leads to a situation where both the
agrarian structure and the various interventions of the
State create conditions where competition by traders for
marketed surplus is actually constraining the long term
expansion of agricultural production.

The specificity of the explanation offered in this
paper is somewhat at variance with the generality of its
title, partly to emphasise that it is only possible to
analyse the role of the money market in rural development
if the relationships between structures of production
and exchange (which are specific to agrarian regions) and
between both of these and the interventions of the State
(which are not specific to agrarian regions) are known.
The general notions embodied in the title are two.
Firstly, it is impossible to consider the role of the money
market in rural development in isolation from the commodity
markets with which it is linked.  Secondly, interventionist
policy options tend to arise from polarity assumptions
about the operation of factor markets: to replace the private
sector where its markets operate monopolistically, and to
regulate its behaviour when its markets operate in a manner
thought "effectively" competitive.  The case study illustrates both money and commodity markets with structural
characteristics of effective competition.  In terms of

performance, however, both are imperfect markets, the commodity market more so that the money market. A multiplicity of bureaucratic interventions in these markets and in the sphere of taxation has the combined effect of maintaining this situation.

1  J. C. Harriss, *Capitalism and Peasant Agriculture: Agrarian Structure and Change in Northern Tamil Nadu*, Monograph 3, Overseas Development Group, University of East Anglia, Norwich, 1979, and Oxford University Press, Bombay, forthcoming.

2  These surveys were undertaken in 1973-4 (with brief revisits in 1976 and 1977) as part of the Cambridge University Project on Agrarian Change (for further details of which refer to B. H. Farmer (ed), *Green Revolution? Technology and Change in Rice Growing Areas of South Asia*, Macmillan, London, 1977; and B. Harriss, *Paddy and Rice Marketing in Northern Tamil Nadu*, Sangam, Madras and J. Harriss, *op. cit.*

3  For example, they allow thumb impressions and do not restrict loans to owners of bank accounts.

4  B. N. Chinnappa, 'Adaption of the New Agricultural Technology in North Arcot Division', in B. H. Farmer (ed), *op. cit.*, Chapter 8.

5  Harriss, *op. cit.*, p. 289.

6  *Ibid.*, p. 291.

7   P. London, *Merchants as Promoters of Rural Development: an Indian Case Study*, Praeger, New York, 1975.

8   R. Venkataramini, 'Distribution-cum-Production Credit Banks Scheme', *Fertiliser Marketing News*, Vol. 4, No. 7, 1973, pp. 10-13.

9   V. I. Lenin, *The Development of Capitalism in Russia*, Foreign Language Publishing House, Moscow, 1960, p. 364.

COMMERCIAL BANKS AND RURAL CREDIT

*Frank A. Wilson*
*Project Planning Centre*
*University of Bradford*

## Introduction

The advantages and disadvantages of commercial banks
as sources of rural credit can be reviewed briefly.  A
recent publication of a large international bank has
summarised the advantages of the private banks as deriving
from their "diversities, competitiveness, international
connections, magnitudes of lending capability, flexibility,
reasonable terms and speed of response".[1]  It is doubtful
whether the *diversity* of commercial bank operations is
a significant advantage to those seeking to utilise the
institutions as a means of providing a major share of
rural credit needs.  However, a recent survey in Kenya
has confirmed that of the reasons given by farmers and
businessmen  for preferring to borrow from commercial banks,
that of "convenience" predominated, arising from the fact
that many customers were already operating current accounts.[2]
The advantages which the diverse nature of operations may
bring are clearly more apparent to larger and more progressive borrowers than to the overwhelming proportion of
potential customers who are unlikely to graduate to the
level of operating a current account and utilising chequing
facilities.

Competitiveness implies the opportunity for borrowers to choose between alternative sources of finance not only on the basis of terms and conditions of repayment but also according to the service provided. Competitiveness is allied to flexibility and speed of response and any deliberate choice between alternatives is based on a complex of factors and not on the terms of repayment alone. If this was not the case it is unlikely that money-lenders and local merchants would be able to operate so effectively in locations where specialist and non-specialist institutions have been able to offer significantly lower borrowing rates. Borrowers have "traded off" higher interest charges against the flexibility and speediness of the informal supplier.

Where commercial banks have been successful in promoting a competitive alternative to the non-formal lenders they appear to have been able to do so by amending their procedures in order to offer the advantages previously only available from non-institutional sources. These amendments, taken together with lower effective rates rather than direct price competition on rates alone, appear to be the main reason (other than in cases where government action has restricted non-institutional activity) why commercial banks have been able to compete with other sources of finance, including the specialist agencies.

As to the magnitudes of lending capability, this can be attributed more to the expanding activities of international banks rather than to the private *or* government-owned commercial banks in developing countries. Where this feature does have a direct impact on the quality and quantity of rural finance as provided by non-specialist agencies, it is as likely to have negative as positive effects due to greatly increasing demand for project, infrastructure and property finance in recent years.[3] A number of large international banks have in consequence had great opportunities to extend their

portfolios significantly without entering into the difficult
area of direct lending to rural people.

It may be suggested that overall this could be to the
longer-term advantage of planners seeking to utilise more
effectively locally owned and/or incorporated non-specialist
institutions; but this is only if a distinction is drawn
between the operations of banks with local branch networks
and those international banks offering the advantages of
their international connections but concentrating on merchant
banking activities. Much of the remainder of this paper
concentrates on the former - commercial banks with local
branch networks - and reviews the ways in which these
institutions are adjusting (and may, in the future be able
to adjust) their operations to service rural credit needs
more effectively.

## The Growth in Institutional Credit

The past ten years has seen an unprecedented rate of
growth in institutional credit. In some countries -
especially in Asia - the commercial banks have developed a
significant role in the provision of rural finance. In
India non-specialist commercial banks increased agricultural
lendings by a factor of 32 between 1968 and 1974. Networks
expanded rapidly elsewhere; the Peoples Bank of Sri Lanka
increased its branches from 27 to 340 between 1967 and 1976
and similar rates of growth in terms of the outlets can
be found in the Philippines and Indonesia.[4] In smaller,
less densely-populated countries with a less developed
institutional base, particularly in some parts of the African
continent and Latin America, the increase in rural branches
and especially loanable funds has been less dramatic but
nevertheless real. Governments have encouraged international
banks to extend their activities into rural areas; they

134

have put pressure on private local banks; and they have
deliberately directed government-owned institutions to
extend their networks. Even though the amount of loans
issued - especially to small rural borrowers - has not
increased everywhere at the same rate as the increase in
the number of rural branches, the potential now exists
for the more effective utilisation of a more developed
banking infrastructure.

If the potential of existing rural banking networks
is to be utilised there will be a continuing need to amend
savings generation, credit delivery and recovery systems
in such a way that viable access to a greater number of
savers and borrowers can be achieved. Commercial banks are
the main channel by which personal savings are mobilised
in many countries. They have often been criticised for
their traditional, inflexible approach to savings generation although as branch banks have increased in number
their accessibility and acceptability as "local" savings
agents has encouraged small savers to open accounts.

In some countries, and especially in government-owned
rural and co-operative banks, the conventional minimum
level deposit limits have been discarded and the majority
of banks now accept and encourage deposits from savings
groups, co-operatives and other organisations. At the
same time it has to be recognised that cost-effective small-
scale savings generation requires an institutional base
which can rarely be adequately supplied by commercial bank
networks. One of the implications is for the development
of the means by which more durable institutional links
between commercial banks and other agencies - which are
more advantageously situated and organised for small-
scale savings mobilisation - can be encouraged and sustained.

*Delivery and Recovery*

Group loan schemes, input finance through credit
provision to intermediaries, and simplification of loan
procedures and documentation are some of the more prominent
methods adopted by both specialist and non-specialist
institutions to improve the delivery and recovery of rural
credit. Despite - or perhaps because of - these innovations,
repayment rates have not improved overall. There are
welcome signs however that credit specialists within and
outside commercial banks are increasingly recognising the
essential and predominant importance of the borrowers'
"management capacity". Too much attention has been paid in
the past to credit morality and not enough to a real understanding of the framework of technical and financial
viability into which credit is introduced. Commercial banks
have been more successful in developing a real understanding
of the borrowers' capacities in larger rather than small-
scale enterprises where credit-worthiness can be assessed
by the more traditional bankers' methods. It is probably
this factor as much as security and even access which has
inhibited commercial bank lending programmes to smaller
farmers and rural businesses. Furthermore, when commitments
to this type of lending programme have been made, this has
resulted in over-ambitious repayment schedules (especially
for medium-term lending), limited control, and consequent
poor repayment performance.

A major problem of lending institutions is the inadequate
number of qualified personnel. At first glance commercial
banks, with their long tradition of professionalism, well-
established staff grading and common approach to training,
might be expected to have a clear advantage over the
specialist agencies in loan assessment and control, if not
credit delivery. It is apparent however that the advantages
they have in respect of loan assessment and control are

only realisable within the limited and somewhat inflexible
framework of lending policies which effectively rule out
a significant rural lending programme. Where commercial
banks have attempted to amend delivery systems and relax
security they have suffered from the same problem as the
specialist agency, namely the lack of sufficient numbers
of suitable trained applied agricultural/rural finance
officers. Where the activities of the banks extend to
assisting in the identification of viable lending proportions at individual and group/intermediary level the
applied nature of the work and the necessity for appointing
specialist loan officers becomes even more apparent.

There has been a belated recognition in recent years
of the need to employ specialist agriculturalists at "head
office" level. In some countries - notably India - the
larger commercial banks have for a number of years employed
staff with technical agricultural training at branch level.
With a clearer approach to the overall viability of commercial bank operations in the rural sector this example could
with advantage be followed by non-specialist institutions
elsewhere in the world as the supply of suitable agriculturalists and agricultural economists permits.

*Government and Private Sector*

Another feature of recent years has been the extent
to which commercial banks have had the opportunity to contribute to lending programmes and project initiatives
planned by government and quasi-government agencies. In
some countries, this has been important as presenting the
opportunity for the first significant input into (small-
scale) rural credit. This in turn has presented challenges
and difficulties which have not always been adequately
overcome, particularly in the areas of the effective use

of intermediaries for delivery and repayment of loans.
There are two beneficial aspects of this type of involvement, however.

The first is that it has encouraged Governments to
develop new approaches to the utilisation of existing
financial institutions as agents to on-lend external (and,
on occasions, internal) funds and to facilitate joint
lending programmes with other institutions such as development banks and specialist agencies. Even where they are
government-owned, commercial banks have tended to fulfil
a distinct and somewhat isolated role relative to other
financing agencies. The increasing degree of direct
involvement in the planning *and* financing of specific
projects and programmes is therefore to be welcomed and
supported.

The second advantage of this type of activity is that
it presents the opportunity for innovative approaches to
risk-sharing between commercial banks and government. The
differential apportionment of unsecured risk according to
the extent of the proven management ability of the borrower,
his access to technical advice and the banks' direct access
to crop or livestock revenues can often be negotiated
within a recognised project framework but not outside it.
Although overall guarantees and the discounting of loans by
Central Banks are procedures which have some value, particularly in a volatile financial market with fluctuating
liquidity, the sharing of risks on the basis of knowledge
of the individual borrower or borrower groups is often a
more realistic approach to the government underwriting of
the least profitable of commercial bank undertakings.

*Implications*

   The final section of this paper concentrates on the
implications of the issues reviewed above for bankers and
also for planners who are involved in determining a policy
on rural credit and advising on the role of commercial
banks within it.

   In many countries commercial banks are well placed to
extend their activities as branch networks  have expanded
to provide banking facilities in rural areas and are in
consequence likely to be operating at under full capacity -
at least in the initial stages.  The successful direct
lending activities of commercial banks are likely to be
concentrated for some time on larger seasonal borrowers
with proven management ability, some security and relative
easy access in both a geographical sense and in respect
of revenues from sales of produce.  Where excess capacity
exists and where suitable intermediaries and/or group lending
schemes can be established there is some evidence to show
that commercial banks can also provide a seasonal credit
service which compares well with that of the specialist
agencies.

   If the banks are to continue to develop this kind of
business - as many banks in countries where there are
sectoral lending quotas will be required to do - there are
serious implications for the training and recruitment of
staff and the development of new procedures.  As far as
staff training and recruitment is concerned the welcome
trend towards the appointment of more technically qualified
officers should be continued and probably accelerated.  At
the same time it will be necessary to train staff up to
branch management level in such a way that they not only
develop a better understanding of the rural sector but will
also be prepared, with the encouragement of head office

managements, to change their conventional approaches to
lending where necessary.

Staff training, or re-training, has to be directed
from the top and should go hand in hand with the formulation
and testing of innovative delivery systems.  The enterprising branch bank manager with a willingness to innovate
is too often at a disadvantage in that his own personal
progress in the organisation may be handicapped rather than
assisted by his preparedness to try out difficult and (at
least in the short term) potentially non-profitable procedures.
In a number of countries there is a considerable wealth of
experience in the formulation of appropriate methods of
credit delivery.  What is needed is not so much the introduction of completely novel approaches to lending but a
commitment initially on a small-scale and with government
support to realistic attempts at the provision of viable
credit to rural peoples.

The crucial expression is "viable credit" and here
government and quasi-government departments from the Central
Banks to district level agricultural officers and marketing
and input supply agencies have a major responsibility.
Legislation enforcing sectoral quotas and even credit
guarantee funds and the establishment of loan discounting
arrangements may be of limited value unless they are based
on a real measure of agreement between the banks and responsible governmental authorities on the costs of effective
delivery and the package of support to borrowers and lenders.
As planners are increasingly encouraged to revise their
original thinking on cheap credit and pay more attention to
the opportunity cost of capital within, if not outside the
rural sector of the economy, it becomes urgently necessary
to clarify thinking on the viability of credit schemes.

Although few would object to the subsidising of credit provision in some form, all credit institutions - including commercial banks - are likely to have difficulty reconciling profit-making or break-even objectives with broadly-stated policy objectives about the role of the institution in "promoting rural development". The rural sectors of almost all countries exhibit a complex of transfer payments from government to individual, individual to government and one government agency to another. Although it is essential to regularly review the extent of financial commitment by government in support of all rural development activity, it is equally important to spell out the operational implications of such support to all parties concerned. Only if this is done on the basis of consultation rather than by edict and tardy confrontation can the real financial and economic costs be adequately assessed. In as far as commercial banks have a role in the provision of rural credit it can only be developed - with all its attendant difficulties - if they are involved from the outset in a much more integrated planning process than has often taken place in the past.

1  I. S. Friedman, *The emerging role of private banks in the developing world*, Citicorp, New York, 1977.

2  M. David and P. Wyeth, *Kenya Commercial Bank Loans in Rural Areas: a Survey*, IDS Working Paper no. 342, Nairobi, Kenya, 1978.

3  C. S. Hardy, "Commercial Bank Lending to Developing Countries: Supply Constraints", *World Development*, Vol. 7, 1979, p. 189.

4  Asian Development Bank, *Rural Asia - Challenge and Opportunity*, Mamla, 1977.

# SMALL FARMER CREDIT DELIVERY AND INSTITUTIONAL CHOICE

*Anthony Bottrall and John Howell*
*Overseas Development Institute*

## Introduction

Research on rural finance and small producers has concentrated largely upon two issues: the use of credit and savings in the small farm economy, and the effect of credit policy upon agricultural development. There has been rather less research on the delivery of credit, although there has been a number of studies of particular initiatives undertaken by banks, co-operative societies, or project agencies. Furthermore (on a theoretical and comparative basis) there has been little attention paid to the institutional aspects of credit provision.

Partly as a result of this neglect, planners and managers of small farmer development projects and programmes can find little guidance from the large body of credit literature when they are called upon to recommend on the organisation of credit and financial services within a particular programme. Small farmer programmes may give priority to a specific crop, land settlement, intensified service provision, farmer service centres, etc, but in most cases there is also a substantial credit component. Obviously, decisions on organising a programme are likely to be determined by the existing patterns of service provision, the strength of private sector institutions, the existence of farmer organisations, etc. Yet even where the range of institutional options is narrow, there are still choices to be made on alternative ways of strengthening those institutions which already exist.

This paper is concerned with the criteria to be employed in attempting to establish or promote financial services as part of small farmer development programmes. The different objectives of such programmes and their political and administrative implications are considered in the first section. This provides a broad framework in which to consider questions of institutional choice from two different perspectives. Firstly, there is the top-down perspective of government agencies and project authorities particularly in the context of new institutions or procedures being established to promote financial services. Secondly, there is the bottom-up perspective of local-level farmers organisations, often already existing, which may be used or adapted to promote savings and credit activities.

*The Objectives of Credit Programmes*

The term 'credit programmes' includes those comprehensive agricultural projects which contain a credit component, and it is in such projects that one of the central problems of credit provision is more often found. Specialist credit agencies, particularly central agricultural banks, are likely to regard the role of credit in such programmes in terms of long-term economic development and are bound to look to the creation of viable rural financial markets as a pre-requisite for project success. From their point of view, the main objective is to move away from a situation where the only depositors are the national treasury and foreign donors, towards a position where the farmer deposits earning commercial interest can lead to an expansion of banking services at the local level.

However, programmes of this sort are only infrequently designed to build local savings capacity. Both government and project staff administering programmes are more likely to regard lack of credit as simply one of a number of deficiencies which impair small farmer productivity and constrain rises in incomes. To them there are two main objectives of credit

provision. The first objective is to provide a general
increase in the resources available to the farmer. Loans
may be intended to have only an indirect effect upon increased
production of cash crops: they may, for example, *reduce the
need to spend time on subsistence food crops*. In many
projects, of course, loans are given specifically for production of a particular crop but in practice the uses of the
loan - even when given in kind - are related to both the
consumption requirements and the production needs of the
farmer, and these cannot be separated. Such loans may be of
a crop season type or an initial capital loan for some technological innovation. In both cases the objective is to
provide what is seen as a stimulus to increased production
which is necessary if the farmer is to take advantage of the
opportunities which may have been offered by initiatives undertaken by other agencies of government (such as the Extension
Department, Marketing Boards, Irrigation Department, etc).

In these circumstances, there is a strong tendency to
attempt to reduce the cost of borrowing to the farmer by as
much as possible. Some of the loan may be converted into a
grant in the case of capital expenditure; much of the administrative cost of borrowing may be borne by an agency
separate from the credit authority; and interest rate charges
will be kept below commercial rates of borrowing. This belief
- that the small farmer should be subsidised, particularly
where he is in the process of fairly rapidly changing his
pattern of production - is widespread, both in agricultural
policy as a whole and in policy towards production increases
within particular projects.

Why is *credit* thought to be one of the most important
inputs requiring subsidy when the long-term impact of low
interest rates is bound to inhibit the development of rural
financial markets? Why subsidise credit rather than other
inputs such as fertiliser, seed, tractor-hire, etc?

The answer to these questions is found in the second main objective of credit provision. This is to offer inducements to the farmer to gain his collaboration in a new project or crop development programme. The *political* importance of credit at low, or even zero, interest is often disregarded by critics of the 'welfare' approach to credit provision. Ideally, a new agricultural development project government department (or project agency) should anticipate farmer response and satisfy itself that the farmer shares its confidence in project success and is therefore willing to match the Government's risk on investment with his own contribution. This contribution involves investing the farmers' own resources, such as labour and capital. In practice, of course, the farmer is unlikely to be willing to share the risk with a Government and he will calculate that the Government, having made a substantial investment - possibly in a mill, or pump scheme, or in crop research - rather desperately needs a corresponding commitment from the small producers.

This dependence on farmer commitment gives the farmer a type of negative 'power' - the power to abandon a settlement scheme, to misallocate water, or to ignore grazing controls. In the face of this threat of producer apathy, governments often see credit as an inducement to the farmer to participate and to commit his own resources. Unlike other subsidised inputs, cheap credit - which has some convertibility - comes close to being a welfare hand-out, rather like providing domestic piped water to nomads as an inducement to settle.

This 'welfare' aspect of credit is also politically important for Governments which have an expressed commitment towards redressing the inequalities within society, between urban and rural sectors, and within the rural sector. In practice, the distribution of credit rarely helps the poorest in rural society, but most Governments' ostensible objectives (reducing the power of the money-lenders, showing a benevolent face to the needy, etc) are an important consideration in determining interest-rate policy in particular.

These differences in objectives between credit provision
as the basis for viable rural financial markets, credit
provision as an encouragement to the adoption of new technology,
and credit as a political inducement lead to a consideration of
a number of other aspects of credit policy which have implications for the choice and design of institutions at both
the government or project level and at the level of farmer
groups.

Firstly, the precise *role* of credit in agricultural
development is not always easy to determine. Even though
credit has often been regarded by governments as a primary
factor in promoting agricultural development, it is now more
generally recognised that credit can have only an ancillary
role following the establishment of *some basis for new investment*, probably new technical knowledge and possibly also a
degree of structural change in rural society. The extent to
which a programme is designed to change the economic, technological and social bases of the rural economy has implications
for choice of organisation or particular institutions, and
is likely to influence the organisation of credit provision
in relation to other components of an 'intervention' strategy.

Secondly, the control over the *use* of credit is similarly
important for institutional choice. It is common practice
among lending agencies to tie credit to production potential
not only by establishing lending limits against production
levels but also by providing credit in kind for production.
Such a policy is likely to neglect alternative credit uses,
including the payment of debts to private moneylenders and
pressing consumption needs, and this confinement of loans to
production often has deleterious effects on farmer investment
and inevitably leads to high default rates.[1] There are two
issues for credit agencies here: the extent to which agencies
should attempt to establish credit requirements and credit-
worthiness using production as only one item of information,
and the extent to which the production process, including

marketing, can be used as a control device, particularly on
loan repayment.

Thirdly, the *target* of small farmer credit programmes
also determines the institutional form of delivery. In many
rural communities there is likely to be a wide spectrum of
producers from low-income farmers (usually in a majority)
lacking in collateral and having only limited prospects of
production increases, to high income farmers regularly
producing a large marketed surplus. Credit programmes may
be designed in such a way that they meet the needs of already
established farmers (particularly if they are producing a
particular high-value crop), or designed to enhance the liveli-
hoods of marginal farmers, or designed for all farmers with
the intention of ensuring that access is not confined to the
successful minority.

A final factor to be considered is the information *needs*
of lenders. A major problem in rural lending is the lack of
information available when considering loan applications and
the cost of obtaining information. The choice of strategy
for agencies confronted with inadequate information will
depend upon the balance of objectives outlined above. If an
overall increase in liquidity is the objective then the risk
of over-financing is likely to be acceptable; if the
stimulation of demand for credit is the objective, then the
more cautious path of underfinancing would be considered a
preferable option.

These different objectives of credit programmes, and
the various aspects of policy which are related, need to be
kept in mind when discussing institutional options.

*Government Agencies and Project Authorities*

In determining appropriate forms of delivering credit
to small farmers there are a number of broad factors which
have to be taken into account. These include

- the level of agricultural development and commercial
  awareness of the farm community;

- the availability of staff resources;

- the strength and potential of the private lending
  sector and the attitudes of Government towards it;

- the distribution of income and resources within the
  farm community and the desire to alter this distribution;

- the type of farm enterprises which the Government
  intends to encourage; and

- existing farmer organisations and their capacity to
  undertake new functions.

Before considering the influence of some of these factors
upon institutions, the nature of different types of project
should be discussed briefly. Project 'types' can be seen
across a spectrum: at one end there are the 'slow-burner' types:[2]
that is, projects which have a long-term perspective and tend
to concentrate upon crop research, 'model' farmers and a
gradual extension effort. There is likely to be a low staff/
farmer ratio and existing field agencies, including credit,
are normally brought into project activities only when necessary.
At the other end of the spectrum are the intensive, accelerated development type of projects which are designed to reach
virtually all farmers in the project area, have a high staff/
farmer ratio, and promote a package of innovations normally co-
ordinated by a single project agency which has direct responsibility for extension, farm supplies *and* marketing and credit.

There is one major institutional issue which is immediately
apparent: when should the credit function be the responsibility
of a single specialised agency and when should credit be
integrated into a multi-functional agency encompassing other
farmer services? There is of course a further, and

closely-related question concerning the extent to which
functions - including credit - can be administered by farmers
themselves, possibly with some professional support.  This
question is discussed fully in a later section but it is
touched upon briefly here to illustrate one of the different
types of multi-function agency.

The term 'multi-functional agency' covers three broad
categories in the context of credit.  Firstly, it can mean a
separate authority with its own sources of credit, its own
loan procedures, control over interest rates, and its own
staff.  This is possible in an area-based project authority
or a special national programme and often occurs where a
substantial proportion of funds come from foreign aid sources.
Secondly it can mean an arrangement whereby an agricultural
bank allows its funds to be administered by an agency such as
a crop board or a settlement scheme authority, which is
responsible for a number of small farmers/borrowers.  In this
case the extension staff, or settlement officers, will have
responsibility for a number of farm-level functions including
credit investigation, debt-collection, etc.  Under such an
agency arrangement the bank is likely to impose a number of
conditions on the administration and distribution of loans.
However in practice the agency - or intermediary - is in a
position to reduce the commercial costs of borrowing to the
farmer by covering management and transaction charges itself.
Finally a multi-functional agency may be a farmer-based organisation, such as a co-operative possibly managing both its own
funds and those of an agricultural bank.

Access to credit and financial services is not always
confined to one agency in fact.  Simultaneously a project
authority may offer the farmer a consumption loan at virtually
zero-interest as a means of stimulating effort and gaining
collaboration, a crop marketing board may offer a crop seasonal
loan against distributed supplies, and an agricultural or other
bank may offer a long-term capital improvement loan.  But in

designing agricultural projects for small farmers, the planner -
especially in parts of Africa - may be confronted by the absence
of rural financial services available to the farmer and by
the need to develop the investment potential and productive
capacity of the farmer so that the provision of financial
services is worthwhile in the long-term.

In circumstances where formal credit services are newly-
established, the main organisational question is whether credit
should be a separate, ancillary service supporting prior farm
innovations or whether it should be integrated into the
package of inputs aimed at inducing change at the farm level.
On the face of it, the case for integration - and a multi-
purpose agency approach - is very strong where a project is
concerned with an intervention in the process of production
which has to be sustained over a period of, say, 10 - 15 years.
Experience in small farmer development points overwhelmingly
to the failure of separate government agencies to co-ordinate
several different inputs.  Where a programme requires a sequence
of supporting activities - for example, land clearing, seed
purchase, credit, crop spraying, collection - there are likely
to be a number of points where delays or inadequacies due to
poor co-ordination undermine the confidence of the farmer in
the public sector delivery capability, especially if the farmer
is expending considerable time in attempting to chase up several
different agencies to provide promised inputs and services.
A multi-functional agency, in theory at least, has the advantage
of ensuring co-ordination of services and reducing the opportunity costs of the farmer in arranging his own supplies.

From the perspective of credit delivery, a multi-
functional agency also has the advantages of information and
control.  The information that is required concerns the
*need* for credit, the prospects of credit being used, directly
or indirectly, for increased production (i.e. the farmer's
investment prospects) and the other inputs which are necessary
to ensure effective use of credit.  When the farming community
reaches a more advanced stage of development and has a greater

degree of self-reliance, and creditworthiness, such questions
do not need to be investigated at length by lending agencies:
the farmer's demand for credit will be based upon his own
calculations which the lending agency learns to respect.
Under such circumstances, credit becomes simply one among
a number of separate service functions upon which the farmer
draws at his own expense.This would suggest as a general rule
that interventionist strategies require a multi-purpose agency;
but for strategies which are 'facilitative' and where the onus
is upon the individual farmer, there are advantages in using a
number of single purpose specialist agencies, including credit.

This general rule seems particularly appropriate where
control over the use of credit is necessary.  In an integrated
approach to small farmer development, ideally there is a flow
of production activities held together by a service organisation
with a single purpose, with credit linked to extension, to
supplies, to marketing etc.  The security of a loan is therefore
established at certain control points in the flow of activities:
planting, harvesting, marketing etc.[3] Operationally this means
that the functions of a loans officer in a specialist agency
are shared between a number of other officers (possibly settlement, extension, processing, marketing officers, etc).

In most rural development projects of this type, credit
is regarded as integral to the project and is not a separate
function.  This approach often means that the existing agricultural banking system is deliberately insulated from the
project, with the problems of high transaction costs, low
repayment security and possibly low-interest rates becoming the
responsibilities of the project alone.  This is less of a
problem where the project evolves into a directly-managed crop
scheme under a permanent authority which is able to reduce
gradually its management costs and raise the costs of borrowing
to commercial levels (possibly by transferring the subsidy
element more towards input or product prices).  But in rural
development projects where the nature and value of the crop,
or crops, produced does not warrant the establishment of a

permanent crop authority, there are limitations to the
multi-purpose agency approach.

Firstly, if credit is regarded as simply one component
of a system of delivery, the long-term objective of developing
viable rural financial institutions can be lost sight of.
This is particularly true in areas where there is a poor record
of service provision and agricultural production. In such
circumstances, it is accepted that the management costs of
loan provision should not fall upon the small farmer but should
be considered as part of overall project costs. The specific
tasks of promoting farm savings and establishing the overall
creditworthiness of the individual farmer are likely to be
subsumed in more general objectives of increasing production
in as short a time as possible, or in gaining farmer support
for new technologies.

Secondly, the integration of credit into a multi-functional
agency can have deleterious effects upon other services. In
many projects, the major credit function becomes, in due course,
loan recovery. This clearly inhibits the efficacy of the
extension effort if the two are closely related. Furthermore,
the initial process of loan application necessarily involves
staff in investigative activities which in many rural societies
are unlikely to enhance a confident working relationship between
the field staff and the farmer.

These limitations are important when considering the major
problem of multi-functional project agency approaches to credit
service provision: the question of eventual organisational
form. In attempts to develop marginal or under-exploited areas,
projects will either organise their own credit services, or
subsidise existing services by bearing transaction costs. The
costs of managing credit are likely to be very high, and
continually rising, as more farmers are brought into the project's
area of operations. In areas of high potential, it is possible
that in due course the level of agricultural production will
allow the multi-purpose project agency to withdraw from credit

provision altogether and allow specialist credit institutions
to take over.  Another alternative is to retain the multi-
functional agency approach, but to transfer much of the
responsibility to farmers' organisations  with extension,
credit and marketing functions.

In practice however, these options do not always present
themselves, and having set up a multi-functional organisation
involved in several aspects of service provision and production support, it is difficult to transfer particular
functions, and the organisation becomes increasingly expensive
to administer.  The likelihood is that in due course the
agency either contracts or fails to expand its operations and
the services that it provides are directed more and more to
those who are already in a position to take advantage of
co-ordinated delivery, and are less costly to administer.

*Organisation at the Village Level and Below*

There are several alternative structures which a credit-
providing agency can have at the local or primary level
(which may be roughly equated with the village or a group
of villages).  The broad character of institutions at this
level is influenced by three main factors: a) whether they
are single-purpose or multi-purpose; b) whether they are
managed exclusively by professional specialists or farmers'
representatives with the assistance of professionals; and
c) whether  they lend directly to individual farmers or to
small 'functional' borrower groups.  This provides a choice
between four distinct types of institution, each of which
may have the option of lending to individuals or to groups:

- single-purpose, professionally managed (eg the branch
  office of a commercial or agricultural bank);

- multi-purpose, professionally managed (eg Farmers'
  Service Centre);

- single-purpose, jointly managed: ie farmer and
  professional staff (eg credit co-operative);

- multi-purpose, jointly managed (eg multi-purpose co-
  operative).

Institutions at the secondary level, whose function is
to provide services and supervision to the primary institution,
are professionally managed in most cases, and the relative
merits of single-purpose and multi-purpose institutions under
professional management have already been discussed.

This section is therefore primarily concerned with joint
management at the primary level. It explores three main
issues: 1) the merits of primary co-operative institutions,
whether single- or multi-purpose, *vis a vis* their professionally managed counterparts; 2) the relative advantages of
single-purpose and multi-purpose co-operatives; and 3) the
possibilities of developing functional groups as a means of
strengthening the effectiveness of rural lending programmes
in general. Each of these issues involves discussion of
some aspect of farmer grouping. It is therefore useful to
begin by looking briefly at the main arguments which have been
advanced in favour of developing farmer groups generally (not
only in the context of credit provision) and at the conditions
which need to be met if the formation of such groups is to
be successful.

It is commonly argued that the stimulation of farmers'
groups of some kind is an essential component of rural development. First, they are needed to extend the coverage of
development services as comprehensively as possible: with very
large populations of small farmers and a scarcity of manpower
resources, government services cannot be delivered unless
groups are established to provide an additional rung in the
administrative hierarchy. Secondly, group formation can give
small farmers longer-term social and political benefits by
stimulating their motivation 'to take an active and increasing
share in the design and management of their own development
process'.[4]

The main conditions for successful group formation and development may be briefly summarised. First, it must be possible through group action to secure a *'collective good'* - i.e. one which can benefit each individual member but which is realisable only if he collaborates with others in an organisation to obtain it. Secondly, the net private benefit to which each person is given access through membership of the group must exceed what he can obtain by any other means. Thirdly, the nature of the group's activity should be such that individuals, in pursuit of their own private benefits, are inclined to do so in a manner which benefits the group as a whole and promotes its long-term growth. Fourthly, each member of the group must agree to share the benefits it yields on the same terms as his fellows. Fifthly, there must be agreed sanctions to protect the group against external harassment or private exploitation by any of its own members. Finally, the group must be a size which is appropriate to its functions and the management capacity of its members.[5]

## Primary co-operative institutions and their alternatives

The use of village-level service co-operatives as a means of promoting the development of small farmers and the rural poor has recently come in for a great deal of criticism. In the post-independence periods, many governments had high expectations that co-operatives could be used to spearhead a process of rural transformation; but as a result of their manifestly poor performance, there has now been a widespread adverse reaction.

The chief criticisms which have been directed against past co-operative policies are:

- that their protagonists have attempted to impose a particular type of organisation with a sophisticated structure and rules, originating from nineteenth century European models,

on a wide variety of local social conditions, to most of
which it is quite unsuited;

- that the resulting institutions have been invested with
overambitious, confused and often conflicting social and
economic objectives;  and

- that they have rarely been supplied with adequate financial
and administrative resources to enable them to be successful
in achieving even a limited number of their intended
objectives.

Much of this criticism relates to the manner in which co-
operatives have been used and only part of it to their intrinsic
structural characteristics.  It is wrong to criticise co-
operatives *per se* for weaknesses in performance which are
attributable to bad policies or inadequate finance and administrative manpower.  For example, co-operatives' performance
has tended to be notably poor where the leading function given
to them has been the provision of credit, often at highly
subsidised rates.  What we should be concerned to ask is whether,
in a particular set of circumstances, any other form of institution, using the same resources of finance and manpower, could
perform a particular function (in this case the provision of
credit) with better results.

The principal criteria to be used in making such institutional
comparisons should include the overall economic benefits
achieved (business efficiency), the extent to which benefits
are spread to poorer members of society (equity) and the amount
of popular participation in decision-making generated.

Policy and manpower weaknesses aside, several different
kinds of argument have been specifically directed against the
widespread use of co-operative institutions.  There is the
general argument that until any village has become relatively
commercialised it is unrealistic to expect a single 'representative'  institution to stimulate participation and business

efficiency.simultaneously. This is essentially an argument
about the different size of institution required for each of
these objectives: effective participation is nearly always
easier to achieve through group action at levels lower than
that of the village, whereas business efficiency usually
requires an organisation at the village level or above. Another
argument often closely associated with this one is that if
co-operatives are to be efficient business enterprises at the
early stages of development they require direction and close
supervision by professional managers with the necessary
commercial expertise. This obviously undermines one of the
main purposes of co-operatives, which is that the members should
have a major say in decision-making.

But the most powerful arguments against village-level
co-operatives relate to their use in those rural societies
which are markedly inegalitarian and/or sectionally divided.
In these cases, one would expect such institutions to fail on
all counts - participation, equity in the distribution of
benefits, and business efficiency; and there is abundant
evidence that this is indeed what happens. In the absence of
legislation or other administrative action specifically designed
to prevent it, the leading positions within the co-operatives
are inevitably captured by the local elites, who then try to
use them as a means of perpetuating or even strengthening their
own influence. These arguments do not always apply: in some
circumstances, even where social stratification is fairly
marked, technical factors and the nature of the co-operative's
commercial activities can to some extent counteract the effects
of social bias - as for example in the case of the marketing
and processing co-operatives for cotton, milk and sugar in
Gujarat and Maharashtra. [6]

What implications do these arguments have for institutional
choice? Clearly, the greater the inequalities and divisions
within a local society, the greater the difficulty of devising
any kind of institutional form which is likely to work
satisfactorily. In all contexts, there must be a point in the

spectrum of inequality beyond which no amount of institutional tinkering is likely to produce any significant change in the existing power structure; only a radical redistribution of assets, through land reform especially, can do so. There are nevertheless many societies in which opportunities exist for assisting small farmers and other sections of the rural poor through the development of forms of local grouping specifically adapted to the needs of each environment.

There are two main approaches to providing such assistance. The first could be described as 'paternalist', and relies on a strengthening of the role of professional staff in 'community development' and co-operative organisation and management.

The principal functions of professional management are to encourage increasing member participation and create the conditions for eventual devolution of management responsibilities. In more unequal and factional societies the paternalist approach requires that co-operative forms of organisation are deliberately designed to minimise elite domination. For this strong technical and 'community development' advisory support has to be provided from the secondary level. Such an approach has been used, with substantial initial success, at Comilla, Bangladesh, and Daudzai, Pakistan, though experience in both cases has shown that where local power is very unevenly distributed political support from the highest level is essential for sustained development. Another alternative is a co-operative or quasi-cooperative organisation, again with very strong management support, whose membership is limited exclusively to smaller farmers (or some other target group).

The second approach rejects the village-level co-operative and instead advocates the formation and support of small functional groups. The two principal advantages claimed for small groups which have come together to perform a particular function is that they have a natural community of interest and that in unequal societies they are much less likely to be subjected to elite domination than a village-level,

committee-led organisation like a cooperative. Such groups
are discussed in more detail below.

*Single-purpose and multi-purpose co-operatives*

Single-purpose credit cooperatives have had a particularly
poor record in ldcs, whereas some multi-purpose cooperatives,
whose principal function has been marketing and processing but
which have also offered credit to their members, have been
more successful. Part of the credit cooperatives' performances
can be attributed to unhelpful policies, but it is also partly
the nature of the credit function itself: there are strong
*a priori* reasons why lending and borrowing are likely to provide
particularly insecure foundations on which to build any kind
of lasting successful group action.

The reasons lie with the motivation of the individual who
wishes to join the group. Where the principal purpose is to
acquire access to credit provided by a source external to the
group, his immediate over-riding interest is likely to be a
short-term private gain and he may have little concern about
the adverse effects which uncooperative behaviour (e.g. default
in repayment) may have on the long-term future of the group
as a whole. Moreover, in stratified and sectional societies
there is no identity of interest among the recipients of credit,
and access to it will tend to be used as a weapon by one sub-
group against another. With reference to cooperative credit
in India, Doherty and Jodha comment: "For large farmers it ...
represented patronage, and for small farmers it represented
independence. Local political/economic leaders sought through
faction-based societies to deny credit to their adversaries or
to those persons whom they wished to see continue as tenants
and agricultural labourers". [7]

By contrast, in the case of a marketing cooperative an
individual will benefit from membership only if it enables him

to get a better price for his product than an alternative
agency. This will not happen unless the group as a whole is
commercially successful and it will therefore be in his own
interest to seek ways of encouraging its long-term expansion
and increasing its market share.

This does not mean that multi-purpose marketing cooperatives
are universally to be preferred to single-purpose credit
cooperatives. There are many conditions, particularly in
predominantly food-crop areas with numerous markets outlets,
where cooperatives are notoriously difficult to establish
successfully. However, where conditions for their development
are favourable - e.g. where a cash crop requires local processing
and lends itself well to a vertically integrated system, or
where perishable fruit and vegetable crops are being cultivated
a long distance from the major consuming centres and transport
costs can be  sharply  reduced through cooperative action -
there are obvious advantages in linking the credit to the
marketing function. Besides the difference in basic motivation
which it inspires, it also ensures that an element of discipline
and control is built into the process of credit provision.
Loans are unobtainable unless members sell through their
cooperative organisation and loan recovery is made automatically
at the point of sale.

Where possibilities for the establishment of marketing
cooperatives are not promising, the best basis for credit
provision may be through a single-purpose cooperative, but
in that case success is more likely if the leading function
initially given to it is the encouragement of savings rather
than the provision of credit, and if savings are subsequently
made the condition on which loans are issued. This again
introduces discipline and control into the lender-borrower
relationship which is often missing from official credit
programmes: the borrower is more likely to respect a contract
with conditions than something which has the appearance of a
handout. A policy of high interest rates obviously assists in
this but there are numerous cases  where savings have successfully

been made the condition of credit provision even though
interest rates have not been high. In Comilla and Daudzai,
for example, credit was not provided at all until cooperative
members had demonstrated a firm commitment through several
years of regular weekly saving. 'Forced savings' programmes
of various kinds have also been used in parts of Africa. For
such programmes, however, where a high degree of externally-
induced discipline has to be imposed on the borrower, strong
paternalist management is needed, at least in their initial
stages.

*Small functional groups*

The main arguments for making much greater use of small
groups in agricultural development policy are based largely
on the observed success which spontaneously formed 'indigenous'
groups have had in performing a variety of functions for the
mutual benefit of their members. However, few attempts have
been made by governments either to incorporate existing groups
into their development programmes or to seek ways of stimulating
new ones. Much of the discussion of the potential role of
groups in rural development must therefore be speculative,
but it may be useful to identify some of the broad distinctions
between different types of group and to consider which of them
seem likely to offer the best foundations for use in future
official programmes, particularly for credit and savings
promotion.

The first distinction is between spontaneously formed, or
indigenous, groups and groups which have been induced as a
result of government action. Among the spontaneous groups
two types of function appear to be most common: savings and
credit; and the management of a shared common natural resource,
such as irrigation water or grazing land. Government-induced
groups cover a wider range of activities. Their purposes include
the provision of points of contact for agricultural extension,
the joint ownership of a new capital investment (eg a well

or a pumpset), the operation and maintenance of watercourse commands on large publicly-operated irrigation schemes, and the joint management of soil and water resources in rainfed catchment areas. Much less widespread have been small groups usually established on a pilot basis, specifically for the purpose of receiving and on-lending credit.

The possible merits of different approaches to group formation may be most simply indicated by examining a) the advantages and disadvantages of trying to link up with already established indigenous groups as against stimulating the development of new groups; and b) the advantages and disadvantages of trying to promote specialist borrowing and saving groups as against groups with multiple functions onto which borrowing and saving could be grafted.

There are two obvious advantages in trying to make use of existing groups. The first is that because they already exist governments do not need to incur the cost of establishing new ones - and, as Adams and Ladman have observed in the case of new borrowing groups, this cost may often be quite high.[8] The second advantage is that, by virtue of having been spontaneously created, indigenous groups (usually with a membership in the 10-30 range) have a community of interest. Common characteristics of indigenous saving and borrowing groups, most of which fall into the category of the 'rotating savings and credit association' (ROSCA), are that their primary focus is on savings; their procedures are simple and flexible, though there are effective mechanisms regulating membership eligibility, credit rating and repayment; and there are powerful sanctions against fraud and defaulting.[9]

The characteristics of indigenous irrigation groups are similar. These are found mainly in upland river valleys where physical conditions make it relatively simple for farmers to collaborate in constructing diversion weirs to irrigate small self-contained systems which they subsequently operate and maintain by themselves. Their common features include an

'accountable leadership' (group leaders are selected by members
of that group, their performance is periodically reviewed by
them, and they are compensated for their services directly
by the group); a high degree of 'management intensity' (each
irrigation system, though itself small, is usually subdivided
into smaller sub-units, each with its own leader); and
particularly where water is scarce, very stringent rules and
regulations, including fines for failure to contribute to
maintenance work and other misdemeanours.[10]

Despite their obvious attractions there are doubts as to
the importance of indigenous groups in rural development.
First, in a large number of environments, such groups do
not exist. In the case of RoSCAs, it is not clear what
conditions have been particularly favourable or unfavourable
to the formation of groups but a low level of capital formation
and a high level of social divisiveness would both seem likely
to act as serious hindrances. In the case of irrigation groups,
it is clear that a favourable physical environment is a very
important determinant. Once rivers or other water sources become
difficult for farmers to control themselves, only outside
agencies can carry out the necessary design and construction
work and there is no scope for the spontaneous emergence of
small self-contained groups. Careful analysis might reveal
that in the more 'difficult' development environments there
are in fact very few successful indigenous groupings in existence
which can be built upon.

A second doubt concerns their social composition. In the
case of groups whose principal common interest has developed
round activities like borrowing and saving one would expect
to find a socially homogeneous membership, with the relatively
prosperous featuring much more prominently than the small
farmers and other poorer sections. There appears to be
greater probability of social heterogeneity in groups which
are dependent on an area-based activity such as the sharing of
a common water source, since anyone whose land happens to fall
within the perimeter of the irrigable command area automatically

becomes a member of the group whatever the size of his holding.
If these assumptions are correct, the policy implications are
that in most social environments a group-based development
programme is unlikely to be effective in reaching small
farmers unless a) new common interest groups are created
specifically for small farmers and/or b) viable groupings
can be developed round activities like irrigation, soil con-
servation and common grazing which for success require farmers
to cooperate across existing social divisions. Except where
groups already exist, success in the latter case nearly always
calls for close official supervision and support.

A further point which must be borne in mind with regard
to indigenous groups is that any attempt to associate them
with an official programme will lead inevitably to some
change in the role and functions of the group; and there is
a danger that greater dependence on government will undermine
the self-reliance which has been the source of much of its
initial dynamism. This emphasises the need for considerable
sensitivity in allocating responsibilities between government
and groups. RoSCAs, in particular, demand creative treatment
if they are to be adapted as intermediaries for official credit
and savings programmes. They have, for example, substantial
flexibility with regard to timing of withdrawals and, in some
systems, there is no interest on savings.

## Conclusion

This review of alternative institutional patterns at the
village level is not conclusive and is not intended to be so.
Each environment is a combination of so many variables that
general prescriptions are impossible. The purpose of this
discussion has been to suggest the criteria on which choices
should be based and to indicate that the range of choice,
particularly with regard to different forms of farmer grouping,
is far larger than is usually contemplated by governments
or development agencies.

The main conclusion to be drawn about the potential
role of small groups in rural development programmes of any
kind is that far more detailed and systematic research needs
to be done if reliable and useful guidelines for official
administrative action are to be developed.  Anthropological
case studies of indigenous groups provide many valuable
insights but they also frequently fail to record information
about certain financial or technical aspects of the groups'
activities which would be vital to anyone wishing to assess
their potential role (if any) in an official programme.  In
the case of newly-formed groups very few attempts appear to
have been made to monitor their performance for the particular
purpose of developing better general criteria for the choice
of appropriate small group strategies.  The extent of our
ignorance on this very important subject may be partly
attributable to lack of interest in it in official government
and aid-giving circles - at least until recently;  but it also
reflects the scarcity of people within the development profession,
whether academics or consultants, who have been trained to
analyse complex institutional questions of this kind.

In examining credit programmes from the government agency
or project perspective, it is clear that one of the major
problems is that the objectives of different parties to a
programme are likely to differ and the relative weight given
to different priorities is likely to alter over time.  The
failure to make such objectives explicit in programme design
is perhaps one of the factors which has inhibited the development
of effective institutions for small farmer service delivery.
In terms of institutional choice, this 'objectives' problem
has implications for the role of credit in delivery and the
need to control the use of credit at the farm level. Questions
of 'style' of delivery, staffing levels and costs of delivery,
and the targets of credit programmes are further variables.  The
importance of all of these is commonly recognised but the
generally low performance of agricultural development programmes

with a credit component suggests that they are not taken
sufficiently into account in the design of projects and
service delivery.

1  For a discussion of this point, see Michael Lipton,
   "Agricultural Finance and Rural Credit in Poor Countries",
   *World Development*, Vol. 4, No. 7, 1976.

2  See H. Ruthenberg, "The Adaption of Agricultural Production Services to Changing Circumstances", *Agricultural
   Administration*, Vol. 4, No. 2, 1977.

3  For an example of the consequences of the failure to link
   the credit function to other input functions, see Alec
   Baird, "Extension and Credit in an Integrated Rural
   Development Project", *IDS Bulletin*, Vol. 10, No. 1, 1978.

4  Guy Hunter (ed), *Agricultural Development and the Rural
   Poor*, Overseas Development Institute, London, 1978.

5  These ideas are adapted from V. S. Doherty and N. S.
   Jodha, *Conditions for Group Action among Farmers*,
   Occasional Paper 19, Economics Program, ICRISAT,
   Hyderabad, 1977.

6  See, for example, N. S. Jodha, "A study of the co-operative
   short-term credit movement in selected areas of Gujarat",
   in G. Hunter and A. F. Bottrall (eds), *Serving the Small
   Farmer*, Croom Helm/Overseas Development Institute, London,
   1974.

7  Doherty and Jodha, *op. cit.*, p. 16.

8   D. W. Adams and J. R. Ladman, "Lending to rural poor
    through informal groups: a promising financial market
    innovation?", *Economics and Sociology Occasional Paper*,
    The Ohio State University.

9   For an excellent survey and analysis of ROSCAs, see
    F. J. A. Bouman, "Indigenous Savings and Credit Societies
    in the Third World - any message?", Paper to ADC
    Conference on Rural Finance Research, San Diego, Cali-
    fornia, 1977.

10  See E. W. Coward, "Irrigation management alternatives:
    Themes from indigenous systems", *Agricultural Administration*,
    Vol. 4, No. 3, 1977; also A. F. Bottrall, "Technology and
    management in irrigated agriculture", *ODI Review*, No. 2,
    1978.

APPLIED RESEARCH AND TRAINING IN
AGRICULTURAL CREDIT INSTITUTIONS

*R. A. J. Roberts*
*Agricultural Services Division*
*Food and Agriculture Organisation*
*Rome*

*Introduction*

When drawing up a plan for the structure of an
agricultural credit institution (ACI), there are some
obvious components: for example a loans department and
an accounts and administration section. Some ACIs also
require a separate recovery department; and if a savings
facility is operated then this too may warrant its own
section. But there are other functions which are not so
obviously appropriate or necessary for an ACI. (Two such
functions are *applied research* and *training*.) Sometimes
other departments have responsibility for research and
training, and in this case they often suffer from releg-
ation of importance. However, in many ACIs they are not
carried out at all on any systematic basis.

In this chapter arguments are put forward for an ACI
to have an applied research capability. A general scheme
is then set out for the organisation of training in an ACI,
together with some suggestions as to how this could be
supported by aid agencies. Then a method is outlined by
which these two functions - applied research and training -
can be carried out in an ACI so that credit performance
objectives can be more effectively identified and achieved.

*ACIs and Small Farmers*

Most lending institutions in any country would
claim that part of their portfolio is at, or approaches
the margin of, acceptable risk for their institution
and for their type of business. In the case of a typical commercial bank, the vast bulk of its portfolio
consists of reasonably sound loans, but at the margin
there would be a small number of rather speculative
loans at relatively high risk, earning a correspondingly
higher rate of interest. This situation does not apply
to ACIs in developing countries. The very nature of
the task of institutions lending to small farmers means
that not just a few, but the vast majority of its loans
are at (or even beyond) the margin of acceptable risk.

The margin of acceptable risk for loans to small
farmers is affected by the adequacy of information available to the lender. It is not possible to make sound
loans when realistic cost/benefit figures, obtained from
data on small farms themselves, are not known or when
they are estimates based on brave but foolish extrapol-
ation from research station or other inappropriate data.
A lack of this type of information can lead a bank to
excessive caution. This, in turn, causes either harmful
under-financing of the small farm sector or - in the case
of a bank with somewhat optimistic policies or management
- over-financing, which is equally undesirable as it
causes diversion of scarce resources.

The small farm sector is worthy of close inspection
by lending institutions. For, despite certain surface
appearances, small farmers can be efficient users of
capital. Moreover, when participating in suitably designed loans programmes, they are not noticeably worse at
repaying loans than are larger borrowers.

The lack of information about the small farm sector is also partly caused by a multi-factor gap between small borrowers and the officers of the lending institutions. The gap is caused by differences in education, income, way of life, housing, means of transport and exposure to other cultures. The differences may even include language; for example, in some North African countries, larger farmers and bank officials commonly use French; small farmers speak only Arabic. There have been some attempts to combine the professional efficiency of commercial banks with a 'village touch'; for example, in India, with the Regional Rural Banks, and by the Bank of Ghana, with its village (or rural) bank programme.

But, on the whole, ACI officials have much more rapport with large borrowers than with small farmers: arrangements of all types, including lending arrangements, can be made much more readily with larger farmers. The large borrower can be treated in a more traditional banking way as the realities of his type of operation are known or can be readily discovered.

To service the small farm sector, on the other hand, a bank needs both a close knowledge of viable types and scales of investment in small farms, and workable procedures for channelling investment funds to this sector and recovering these funds. These put particular demands upon the working of ACIs.

The small farm sector is not static. Crop and livestock enterprise possibilities change through developments in technology, in level of knowledge and education of farmers and because of market changes. Changes also occur in terms of feasible scale of operation and of cost and return figures. Moreover, because of development planning requirements, lending policies cannot always be

set down rigidly on a national basis. Terms and conditions of loans, and any necessary subsidies must be determined according to the need or otherwise to favour a
particular geographical area. Realistic loans programmes
for each area can only be drawn up on the basis of typical cost/return figures for particular categories of
farm. Data on these can only be obtained through field-
level surveys, since it is unrealistic and misleading
to estimate small farm production costs and returns on
the basis of research station trials data, even though
it is tempting to use such data when no other figures
are available.

An investigatory aspect of great potential value
to an ACI is the comparison of different lending systems,
in terms of cost per unit sum lent, cost per client,
recovery rate and, where possible, loan productivity.
Perhaps the most obvious comparison in small farm lending
operations is that between individual and group borrowing,
with further comparisons possible between various types
of groupings and operational procedures for dealing with
them. An obvious, but as yet little utilized method by
which an ACI can obtain the kind of information mentioned
above, is to establish a special applied research or
performance monitoring unit.

## Applied Research Units

An ACI is in a good position to obtain valuable
information through monitoring the operations of its
small farmer clients. By doing so it assists itself by
building up a knowledge of its clients and their potential
for viable credit-financed investment. It can also make
a valuable contribution to the national development effort
by providing information on the small farm sector, inform-

ation which may not otherwise be readily available to Government ministries or to other institutions.

The task of such a unit in an ACI would be some or all of the following types of investigation:

*Lending opportunities:* it would investigate the role of investment in a range of crop and livestock enterprises, including obtaining typical input/output data. In India this task is carried out by Crop Loan Technical Committees, which have representation from banks, farmers and appropriate Government departments. In many other countries ACIs have no such data base from which to work.

*Lending recovery methodology:* investigation here would include an appraisal of existing lending procedures with the provision of ideas for new situations such as an improved loan programme, lending to groups, lending to small farmers producing for a central processing plant, etc.

*Effect of lending policies (vis-a-vis national agricultural production targets):* the research here would involve close liaison with government development planning authorities in order to determine the potential and actual role of the agricultural bank in steering agricultural production towards various specified enterprise, varietal and quantitative goals.

An applied research unit within an ACI needs to operate through a number of different mechanisms. There should be direct monitoring of lending operations. This involves following closely the operations of the bank at head office, in branch offices, and above all, through sampling at farm

level on the farms of the bank's clientele. In addition,
an ACI can draw upon information obtained from Departments of Agriculture, research stations, from marketing
boards and agencies and from other non-bank sources within
a country. Finally, there should be exchange of experience with similar banks both in the same country and in
other countries. Such an exchange is the type of mechanism
facilitated by the regional agricultural credit associations recently established by the FAO in Asia and the
Pacific, the Near East and Africa. In this case the
exchange is effected through technical workshops and sem-
inars, through the exchange of personnel and through joint
programmes for staff.

It is not possible to set out an ideal structure for
an applied research or monitoring unit, for what is suitable will very much depend on the individual bank, its
size and the way in which it is presently structured.
Generally speaking, however, a research unit needs to
have two main characteristics.

First, it must be independent from the operational
section of the bank; second, it must be staffed with
persons who have sufficient outside experience and exposure to general developmental issues to enable them to
bring to bear an imaginative approach to the role of an
agricultural development bank. Such persons might be
expected to have a university training followed by practical experience in development planning, in an agricult-
urally-based commercial firm, or in a marketing board.
Conversely, the staff must not be so removed from practical
banking that they are unable to present recommendations
which are consistent with the necessary disciplines associated with accepting deposits and lending money.

*Training*

Training has had more general acceptance with ACIs
than has been the case with applied research. Most
ACIs have a training department or at least provide the
opportunity for staff to attend courses at local training
colleges and universities, or to participate in training
programmes such as those offered by the Economic Development Institute of the World Bank, the International
Co-operative Training Centre in Loughborough, FINAFRICA
in Milan and the Project Planning Centre, Bradford.

Senior level staff are more likely to be sent to
centres such as those listed above. The mass of employees
in the ACI, those who can probably aspire no higher than
field credit officer or district supervisor, have to rely
on local training.

A survey carried out in the 1970s by FAO (with the
support of Barclays Bank International Development Fund),
which involved 42 ACIs in a broad range of developing
countries, indicated that the training of junior and
medium level staff is generally weak. In only one institution of those surveyed, was there any systematic
training. In this case the policy was to use loan case
histories (especially case histories of problem loans)
as participatory training material.

There is probably no simple or single explanation
for the lack of satisfactory training in the other institutions. Part of the reason may be that agricultural
banking is not a technical area which flows naturally
from one of the traditional study disciplines. It is a
hybrid animal, requiring a background in agriculture,
farm management, banking and rural sociology.

This means that most experienced agricultural bankers come from a background in one or perhaps two of these subjects, and pick up the others on the job. The end result is not necessarily poor, but the process is time-consuming and reduces the numbers of fully-experienced persons in the field. Thus trainers in agricultural banking are not readily found, for essentially the task has to be carried out by a person with both the necessary technical knowledge and the ability to impart that knowledge.

The staff of an ACI are its most precious resource. The development implementation of effective personnel policies should therefore receive a great deal of attention from senior management. That this is not often the case is hardly surprising, for two reasons. First, this type of management concern is not easy in the risky or often loss-making environment of an ACI. Second, the senior management itself is frequently unclear as to the components of a desirable personnel policy. Such personnel policies cannot be suggested in detail, but invariably it is necessary to ask: 'do career prospects within the ACI depend to a large degree on competence, and do staff members have the opportunity to improve their competencies through systematic in-house training?'

*Regional Associations*

The regional agricultural credit associations established in recent years in Asia/Pacific, Africa, North Africa/Near East and the Caribbean provide a convenient means whereby ACIs can collaborate for senior level training. As mentioned earlier, much of the present senior-level instruction is carried out in developed countries. Whilst not decrying in any way the effect-

iveness of such courses, it is at the same time likely
that very useful supplementary courses can be developed
at the regional or sub-regional levels.

Indeed the regional agricultural credit associations
mentioned above have realised this and are, at present,
involved in establishing a number of sub-regional training
centres to permit courses to be held at intervals,
for senior staff of institutions from a group of neighbouring countries. Such centres are now being planned
for Poona, Amman, Nicosia and Dar-es-Salaam with further
centres likely in South East Asia, South West Pacific,
Coastal West Africa, Central Africa, Sahelian zone and
the Caribbean.

Although the overall shape of such courses will be
determined locally, they are likely to be on specific
technical subjects where some outside assistance is highly
desirable. Topics might include: the management of staff,
control of fraudulent practices, setting up specifically-
targeted lending programmes.

*Applied Research and Training*

We now turn to the linkages between applied research
and training departments. Effective on-the-job training
is largely a combination of two factors. Firstly, the
identification of suitable technical material to be taught,
in the same sense that it is relevant to the immediate
post-work performance, and secondly, the imparting of this
knowledge on the basis of what is already known and accepted
by the trainee.

The second factor is simply sound instructional
practice. The first requires a special effort by the

176

employing institution.  This effort has to be directed
both to the modification of existing training materials
and courses, and to the formulation of new material.
The scope and need for this modification of existing
material and the generation of new material are greater
than is sometimes realised.  Virtually every ACI is
faced with a set of problems peculiar to its area of
operations and to similar areas.

Consider the following examples:

- large-scale smuggling of hypothecated farm produce
  from a border district to an adjoining country;

- a large proportion of the potential clientele, in
  a given area, being nomads;

- a history of poor repayment followed by writing-
  off debts by a Government decree;

- difficult terrain greatly hindering communication
  between bank and clients and thus affecting all
  banking operations;

- a Government establishing a cotton mill and charging
  the bank with the task of quickly promoting cotton
  production so that the mill can have sufficient
  throughput to be viable;

- large numbers of borrowers being involved with
  local money lenders.

These problems are just a sample from countries as
diverse as Papua New Guinea, Bangladesh, Greece, Somalia,
Ghana and Zambia.  All require special instruction to staff
if the effects of the problem are to be minimised or the

performance objective achieved.

Initially, considerable work must be carried out by applied research personnel. This would be followed by researchers/trainers jointly preparing specific training programmes. Finally the course programme would be implemented and on-the-job performance of trainees monitored.

Most general credit issues also deserve action by both researchers and trainers to ensure that performance priorities, outlined broadly by management can be tackled effectively by the operational units of the bank. Input material for training courses on general issues can usually be generated by the on-going monitoring of lending operations and the borrowers' use of loaned funds.

During the survey referred to above, the training which appeared to be most effective was that carried out by the Bank Pertanian Malaysia. Here the basis of training course material was a set of case histories of problem loans. Trainees considered each case in detail, making and discussing suggestions as to what the ACI might have done in order to assist the farmer make productive use of the loan on the one hand, and help the bank safeguard its portfolio on the other.

Whilst an applied research unit within a bank provides the information necessary to bring about improvements in bank operations, effective implementation of new loans programmes, better lending operations and improved loan recovery procedures depend to a large degree on the ability of staff to handle them. Specific short training courses based on material generated by the applied research unit are the obvious remedy.

AGRICULTURAL CO-OPERATIVES AND CREDIT

B. J. Youngjohns
*Overseas Development Administration*
*London*

*Introduction*

Among developing countries, the co-operative movement
originated in India around the turn of the century. At the
time, a conscious decision was taken to give priority to
Agricultural Co-operative Credit Societies, loosely based
on the Raiffeisen model in Germany. The Rochdale system,
which had been so successful in Britain since 1844, was
rejected as being more suitable for urban than rural conditions and as being too sophisticated for India. The
introduction of co-operatives to India was seen, in fact,
primarily as an instrument for dealing with the problem of
credit. It was one of a series of policy decisions which
followed in the wake of the Famine Commission of 1880,
including the Land Improvements Act of 1883 and the
Agriculturalists' Loans Act of 1884, setting up the "takkavi"
system. The first Law providing for the registration of
co-operatives was the Co-operative Credit Societies Act of
1904 and, as its name implies, provided only for co-operative
credit societies.

The manner in which co-operatives were first introduced
in India has set a pattern which has been followed throughout
the Third World. The Co-operative Societies Act of 1912

permitted the registration of other types of co-operative,
and became a model for co-operative legislation throughout
the former British dependencies and in many other countries
as well. It set the pattern of a co-operative movement
under the supervision of a government department, headed
by a Registrar of Co-operative Societies. Moreover, it
set the pattern of co-operatives as instruments for public
policy rather than as worthwhile institutions in themselves.
This "instrumental" approach to co-operatives has persisted
and has been taken up by planning and development offices
and by the bilateral and international aid agencies. In
some countries, co-operatives have been introduced to
supply agricultural inputs or market produce, rather than
credit, but the approach is the same. In the Indian sub-
continent, the credit base to the movement has survived.

The central contention of this paper is that, no
matter how worthy the intentions, the instrumental approach
to co-operatives is mistaken, and is the root cause of
failure and disappointment. It misconstrues the fundamental
principles on which a co-operative is based. The allegation
that the colonial powers uncritically tried to transplant
an organisational form from industrial Lancashire to rural
India and Africa, misses the point altogether. This is
precisely what they did *not* do - if they had done so, the
result might well have been better. To develop this
argument further, it is necessary to review the basic
principles of co-operative organisation.


*Co-operatives as Businesses*


A co-operative is a voluntary, democratically-controlled
association of people with the specific purpose of conducting
some kind of business. Voluntary associations are established
for all kinds of social, political, cultural, recreational

or defensive purposes. A co-operative differs from all the others in being an association especially set up for the purpose of going into business. Furthermore, once established and registered, the co-operative becomes a body corporate, with perpetual succession, which means that it has an identity of its own, separate from that of its individual members. In one sense, a co-operative belongs to the class of voluntary associations: in another sense, it belongs to the class of business organisations. There are many types of business organisation, from one-man firms, through family firms, partnerships, private companies to public companies and nationalised corporations. Co-operatives constitute another type within this general class of businesses. They differ from the others only in the manner in which they are owned, raise capital and distribute profits. The purpose of establishing a co-operative is to apply principles of voluntary association to business.

The essence of a co-operative business is that it is owned by its members, who are either its customers or (in the case of workers' co-operatives) its employees. Concentrating on the former it follows that, since the members are the customers, and the customers are the members, the co-operative must be concerned with promoting, not only its own business interest, but also that of its members. This is not an ethical proposition: it is a matter of logic. It would be illogical for a person to be a member of a co-operative which conducted its business against his interests: it would be equally illogical for the co-operative to favour the members at its own expense. There are, of course, plenty of examples where a co-operative does conduct its business contrary to the interests of its members and vice-versa. The point being made is that in both cases, this is an offence against logic rather than against ethics. A co-operative which makes a large profit by underpaying for its members' produce or one which overpays its members and makes a loss are both

behaving illogically.  A balance has to be maintained: a
co-operative should aim to be a sound business, but not at
the expense of its members; and it should promote its
members' interests, but not at the expense of its own
business.


## Co-operatives and Profit

The test of success in business is profitability.  It
is sometimes argued that a co-operative does not make a
"profit", because this can only be made by one person out
of another and the members of a co-operative cannot be
said to make a profit out of themselves.  In co-operatives,
profit is frequently referred to as "surplus".  Either way,
it must be made.  A co-operative which runs at a loss is
not a successful business and will not survive, without
external support.

Profit or surplus in a co-operative is (i) ploughed back
as reserves, (ii) paid out as a limited flat rate dividend
on share capital and (iii) distributed to the members as a
patronage bonus.  When operated properly, this system has
great economic strength.  It provides for interest to be
paid on capital, sufficient to attract investment in shares;
it builds up reserves and, through the patronage bonus, it
attracts custom.  If the members are encouraged to leave some
of the patronage bonus on deposit, this is a further method
of building up capital.  In order to be profitable in the
first place, and bearing in mind the need to keep a balance
between the co-operative's interests and that of its members,
the co-operative should operate at normal market prices.

An examination of the record of co-operatives in
developing countries shows how often these basic principles
concerning the profitability of co-operatives have been

disregarded - because of the instrumentalist approach
adopted. Marketing co-operatives have been required to
operate narrow margins laid down by marketing boards and
governments, while credit co-operatives have always been
required to lend at artificially low rates of interest.

*Open Membership*

The principle of open membership has been misconstrued
widely. It does not mean that any co-operative must be
wide open to anyone who wants to join: what the principle
really means is that a co-operative should not do business
with, or give services to, persons who are debarred from
membership. Again, this is a matter of logic and not ethics.
If a co-operative habitually trades with persons debarred
from membership, it ceases to be a co-operative within the
definition of the word and becomes a kind of company instead.
The members are making a "profit" out of the non-members.
That is all the principle of open membership - which originally
applied to consumer co-operatives - ever meant. It is frequently enforced by law, because otherwise a co-operative
could be a device for evading tax.

There is no reason why a co-operative should not restrict
its membership to defined classes of persons such as small
farmers, fishermen, or residents in a particular village,
provided it does not give regular services to persons outside
these groups. The Credit Union Movement has the concept of
the "common bond", which means that membership should be
open and confined to particular classes of person, such as
the employees of a particular company or department, or the
inhabitants of a particular neighbourhood. The principle
of the common bond could be much more widely applied. The
complaint that rich farmers are allowed to dominate village
co-operatives could be met by establishing the common bond
as all farmers with less than (say) five acres of land.

*Co-operatives and the Law*

Co-operatives are legally constituted bodies, registered
under the Co-operative Societies Act. Registration makes
them bodies corporate, necessary for sound business practices.
Unregistered, informal associations are best for doing
informal things, but are at serious legal disadvantage for
the conduct of business, such as borrowing and lending,
buying and selling. The Co-operative Societies Act is
mainly concerned to prescribe the fundamental principles
and to require any co-operative registered to conform to them.
For example, most Acts lay down that a proportion of net
profit or surplus must be carried to reserves, that interest
on shares must be at a limited rate and that any other
surplus must be distributed as a patronage bonus.

Administration of the law, following the precedent of
the Indian Act, is vested in a government department headed
by a Registrar of Co-operative Societies.[1] He is, in fact,
much more than a Registrar: he is also expected to provide
supervision, assistance, counsel and control. This peculiar
relationship between a government official and an independent
movement originated in the paternalism of colonial rule and
has survived into the era of state planning and intervention.
There has been a marked tendency to strengthen the powers of
the Registrar.[2] The Registrar has been given powers to
approve or disapprove expenditure, remove committees from
office, appoint managers, order amalgamations and so on.
Combined with the "instrumentalist" approach, excessive
bureaucratic control tends to produce a kind of hybrid
between the public and private sectors. Practice varies
greatly, however, from one country to another, and nowhere
is the trend completely irreversible. Recognition that co-
operatives ought to be independent, profitable businesses
is, in fact, regaining ground.

*Credit as Business*

Much of the discussion heard on the subject of credit gives the impression that it is some kind of charity or system of welfare. In fact, credit in its very essence, is a commercial concept. Banks allow credit, because they make profits from the interest earned. Merchants give credit because it increases the demand for their wares. Introducing charitable or welfare considerations into credit is bad for both lender and borrower. If there is a case for "helping" small farmers, over and above what is commercially sensible, it should be done by grants and subsidies, and not by credit. Credit belongs to commerce and should be practiced only if it can be made a commercial success. The real question then is not whether co-operatives can be used as instruments to get credit to the people but under what conditions can co-operatives make credit into successful business.

*Single Purpose Credit*

The original credit co-operative introduced into India at the turn of the century was the Primary Agricultural Co-operative Society (PACS) whose sole purpose was to make loans. Later, the Co-operative Land Mortgage Banks or, as they are now called, Land Development Banks (LDB) were introduced to make long-term loans against mortgage security. In some countries, primary co-operatives make both short and longer-term loans, but remain single-purpose credit societies. They do nothing else except lend money. The members may contribute minimal amounts of share capital, but do not use the societies for savings. The essence of the societies is collective borrowing. The principle behind them is that a group of small farmers, legally constituted as a co-operative society, can borrow on better terms, can shoulder some of the costs of loan administration and can offer better security

186

than the individuals borrowing on their own account.

In a paper of this length it is not possible to set
out the massive evidence, but it can hardly be denied that,
after nearly a century of experience, single-purpose credit,
under *any* institution (and not only co-operatives), is not
good *business*.  The record of direct government loans,
whatever the lending mechanism, all tell the same story of
overdues, default and losses.  In fact, the only mechanism
to have made a success of credit is the much-maligned
village money lender, and  even he is usually in other
businesses as well.

These are some of the reasons why small farm credit is
a commercial loser:-

- *High administrative costs*.  The work involved in
  appraising, supervising, recording and recovering
  a small loan is not much less than doing so for a
  larger one.  Proportionately, the cost is very much
  higher.  While bank branches may carry a few small
  loans and absorb the costs along with those of their
  normal business, they would need great increases of
  staff to be able to cope with large numbers.

- *High risk*.  Small farmers are bad risks.  They are
  unlikely to have a good money sense, do not keep
  accounts, are under social and family pressures to
  mix up the farm money with their own, and they are
  prone to disasters, such as crop failures, sickness
  and death.  They have few resources to cushion them
  and little to offer as collateral security.

- *Lack of Equity Involvement*.  With single-purpose
  credit, irrespective of the institution handling
  it, the borrowers have little or no equity stake
  themselves, and therefore no sense of personal

responsibility.  In single-purpose credit co-operatives
and similar institutions, loans are approved by
committees who have no financial stake in what they
are doing.

- *Low Interest Rates*.  Either because the borrower
  cannot pay more or because of political and moral
  pressure, interest rates are usually below cost.[3]

- *Infrequent Cash Flow*.  The secret of a successful
  financing business is a regular and strong cash flow.
  Commercial banks thrive on fluctuating overdrafts
  with frequent, even daily, deposits and withdrawals.
  Short term small farm credit means one trickle out
  before ploughing and (if lucky) a trickle back after
  the harvest.  No business can be viable on this basis.

It is hardly surprising that large numbers of single-
purpose credit societies have failed.  There is, simply,
not the basis for a commercial operation.  It is significant
that even in Botswana, where consumer and marketing co-operatives have been conspicuously successful, the experiment
in single-purpose agricultural credit societies was a failure.[4]

The single-purpose credit society, and its variants,
are consequences of two errors.  Firstly, co-operatives
are seen as instruments of government policy, and not
businesses in their own rights.  Secondly, it is held that
the simplest forms of organisation are the easiest to run.
In business, this is conspicuously untrue.  If there is a
hot summer, what the shopkeeper loses on the sale of
umbrellas he makes up on the sale of swimsuits, provided
he is in both businesses.  In business, diversification (up
to the limits imposed by management capacity) produces
strength: it spreads the costs and it spreads the risk.

The single-purpose credit society, conceived as an
instrument of government policy, has done very serious harm
to the co-operative movement.  The overwhelming majority of
individual society failures are either single-purpose credit
societies or those, although nominally diversified, which
are mainly in business for credit.  What is more, their bad
reputation has affected and hindered other types of co-operative.  Finally, their recurrent delinquency has provoked an
official reaction of throwing in more and more supervisors
and controllers, which has not only been self-defeating, but
has enveloped the entire co-operative movement in government
bureaucracy.

*Savings and Credit (Credit Unions)*

Nowadays, the best known savings and credit co-operatives
are the credit unions, and it is convenient to use that term.
Like the single-purpose societies, the credit unions owe their
origin to the Raiffeisen movement.  They differ radically,
however, in that they are firmly based on regular savings by
the members.  The collectively-owned savings constitute a
fund from which the members can borrow.  As in an ordinary
bank, the underlying principle is that not everyone borrows
at the same time.  The security for loans is the savings of
the borrower plus those of up to two other members whom he
can persuade to act as guarantors.  Under this system, the
credit union is fully covered.

Once they become well established, credit unions use
more conventional forms of security, such as committee scrutiny
of 'character', and collateral.  Interest on loans is trad-
itionally fixed at 1% per month, a rate which, at least until
recent inflation, was more than adequate to make the union
profitable.  When a profit is made, it is handled in accordance
with co-operative principles.

The Credit Union Movement is based in North America
and has procedures codified with characteristic thorough-
ness.  The Credit Union National Association (CUNA) is a
vigorous and enterprising organisation with a strong
interest in developing credit unions overseas.  There
has been very considerable success in exporting credit
unions to Latin America and the Caribbean, where credit
unions are the most conspicuously successful of all co-
operatives.  They have, more recently, been introduced into
Africa and there is evidence, for example in Cameroon and
Lesotho, that they can be made to work.  Education is
an important part of the preparatory work, and the standard-
ised procedures and record-keeping systems facilitate
training.  Advice is readily available from CUNA and through
the World Organisation of Co-operative Credit Unions (WOCCU),
and there is an insurance service to safeguard loans.

In some countries, for example Fiji and the UK, credit
unions have a special law, but the more common practice
is for them to be registered under the ordinary co-operative
law.  They are very jealous of their independence and, in
most countries, have successfully resisted encroachments
by the bureaucracy.  Where they are registered as co-operatives, the Registrar is responsible for audit, inspection,
arbitration in disputes and for ensuring that they operate
in accordance with the provisions of the law but, otherwise,
he does not usually interfere.

It would be a mistake to claim *too* much for credit
unions, because they have their limitations, and there
have been failures.  Nevertheless, they make much better
commercial sense than the single-purpose credit societies
and, in the countries where they have become established,
they are among the best examples of non-state enterprise
by the less well-off sections of the population.  While
credit unions have received some state aid, this has been

much less than for many other, less successful, organisations; and it is significant that they are reasonably well-managed, without excessive government supervision.

The real debate about credit unions is not whether they work or not, but whether they are really suitable *for agricultural* credit. The largest and most successful credit unions have been either urban-based, or based upon salaried groups in rural areas. The system of regular savings works best among regular wage earners, especially where arrangements can be made for savings, and loan repayments, to be deducted from the payroll. Where this is not possible, the members have to bring in their savings voluntarily and this inevitably produces a weaker performance. Small farmers do not receive a regular income, and the organisation of regular savings and loan repayments is much more difficult. Nevertheless, there is some evidence (from Cameroon and Lesotho for example) that credit unions can be made to work in rural areas. The core membership may well be school-teachers, civil servants and the like, but small farmers can be brought in. There are difficulties, of course, in making loans for agricultural purposes where credit is risky. Farmers do not find it easy to persuade other members to act as guarantors, and with good reason. Nevertheless, in some countries (for example in Belize and Lesotho) a determined effort is being made to involve credit unions in agricultural production.

Another problem derives from the very nature of credit unions themselves. Their undoubted success is explained by the fact that the members have a financial stake in the credit union. Individuals on committees who approve loans know that their own money is at risk. This very self-sufficiency makes it difficult to use credit unions as instruments for government credit policies. If a credit union raises a large external loan, its self-reliance is

undermined.  Obviously, the aggregate guarantees available
cannot exceed the total amount of self-owned resources.
External loans cannot be covered by guarantee, but must
have some, probably less satisfactory, form of security.
If the external money greatly exceeds the self-owned resources,
there is a danger that credit unions will go the same way as
single-purpose credit societies.  There have been examples
where the performance of credit unions with their own money
has been so impressive  that aid agencies have swamped them
with external funds and brought about their bankruptcy.
This is not to argue that credit unions should not receive
any external aid: only that there must be a reasonable ratio
between external and internal funds.  Another approach to
external funds would be to use credit unions, with their
intimate knowledge of their members and their skill in
managing loans, as agents for credit schemes, without
saddling them with the whole of the risk.


*Multi-Purpose Co-operatives*


     A multi-purpose co-operative is one which provides two
or more different classes of service to its members.  There
are a number of possible combinations, but the relevant one
for this discussion is the co-operative for credit, input
supply and marketing.  The member is supplied with fertiliser
and other inputs on credit before planting, and, after the
harvest, delivers his crop to the co-operative, which deducts
the loan from the proceeds, before paying him the balance.
In the better-organised, such as the coffee co-operatives
in Kenya, there is also a deposit system, so that the member's
passbook account is active throughout the year.  It goes
into the black after the harvest when the proceeds are credit-
ed to his account; withdrawals follow until around the time
of planting and the purchase of inputs when the passbook goes
into the red, where it remains until the next harvest.

While there is much to be said for the multi-purpose
co-operative (and there are plenty of examples where it has
been made to work) it is by no means fool-proof. It depends
upon either the members having no alternative to marketing
their produce back through the co-operative from which they
got a loan, or on their being sufficiently enlightened and
disciplined to do so. There are two provisions in the co-
operative law which ought to help. The first is the so-
called "binding clause" in terms of which a member of a
marketing co-operative can be obliged to dispose of all his
produce through that co-operative; the second is the provision for "first charge", in terms of which a co-operative
has the first charge over any asset, created directly or
indirectly by a loan. A crop counts as an asset created
by a loan for agricultural inputs. Combined, the two provisions, in effect, constitute a crop lien.

It is frequently argued that the crop is useful as
security only if there is one-channel marketing. This view
is too extreme. The multi-purpose co-operatives in the
Gambia do *not* have sole purchasing rights over the crop, but
do have a consistently high record of loan recovery. On the
other hand, even when there is single-channel marketing,
there are still means of evasion for the borrower determined
to default. He can send the produce to the co-operative in
someone else's name; he can send it to a different co-
operative; he can even send it across the border into a
neighbouring country. In spite of these difficulties, the
multi-purpose system is less insecure than most others, and
ought to be persevered with. There is evidence, too, that
this is a field in which education can help. Members can
learn that it is not in their long-term interests to dodge
repayment.

While the security argument is the one mostly quoted,
and sometimes challenged, for the multi-purpose system,

there is another argument in favour. The diversity of
operations makes for a much more viable business. The costs
of management are spread over a wider range of activities.
A full-time book-keeper can be afforded. There is a much
more consistent cash flow. If credit is seen, as it should
be, as a part of the whole business enterprise, some of the
risk can be absorbed as operating costs on the supply and
marketing business. After all, this is what all other businesses do. If multi-purpose co-operatives give credit,
they should do so as part of a profit-making business and
calculate the risk as a cost.


*Security and Loan Discipline*

   The original agricultural credit societies had unlimited
liability. This meant that when a society went into liquid-
ation, the members could be forced by the liquidator to
contribute from their own resources sufficient to pay all
the society's debts. In practice, it hardly ever happened.
With societies of limited liability, it is frequently the
practice to enforce some kind of collective responsibility
by not allowing a society to have a new loan until it has
paid a stipulated proportion of its previous debts.

   While some kind of discipline is necessary, this has
the disadvantage of punishing the good payers along with the
bad. Furthermore, where the co-operative is treated as an
instrument of credit policy, it has the consequence of
putting other channels of credit out of action. If the other
institutions also have overdues, as they will, the same
discipline will have to be applied to them, with the consequence that the whole credit system will stop operating.
Artificial and arbitrary limits are, of course, a product
of artificial and subsidised credit. The proper way to
judge a co-operative is in business terms. Overdue debt

may be perfectly respectable, provided the co-operative has
the reserves to carry it. Persistent debt, however, is
evidence of commercial failure and such co-operatives are
not worth further credit.

Some types of security, such as crop liens and guarantors
have already been mentioned. Among others are land, chattel
mortgages, character assessment and penal sanctions. Land
is normally used as security for long-term loans, either to
purchase land, or to pay for improvements such as irrigation,
permanent crops and buildings. While, theoretically, land
provides complete security, in practice it is not easy to
realise. If there is default, the institution may become
the proprietor of land which it cannot sell. There may be
great political difficulties in repossession, for the repossession and sale of land may lead to retrograde redistribution from the poor to the better-off. Meanwhile, the
cash flow of the lending institution is stopped.

Chattel mortgages have mostly been used for urban credit,
but could be used for farmers as well, especially when the
loan is paying for something durable, such as a piece of
agricultural machinery. Under co-operative law, a lending
society can simply take a first charge over it. Character
assessment is frequently used by credit unions and is likely
to be effective provided the persons assessing character
have their own money at stake. Penal sanctions are not so
much a form of security in themselves, as a reinforcement of
other forms, particularly the "binding clause" and the first
charge. They can operate either against the borrower, in
which case it is usually necessary to prove deliberate or
fraudulent evasion or, more likely, against other traders,
who can be forbidden to purchase produce already pledged
to a co-operative.

It is a curious fact that while there are several
potentially effective systems of security, there is a
widespread reluctance to enforce them. Under co-operative
law, a society can refer a debt to the Registrar as a
dispute, and can get an award which has the force of a
court judgement. The legal framework is comprehensive.
The failure to make use of it can only be explained by
the fact that the money on loan does not usually belong
to the society itself, but has come from a government
agency. When a co-operative is run as a members' business,
it has a normal business's motivation to collect its debts
and improve its cash flow.


*Rate of Interest*

The "Rochdale" principle of trading at current market
prices and distributing any resultant profit or surplus as
a patronage bonus, has hardly ever been applied to agricultural credit. If it had been the original agricultural
credit societies would have charged the same rate as the
money-lender, and possibly made a large profit which would
have been refunded after the end of the financial year to
produce a genuine net going rate. It has been impossible
to do this, because a "low" rate of interest became part
and parcel of agricultural credit society policy.

Since the alternative is to borrow from the money-
lender anyway, and the borrowers have to go back to him
when co-operatives have collapsed, the argument against
market rates of interest has no ethical basis. Artificially
low rates of interest have been forced on the co-operatives
and other credit institutions for political and pseudo-
ethical reasons, and have pauperised entire credit systems,
with only trivial and transient advantages to the ultimate
borrowers. The whole credit system is static and dependent

on everlasting financial replenishments from government
and international aid.  The proper source of payment for
credit is the additional production or trade which it
ought to produce.  If it does not result in gains to the
borrower more than enough to repay the loans plus the
going rate of interest, it should not have been granted
in the first place.

   Artificially low rates of interest are not only
responsible for operational losses in the lending institutions, they are the cause of corruption and misuse of
loan funds.  Because the rate of interest is low, demand
for credit exceeds supply, necessitating some kind of
rationing.  The richer and more powerful members of the
community have an incentive to borrow, because it is
cheaper to do so than use their own funds or go to ordinary
commercial channels, and use their power to manipulate the
rationing in their own favour.  If supply and demand were
equal, there would be no need for rationing, and the rich
would have no incentive to muscle in.  Corruption, and the
misuse of power are *consequences* of unsound credit policies,
not - as is frequently alleged - the causes.


*Conclusion*

   This paper is concerned with the credit performance of
co-operative institutions, but a glance at the record of
other institutions shows that in the same type of credit,
their record is no better.  Development Banks either keep
out of agricultural credit, or try to lend through co-
operatives and other groups, or have large overdues.  At
the other end of the scale, informal groups may have some
advantage over co-operatives in being more homogeneous
and cohesive, but they have no legal status, cannot proceed
against defaulters and cannot be proceeded against, and

have no provision for book-keeping and audit. Their record
of failure is beginning to mount. The truth is that unsupported low-cost agricultural credit, whatever institutional
form it takes, is unsound business in itself. It mixes the
commercial concept of credit with charity and welfare. If
governments feel that it is necessary for political, social
or macro-economic reasons, they must be prepared to subsidise it *ad infinitum*. It would be better, however, to
assist small farmers by direct grants or the subsidising of
inputs, rather than perpetuate the farce of pretending that
unsupported credit can be organised on a commercial or quasi-
commercial basis.

The best hope of establishing dynamic and self-supporting
credit systems in rural areas is through commercially viable
organisations such as credit unions, multi-purpose co-operatives and private enterprise. Multi-purpose co-operatives
should go into credit only if they can, taking one thing with
another, be made to pay. This approach may be slower than
pouring out subsidised public money, but it will prove to
be sounder and more durable in the long run.

---

1  A number of countries have changed this title to
   "Commissioner for Co-operative Development", and there
   are some other variations such as Director of Co-
   operatives, but the principle remains the same and the
   officer concerned is always appointed under a section
   of the law. For convenience, the title Registrar is
   used in this paper.

2  See, for example, the Co-operative Societies Acts,
   Swaziland (1964), Kenya (1967) and Sri Lanka (1970).

3   A consultancy document for USAID, prepared by Public
    Administration Service, Washington, January 1979 quotes
    the costs of Long-Term Credit Under ARDC II in India
    as:

|   |   |
|---|---|
| Co-operative Banks | 18.75% |
| Commercial Banks | 20.50% |
| Co-operative Land Development Banks | 16.00% |

The highest rate charged to ultimate borrowers is 10.5%.
The figure for costs includes only a token allowance for
default.

4   See Helen Kimble, *Report on Agricultural Co-operative
    Credit in Botswana,* Plunkett Foundation, 1978.

*Part Three:*

**FARM HOUSEHOLDS AND CREDIT USE**

# MEASURING THE FARM LEVEL IMPACT OF AGRICULTURAL LOANS

*Cristina C. David and Richard L. Meyer*
*Department of Agricultural Economics and Rural Sociology*
*The Ohio State University*

This paper reviews selected studies of the impact of agricultural credit programmes in low income countries. The objective is to summarise key conceptual problems and analyse important methodological alternatives. We first briefly present a conceptual framework of the potential impact of credit on farm resource allocation. This framework is used to identify general methodological problems encountered in empirical research. The second section reviews the empirical literature including descriptive, econometric, and mathematical programming studies. Finally, research suggestions are given to improve estimates of benefits obtained from agricultural credit programmes.

## The Role of Credit in Resource Allocation

An important problem in analysis of the impact of borrowing on a farm-household is the lack of a sound theoretical framework to guide empirical research.[1] Errors in specification of empirical models and misinterpretation of results are logical outcomes. Two issues are particularly troublesome. First, farm households are complex units simultaneously making production and consumption decisions. Secondly, given fungibility in farm-household cash flow management, it is difficult to identify the effects of loans on the farm versus the household. But since formal credit is usually intended to increase production, not consumption, many researchers assume that production loans are actually used for production. As background for the research review, we present therefore a conceptual role of credit in farm production which seems to underlie available studies of loan impact.

In the typical neo-classical production model, the cost of working capital does not enter the decision process. However, in farm-households in less developed countries, supply of working capital from household saving may be limited and the cost of short-run borrowing significant. To take this into account, let us introduce a savings constraint represented by S in the standard maximisation model. Given product price P, input prices $P_i$'s, and a continuous, twice differentiable production function $f(X_1, X_2 \ldots X_n)$, the farm is assumed to maximise profits subject to the condition that production costs do not exceed savings. The profit equation is:

$$\Pi = \{P*f(X_1, X_2, \ldots X_n) - \Sigma P_i X_i\} + \lambda(S - \Sigma P_i X_i)$$

where $\lambda$ is the Lagrange multiplier. The equilibrium conditions are:

$$Pf_i = P_i(1 + \lambda),$$ where $f_i$ is the marginal product for each input i from 1 to n, and

$$S = \Sigma P_i X_i$$

Normally, $\lambda$ is assumed zero and the farm equates marginal value product to input price. When savings are limited, $\lambda$ denotes the farmer's marginal time preference for present over future consumption or, if a financial market exists, the effective cost of borrowing. Optimal input use, output, and net farm income are expected to be lower when $\lambda$ is not zero.[2]

The implications of these equilibrium conditions on farm resource allocation are shown in Figures 1a and 1b

203

relating output to input $X_i$ and marginal value product of
$X_i$ respectively, other things being equal. With no financial
constraint, optimal levels of output and input use are
Q* and $X_1$* respectively. Financial constraints, imperfect
knowledge and risk factors may cause departure from these
optimal levels. Assuming perfect knowledge and certainty,
input usage of $X_i^o$ and production of $Q^o$ implies an effective
cost of credit or marginal time preference between present
and future consumption of $\lambda$. A credit programme which
lowers the effective cost of borrowing to r increases
optimum input use to $X_i$', production to Q', and net
farm income by YXZ. The increase in net farm income
represents the benefit of borrowing to the individual farm.
Private benefits equal social benefits if r is the equilibrium interest rate determined by market forces.

The empirical measurement of the total benefits of
borrowing is much more complex than implied by this simpli-
fied model. Focussing on the farm rather than the farm-
household ignores possible welfare effects of borrowing
through increases in consumption and non-farm activities.
The true effect of borrowing is the additionality which
occurs in farm input use and output but, due to fungibility,
loans from a formal programme may simply substitute for own
savings or other sources of loans. Accounting for substitution, however, may improve measurement of the impact of
loans on the farm, but may understate the overall impact
on the farm-household. If no impact can be detected on
the farm, the additional liquidity due to credit may have
substituted for savings or other loan sources or diverted
to other non-farm or household uses. A more complete
evaluation requires information about the household's
marginal use of additional liquidity obtained from borrowing, not just the impact of the direct expenditure of loans.
Such information is extremely difficult to collect through
the cross-sectional farm surveys which are usually conducted.

204

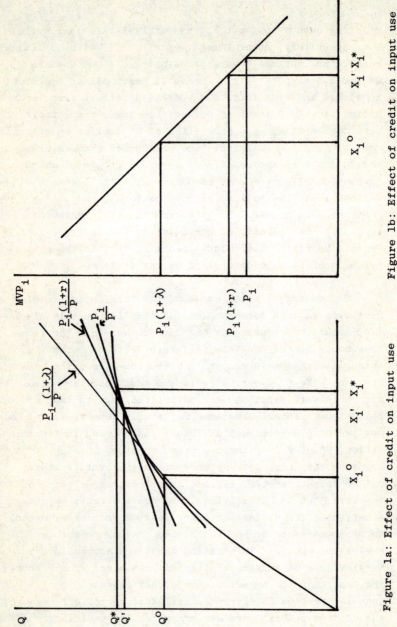

Figure 1a: Effect of credit on input use and production

Figure 1b: Effect of credit on input use and marginal value product (MVP)

Even with more comprehensive data, the problem remains of isolating the effect of loans on observed differences between borrowers and non-borrowers or before and after borrowing. This has been referred to recently as the attribution problem.[3] At least four factors other than credit can explain differences between borrowing and non-borrowing households:

- differences in shifters of the production functions, such as technology, technical information, irrigation, weather, and other variables not easily quantified in production models;
- differences in factors explaining non-optimal input use, such as yield and price uncertainty, and management ability;
- differences in product and input prices; and
- differences in own financial constraints or savings.

Multipurpose agricultural credit programmes contribute to the attribution problem. Although credit is the central component of these programmes, intensive extension services and input subsidies are frequently involved. Many studies assume that extension explains little of the differences found between borrowers and non-borrowers.[4] However, the effect of input subsidies on input use and production may be significant and needs to be separated from the impact of credit.

Concessionary interest rates, characteristic of most credit programmes, further complicate research. The resulting excess demand for loans implies non-price rationing which typically favours large loans to farmers with greater factor endowments, access to better technical information and better management. Therefore, borrowers may be systematically different from non-borrowers with borrowing the result rather than the cause.

Surprisingly little research has evaluated the impact of the vast sums spent on agricultural credit programmes. For example, the comprehensive 1973 AID Spring Review contained about 60 papers describing various credit programmes but no papers systematically assessed the farm level impact of loans. Some studies reported trends in aggregate output, use of inputs, and adoption of new varieties, while lamenting the scarcity of data to conduct more detailed analysis.

## Descriptive Studies

The most common analysis of credit programmes is the comparison of farm inputs, production, and productivity before and after borrowing by borrowers or between borrowers and non-borrowers. Few descriptive studies are widely available, but many undoubtedly exist as unpublished reports or graduate student theses. Table 1 summarises the results of selected descriptive studies to illustrate the variables examined and the impact usually attributed to borrowing. Additional analysis was performed using econometric techniques (Colombia) or by investigating factors affecting demand for credit (Korea, Brazil).

Except for Colombia, these studies were cross-sectional analyses of borrowers and non-borrowers. (In the Philippines and Taiwan, the data included several years, but the sample changed from one year to another.) Longitudinal data from panel farms would minimise some attribution problems, but would magnify the influence of weather, insects and diseases which often dominate year to year yield variations. "Before and after" comparisons are fewer because evaluation is generally initiated after the programme begins so quantification of the "before" situation is based on questionable farmer recall.

These studies represent widely different types of
agriculture and credit programmes. The Latin American
studies cover relatively large farms producing multiple
crops and programmes including both short and medium term
loans. Asian studies refer to small monoculture rice
farms receiving only short term credit. Despite these
differences, several common patterns emerge. Borrowers
had larger farms than non-borrowers: but farm size
differences in Asian countries were considerably smaller
than those in South America. (The Guatemalan farms were
of similar size due to the sampling procedure.) Operating
expenses and investment per hectare were higher for
borrowers, but production differences were less marked.
Moreover, net farm income per hectare, when reported, was
roughly the same.

Inferences about impact of loans must be treated with
caution due to the attribution problem. Small differences
in production and net farm income do not necessarily imply
that borrowing leads to misallocation or that loans have
been diverted. The impact of loans is ordinarily expected
to be overstated in simple comparisons of selected variables.[5]
However, uncontrolled production problems may cause under-
estimation as *ex post* yields are lower than *ex ante* yields
for borrowers using high levels of inputs. Thus, net
profits per hectare may be similar for both groups or
higher for non-borrowers.

In Guatemala, a sampling and a decomposition technique
was used to reduce attribution errors. The sampling procedure was designed to control for potential effects of
farm size and region-related factors. Differences in value
of production between borrowers and non-borrowers were
decomposed into price, yield, crop mix, and crop area
effects. The contribution of each factor was estimated by
calculating the effect if only one factor varied, implicitly

Table 1

Percentage Differences in Selected Measures Between Borrowers
and Non-borrowers, Selected Countries

| Countries/Years | Number of Observations | Farm Size | Operating Expenses per Hectare | Percentage Differences In: | | |
|---|---|---|---|---|---|---|
| | | | | Investment per Hectare | Production per Hectare | Net Farm Income per Hectare |
| Brazil (1965) | 132 | 78 | 112 | n.a. | 30[a] | 2 |
| Southern Brazil (1965) | 954 | 94 | 127 | 80 | 62[a] | n.a. |
| (1969) | 732 | 68 | 281 | 338 | 133[a] | n.a. |
| Colombia (1968) | 52 | 74 | 104 | n.a. | 6 | n.a. |
| (1968/1965)[b] | 25 | 30 | 56 | n.a. | 35 | n.a. |
| Guatemala (1975) | 1600 | 5 | 39 | n.a. | -3 | 0[c] |
| Philippines (1975/77) [d] | 577 | 16 | 15 | n.a. | n.a. | 4 |
| [e] | 497 | 2 | -15 | n.a. | n.a. | 0 |
| Korea (1970) | 438 | 3 | 5 | 5 | n.a. | -1 |
| Taiwan (1965, 1970, 1975) | 1373 | 16 | 21 | n.a. | 8 | -2 |

a  Gross farm income per hectare.
b  Comparison of borrowers before (1965) and after (1968) the credit programme.
c  Based on lower 75% of farms in size.
d  Non-borrowers include those who borrowed from non-formal institutions.
e  Comparison of borrowers from non-formal sources and non-borrowers.

Sources:

Brazil – P. F. de Araujo, "An Economic Study of Factors Affecting the Demand for Agricultural Credit at the Farm Level", unpublished Master's thesis, The Ohio State University, 1967.

Southern Brazil – G. Singh, "Farm Level Determinants of Credit Allocation and Use in Southern Brazil, 1965–69", unpublished Ph.D. dissertation, The Ohio State University, 1974.

Colombia – D. Colyer and G. Jimenez, "Supervised Credit as a Tool in Agricultural Development", *American Journal of Agricultural Economics*, Vol. 58, No. 4, November 1971.

Guatemala – S. R. Daines, "Guatemalan Farm Policy Analysis, The Impact of Small Farm Credit on Income, Employment and Food Production", Analytical Working Document No. 10, Bureau for Latin America, AID, Washington, April 1975.

Philippines – V. Cordova, P. Masicat and R. W. Herdt, "Use of Institutional Farm Credit in Three Locations of the Philippines: 1975–1977", Unpublished Paper, International Rice Research Institute, Philippines, 1978.

Korea – O. O. Nyanin, "Credit and Small Farmers in South Korea, 1968–70", unpublished M.S. Thesis, The Ohio State University, 1978.

Taiwan – Data available at the Department of Agricultural Economics and Rural Sociology, Ohio State University.

assuming independence among factors and constant returns
to scale.  It was concluded that the substantial expansion
in crop area, which explains most production differences,
was largely due to credit.

A decomposition technique was also used in a World
Bank evaluation of projects providing medium and long term
credit to crop farms in the Philippines, Pakistan, and
Morocco and to livestock farms in Uruguay and Mexico.
Crop production changes were accounted for by changes in
cultivated area, cropping intensity and yields, and changes
in livestock production by changes in breeding cattle,
feeders, reproduction rates and beef yields.  Judgements
were made about the probable effects of the project on
each source of growth.  For example, on crop farms loans
were assumed to explain 20, 75 and 100 per cent of the
increases in yields, cropping intensity, and cultivated
area, respectively.  Adjustments were also made for the
possible effect of other loan sources.  The study concluded
that the projects raised crop production by 67% instead of
the observed unadjusted 82%.

The World Bank study also dealt with substitution by
speculating on the farm investment that would have occurred
without the project or, conversely, the additional farm
investment due to the project.  Three sources of information
were used to derive an adjustment factor.  First, borrowers
were asked to estimate the investments they would have
made without the programme and the probable source of
finance.  Second, investments between borrowers and non-
borrowers were compared.  Third, assets financed by the
project were related to the borrowers' total assets.  Based
on these data, a crude substitution factor of 40% was
assumed.  Thus, the credit projects explained approximately
28% of the net production increase rather than 67%.

*Econometric Studies*

Recent studies have used econometric techniques to
analyse the impact of borrowing.  Three different models
have been used: a production function, an input demand
function, and an efficiency gap function.


Production Function

Colombian, Brazilian and Ghanaian studies hypothesised
that loans influence the farm production relationship.  The
credit variable was specified in several ways (Table 2).
The Colombian studies treated credit as a separate unit.
The later Colombian study further hypothesised that borrowers have a completely different production technology so
separate production functions were estimated for borrowers,
non-borrowers and borrowers prior to the supervised credit
programme.  A modified Cobb-Douglas production model was
used in the Brazilian model where credit was assumed to
shift production coefficients for operating expenses,
modern inputs, and machinery, but not for land, labour or
animal power.  Similarly, the Ghanaian study assumed all
production parameters, except the intercept, were affected
by credit.  The Ghanaian study used time series aggregate
data, while the others used cross-section farm level data.

These production function studies assume a different
role for borrowing than presented in the first section of
this paper.  First, specifying credit as a separate production input presents a conceptual problem because loans
may permit purchasing optimal input levels, but do not
directly generate output.  Double counting of inputs may
also occur with credit as a separate variable.  An example
exists with the Colombian results where a higher production

Table 2

Estimates of the Effect of Borrowing on the
Cobb-Douglas Production Function, Selected Countries

| Item | Colombia 1960 | Colombia Borrower[a] 1965 | Colombia 1968 | Non-Borrower 1968 | Brazil 1971/72 | Ghana 1962-74 |
|---|---|---|---|---|---|---|
| Log a | | 1.174 | 2.899 | 0.740 | 1.514 | 0.006 |
| Land | 0.303[b] (1.620) | 0.379* (1.560) | 0.777* (3.964) | 0.418* (1.742) | 0.293* (4.420) | -2.127 (1.217) |
| Labour | -- | 0.396* (1.472) | 0.049 (0.383) | 0.456* (2.505) | 0.009 (0.880) | 4.248* (1.977) |
| Farm Equipment | -0.103 (-1.873) | 0.144 (1.043) | 0.048 (0.533) | 0.034 (0.354) | 0.045* (1.340) | -- |
| Livestock | -- | -- | -- | -- | 0.009* (1.830) | -- |
| Operating Expense | 0.115[c] (1.885) | 0.314* (1.377) | 0.279* (1.898) | 0.405* (3.092) | 0.246* (4.300) | 0.336 (0.269) |
| Modern Varieties | -- | -- | -- | -- | 0.356* (5.020) | -- |
| Credit | 0.641 (3.705) | 0.064 (0.877) | -0.084 (-1.000) | 0.104* (1.825) | -- | -- |
| Credit x Land | -- | -- | -- | -- | -- | 1.559 (1.505) |
| Credit x Labour | -- | -- | -- | -- | -- | -1.941 (-1.691) |

| | | | | | | |
|---|---|---|---|---|---|---|
| Credit x Operating Expense | -- | -- | -- | -- | 0.0001* (1.970) | -0.395 (-0.297) |
| Credit x Modern Inputs | -- | -- | -- | -- | -0.00003 (-0.370) | -- |
| $R^2$ | 0.89 | 0.57 | 0.90 | 0.80 | 0.96 | 0.85 |
| Number of Observations | 17 | 27 | 27 | 25 | 129 | 13 |

a   Borrowers are participants in supervised credit programmes. Non-borrowers are non-participants including farmers borrowing from non-formal sources.

b   Figures in parenthesis are t-values. Asterisk indicates statistical significance at 10% or better confidence interval.

c   Includes fertiliser only.

Sources: Colombia — W. S. Becker, "Agricultural Credit and Colombia's Economic Development", unpublished Ph.D. dissertation, Louisiana State University, 1970, and D. Colyer and G. Jimenez, "Supervised Credit as a Tool in Agricultural Development", *American Journal of Agricultural Economics*, Vol. 58, No. 4, November 1971.

   Brazil — P. B. Rao, *The Economics of Agricultural Credit-Use in Southern Brazil*, Andhra University Press, Andhra Pradesh, India, 1973.

   Ghana — A. B. Gyekye, E. T. Acquah and C. D. Whyte, "An Evaluation of Institutional Credit and its Role in Agricultural Production in Ghana", Bureau of Economic Research and Development, Virginia State College, 1977.

coefficient for credit was found in the earlier study. In
this study the credit variable in effect captures the contribution of labour and other variables explicitly specified
in the later model.

Second, attributing differences in production functions
between borrowers and non-borrowers to borrowing implicitly
assumes a relationship between source of liquidity and production function. A slight difference exists between
borrowers and non-borrowers in the operating expense coefficient in the Colombian and Brazilian studies, but not
in coefficients for modern inputs also expected to be
influenced by loans. The direction of the differences,
however, is inconsistent. Insignificant coefficients in
the Ghanaian study, except for the very high labour coefficient, probably reflect aggregation and specification
problems.

The somewhat unclear picture of loan impact is not
surprising. Short term credit programmes attempt to encourage
adoption of new seed-fertiliser technology, but there is
little reason to expect adoption and, therefore, a shift in
production function to be conditional upon borrowing.
Modern varieties frequently imply greater operating expenses
for optimal chemical use. However, the costs of seed are
similar; the response of modern varieties to fertiliser is
usually higher at all levels of fertilisation; and fertiliser
itself is highly divisible. Therefore farmers with varying
financial constraints should simply be located at different
points on the modern technology function. On the other hand,
medium and long term credit may be more closely associated
with changes in the production relationship because these
loans frequently finance large inputs more difficult to fund
internally. For example, increasing farm size introduces
scale economies; expanding irrigated area raises the productivity

of fertiliser, land and modern varieties; and mechanisation changes land-labour relations.

The apparent difference in production coefficients between borrowers and non-borrowers, such as in land and labour in Colombia, may be due to omission of other inputs associated with loans like technical information or irrigation. Short term loans would not be expected to have a major impact on these variables. A more plausible explanation is that progressive farmers with irrigation and better technical information borrow more. Thus, causality is as likely from higher inputs, output, income, etc to loans as it is from loans to these changes.

Input Demand Function

Input demand studies directly test the resource allocation model presented in the first section. Schluter's comprehensive analysis of the impact of credit and uncertainty on resource allocation is an example.[6] Input demand functions for labour, modern varieties, fertiliser, crop area, and animal and machine power were estimated. The explanatory variables included financial constraints represented by credit availability and income; ability to bear risk, measured as non-farm assets and farm size; technology and knowledge. No significant input and output price variations were assumed to exist across the farm sample.

Table 3 presents Schluter's results only for modern varieties and fertiliser, the main targets of supervised credit programmes. Access to loans, dairying income, acreage cropped, and assets were significant explanatory variables for adoption of rice varieties and fertiliser use. Schluter regards assets and farm size as indices of farmers' ability to bear risk. Farmers more able to cope with uncertainty

216

## Table 3
### Linear Regression of Factors Affecting
### Use of Modern Rice and Wheat Varieties and Fertiliser
### in Surat District, India, 1971-72

| | Modern Varieties[a] | | |
| | Rice | Wheat | Fertiliser |
| --- | --- | --- | --- |
| Credit[b] | 0.182* (2.020)[c] | -0.114 (-1.570) | 82.676* (4.280) |
| Assets | 0.020* (2.520) | -0.005 (-0.890) | -0.585 (-0.340) |
| Non-Agricultural Income | 0.089 (1.380) | -0.016 (-1.280) | 8.575 (1.180) |
| Dairying Income | 0.100 (1.540) | 0.073 (1.530) | 25.656* (2.490) |
| Acreage Under Crop[d] | 0.661* (6.590) | 0.541* (3.840) | 66.998* (4.780) |
| Gross Cropped Acreage | -0.056* (-2.170) | 0.006 (0.290) | -- |
| Acreage Under Improved Rice | -- | -- | 54.359 (2.480)* |
| Acreage Under Traditional Rice | -- | -- | 18.513* (2.500) |
| Acreage Under Unirrigated Crops | -- | -- | -8.991 (-0.890) |
| Education | -0.005 (-0.120) | 0.076* (3.230) | -5.129 (-0.970) |
| $R^2$ | 0.76 | 0.74 | 0.63 |
| Number of Observations | 59 | 56 | 25 |

[a] Two other variables, number of family workers and home consumption requirements were included in these equations but were not statistically significant.

[b] Refers to maximum amount the co-operative would be willing to lend the farmer for variable inputs based on acreage, cropping pattern, assets, and character of the farmer.

[c] Figures in parentheses are t-values. Asterisk indicates significance at 1% level.

[d] For fertiliser, this represents acreage under high yielding rice varieties.

* Statistically significant at 1% level.

Source: Schluter, *op. cit.*, 1974.

and with more access to institutional loans were more
likely to adopt modern rice varieties. Interestingly,
these variables did not explain adoption of wheat varieties.
Access to loans and technology (acreage in modern varieties)
were the most significant factors explaining fertiliser use.
Access to loans appeared to be less important, however, in
explaining demand for other inputs not reported in Table 3.

Although the input demand approach does not directly
test loan impact on farm production or income, it does
avoid the conceptual problem of relating loans to the
production function. The importance of borrowing in
achieving optimal input use, however, can be better analysed
by developing a more appropriate measure of the opportunity
cost of liquidity, eg effective cost of credit for borrowers
and rate of return on next alternative use of liquidity,
instead of the usual dummy variable representation of
borrowing or borrowing limits.

Efficiency Gap Function

The third econometric approach relates credit not
directly to input levels but to the farmer's ability to
efficiently allocate resources. These studies attempt to
determine if loans explain differences in ability to use
optimum levels of inputs. Some studies simply compare
whether borrowers and non-borrowers equate prices of
inputs to marginal value products for inputs frequently
financed by loans.[7] Separate production functions are
estimated for borrowers and non-borrowers but differences
in initial level of savings, managerial ability, and perception of risk are usually not considered. A Malaysian
study is an exception as farmers were classified by capital
availability index, rather than borrower and non-borrower,
to correct for differences in financial constraint.[8]

A study by Mandac and Herdt was mainly concerned with
identifying efficiency constraints on Philippine rice
farms, but it represents an alternative approach to
measure loan impact.[9] They used a unique data set, including production activities from normal farming operations
as well as from experimental trials conducted on the
farmers' same fields. Measures of technical versus allocative inefficiencies were identified for each farm.
Level of technical knowledge, and environmental factors
such as irrigation and soil fertility were expected to
influence technical efficiency; while managerial ability,
uncertainty and perception of risk, financial constraints,
and credit availability would likely affect allocative
efficiency, which refers to equating marginal value product
to input price.

Table 4 reports the regression analysis explaining
differences in allocative efficiency among sample farms.
Considering the cross-sectional nature of the data and
the measurement problems in estimating efficiency, a
remarkably high percentage of variation in efficiency was
explained by the model. Most of the significant variables
are measures of financial constraint - total area, gross
family income, and credit - and the signs of the coefficients were as expected. Farm size reduces supply of
liquid capital per hectare, while family income and credit
increases the supply. The highly significant coefficient
for irrigation indicates the importance of risk factors
in farmer decisions. Variables reflecting farmers'
knowledge seem to be relatively less critical, although
the information index and days worked off-farm had significant coefficients.

Efficiency gap models are conceptually appealing and
future analysis can be extended to estimate loan impact on

Table 4

Regression Analysis of Factors Affecting Variation in
Allocative Efficiency Among Philippine Rice Farmers

| Variable | Coefficient | t-value |
|---|---|---|
| Intercept | 1.7490 | |
| Intercept Dummy Variables | | |
|   Credit (1 = non-borrowers) | −0.4369* | −2.1260 |
|   Labour Scarcity (1 = scarce labour) | 0.0249 | 0.0913 |
|   Tenancy (1 = share tenant) | −0.2836 | −0.8203 |
|   Irrigation (1 = unirrigated) | −0.0075* | −3.2051 |
|   Risk Index (1 = higher risk) | −0.1302 | −0.6500 |
| Gross Family Income | 0.00003* | 3.0000 |
| Total Area | −3.0731* | −9.5497 |
| Information Index | 0.1713* | 1.8013 |
| Age of Farmer Operator | −0.0091 | −1.0225 |
| Years of Education | −0.2418 | −1.2002 |
| Number of Days Worked Off Farm | 0.0026* | 2.0813 |
| Technical Knowledge Score | 0.0397 | 0.4091 |

$R^2 = 0.77$

n = 336 (56 farmers from wet season of
1974 to dry season of 1977)

\* Statistically significant at 10% level or higher.

Source: Mandac and Herdt, *op. cit.*, 1978.

farm production or income. However, use of experimental
data to establish the frontier production function and
thus distinguish technical versus allocative efficiency
is rarely possible. In many cases, farm practices of the
"best" farmers may have to be used as in other empirical
studies of technical efficiency.

*Programming Studies*

Several studies of loan impact and demand have used
some type of mathematical programming. Part of the attraction
is that these studies provide estimates of normative behaviour; that is, they suggest what farmers should do to
achieve a goal specified in the model's objective function.
Therefore, they are frequently used to simulate the impact
of alternative policy changes.

Modelling Alternatives

Table 5 lists examples of the evolution in programming
studies dealing with some aspect of agricultural finance.
Single period linear models are most commonly used. Typically, a representative model is developed for reasonably
homogeneous farms with respect to size, enterprises, technology, resource endowment and other characteristics.
Profit maximisation is normally assumed, subject to
maximum and minimum farm and/or household constraints.
The activities included represent what exists or what is
expected under alternative scenarios. Formal and informal
loan sources supplement internal funds to finance operating
costs.

Multi-period models, with and without discounting
future cash flows, provide important advantages for the
study of impact of. loans on investment, firm growth and
liquidity management.  First, monthly or seasonal constraints for borrowing or consumption may be specified
within a model for a longer planning horizon.  Sales
activities can also be incorporated to furnish funds for
the capital constraint.  Second, periods can be linked to
show how current activities influence future activities.
Third, future cash flows can be discounted to account for
the time preference of consumption when the planning
horizon is several years.

In addition, some specific issues have been studied
with multi-period models.  For example, Boehlje and White
compared results of maximisation of income versus net
worth.  Baker and Bhargava, Tewari and Sharma, and Hadiwigeno
tested how the value of unused cash and credit could
influence liquidity management.  If the value of credit
reserves is high, farmers may engage in internal credit
rationing and borrow less than the full borrowing limit.
Likewise, when the reserve value of cash is high, farmers
may borrow even while holding cash.

Recursive models have been used to model both representative farms and agricultural regions.  Unlike other
multi-period models, the objective function is solved each
year with the results for one period linked to previous
periods by feedback constraints.  These constraints are
specified to reflect farmer behaviour, such as accounting
for risk aversion by safety first objectives.  Some tests
exist for verifying model results relative to historical
experience.  Another feature of regional models is farm
size decomposition to test competition for resources, such
as a fixed regional credit constraint, among different size
farms.[10]

Table 5:   Characteristics and Selected Results

| Authors & Study Area | Study Objectives | Objective Function | Selected Model Characteristics |
|---|---|---|---|
| *Single Period Linear Models:* | | | |
| Agarwal & Kumawat; Rajasthan, India | Estimate credit requirements of new technology | Maximise net farm income | Three farm size groups; wet & dry seasons; simulations with & without formal credit and new technology |
| Patrick; N. E. Brazil | Analyse possible effect of government policies | Maximise net farm income | Various sizes; three counties; crops & livestock; simulation of alternative technologies, fertiliser & crop prices, land purchase & interest rates |
| Whitaker, et al.; INCORA borrowers, Colombia | Analyse impact of credit programme | Maximise profits or production | Twelve technology classes of farms; corn enterprises only; simulations with & without credit, and with & without credit tied to inputs |
| White; Minas Gerais Brazil | Analyse regional development potential | Maximise net farm income | Twelve typical farm situations; crop & livestock; simulated technology, borrowing limits, interest rates & specialised credit programmes |
| *Multiple Period Linear Models:* | | | |
| Ahmed; Gezira, Sudan | Analyse supply & demand for credit | Maximise profits | Six farm types; 24 semi-monthly periods; minimum consumption constraints; production & marketing; parameterised interest rates & borrowing limits |
| Alexander; West Java, Indonesia | Analyse policy alternatives for Bimas programme | Maximise net farm income | Six farm types by liquidity & size; consumption constraints; off-farm business specified; three crop seasons; parameterised interest rates, credit allocation rules, payback period & credit in-kind |

of Mathematical Programming Studies of Agricultural Credit

| Financial Component | Illustrative Results | Source |
|---|---|---|
| Initial cash balance; operating credit borrowing limits | Optimum farm plans with existing technology require borrowing; borrowing requirements sharply increase with new technology | N.L. Agarwal & R.K. Kumawat, 'Green Revolution & Capital and Credit Requirements in Semi Arid Region of Rajasthan' *Indian J. of Agric. Econ.* Vol.XXIX, 1974 |
| Operating & investment credit from formal sources | Reductions in fertiliser prices & interest rates had little impact except on income distribution | G.F. Patrick, 'Efectos de Programmas Alternativos de Governo Sobre a Agricultura do Nordeste' *Pesquisa e Planejamento Economico* Vol.4, No.1, 1974 |
| Working capital borrowing limits | Working capital is a constraint; INCORA loans had significant impact on profits, production, factor use & technological change | M. Whitaker, J.R. Loidan & T. Walker, 'Supervised Credit', Analytic Working Document No.8, Sector Analysis Division, Bureau for Latin America, AID/Washington March 1973 |
| Operating & investment credit from formal sources | Borrowing capacity limited adoption of technology; results insensitive to interest rates | T.K. White, 'Credit & Agric. Development – Some Observations on a Brazilian Case' in G. Patrick, *Small Farm Agriculture: Studies in Developing Nations* Station Bull. 101, Dept. of Agric. Econ., Purdue University, 1975 |
| Initial cash constraint; formal & informal credit | Borrowing required to reach optimum income; increased interest rates had little effect on income | S.E.M. Ahmed, 'The Integration of Agricultural Credit & Marketing in the Gezira Scheme of the Sudan' unpublished Ph.D. Thesis, Wye College, Univ. of London, 1977 |
| Borrowing & savings activities; borrowing limits for each type of credit | Interest rates could be raised to 5% per month with little effect on borrowing; increasing credit cost altered marketing practices | C.D. Alexander, 'Production Credit for Farms in a Javanese Village' unpublished Masters Thesis, Univ. of Hawaii, 1975 |

| Authors & Study Area | Study Objectives | Objective | Selected Model Characteristics |
|---|---|---|---|
| *Multiple Period Linear Models - continued* | | | |
| Baker & Bhargava; Uttar Pradesh, India | Analyse liquidity management | Maximise farm returns plus values of cash & credit reserves | Small farm; wet & dry season; minimum crop & cash requirements; reserve values for cash & credit |
| Hadiwigeno; East Java, Indonesia | Analyse effect of changes in credit policy | Maximise farm net income plus value of cash & credit reserves | Small farms in four villages; one year planning horizon; six seasons; padi & other annual crops; minimum household padi; simulated changes in Bimas credit |
| *Multiple Period Linear Models (Discounted Future Income):* | | | |
| Dean & Benedictis; Southern Italy | Analyse optimum investment behaviour | Maximise discounted future net farm income | Small farm; 60 year planning period; annual & orchard crops; exogenous consumption requirements |
| Naseem; Punjab, Pakistan | Analyse effect of government policies on growth | Maximise discounted future net farm income | Small farm; four year planning model; winter & summer seasons; simulated borrowing limits, savings rates, interest rates, product prices & farm size |
| *Multiple Period Recursive Linear Models:* | | | |
| Day & Singh; Punjab, India | Analyse agricultural transformation | Maximise regional net farm profits each year | Regional model; regional cash & consumption constraints; feedback constraints; historic behaviour 1952-1965; projections to 1980 |
| Heidhues; Northern Germany | Analyse policy alternative effect on firm growth | Maximise net farm returns each year | Eleven farm size-types; year planning period; feedback constraints; simulated grain & milk prices |

| Financial Component | Illustrative Results | Source |
|---|---|---|
| Borrowing from money-lenders & small farmer credit programme; para-meterised cash & liquidity require-ments | Models with reserves concept approximate farmer plans; reliable sources of small farmer credit increase out-put & income | C.B. Baker & V.K. Bhargava, 'Financing Small Farm Devel-opment in India' *Australian Journal of Agricultural Eco-nomics*, Vol.18, No.2, 1974, pp.101-118 |
| Borrowing from money-lender, bank & Bimas programme | Changed terms for Bimas loans, affected marketing; little effect on production; little effect of increased interest rate | S.S. Hadiwigeno, 'Potential Effects of Modification in the Credit Program for Small Farms in East Java, Indonesia' Un-published Ph.D. Thesis, Univ-ersity of Illinois, 1974 |
| Government prod-uction grants & interest subsidies; 8% discount rate | Rapid conversion to orchards with/without grants; a dis-count rate of 16% would lead to annual crop production | G.W. Dean & M.de Benedictis, 'A Model of Economic Develop-ment for Peasant Farms in Southern Italy' *Journal of Farm Economics* Vol.46, No.2, 1964 |
| Borrowing & savings activities | Credit constrains full use of resources; farmers would bor-row triple initial credit availability at prevailing interest rates; shift to higher value crops & imp-roved technology with credit | M. Naseem, 'Credit Availability & the Growth of Small Farms in the Pakistan Punjab' *Food Res-earch Institute Studies*, Vol. XIV, No.1, 1975 |
| Borrowing & savings activities; credit tied to gross sales; operating & invest-ment credit | Increasing internal finance over time; elasticity of demand for loanable funds increases | R.H. Day & I. Singh, *Economic Development as an Adaptive Pro-cess: The Green Revolution in the Punjab*, Cambridge University Press, Cambridge, 1977 |
| Several money & capital constraints; investment & sav-ings activities | Investments lower on farms with reduced internal finance | T. Heidhues, 'A Recursive Pro-gramming Model of Farm Growth in Northern Germany' *Journal of Farm Economics*, Vol.48, No.3, Part I, 1966, pp.668-684 |

| Authors & Study Area | Study Objectives | Objective Function | Selected Model Characteristics |
|---|---|---|---|
| *Multiple Period Recursive Linear Models - continued* | | | |
| Singh & Ahn; Rio Grande do Sul, Brazil | Analyse regional development process | Maximise regional net farm income | Three farm size models; crops & livestock; 10 year period; feedback constraints; simulated alternative credit & price policies |
| *Single Period Quadratic Models:* | | | |
| Peres; Sao Paulo, Brazil | Estimate derived demand for credit under risk and inflation | Minimise variance of farm income | Small and large farm models; crops & livestock; price expectation model; parameterised interest rates & labour supply |
| Schluter; Surat District India | Analyse cropping pattern | Minimise mean absolute deviation of cash income (MOTAD) | Typical farms; irrigated & non-irrigated farms; annual crops; minimum consumption constraints; parameterised family size; farm size; wage rates & interest rates |
| Soares; Northeast Brazil | Determine optimum resource use under risk | Minimise variance of farm income | Large farms; one cropping season; simple & inter-planted crops; sharecropping; parameterised technology, cotton prices, wages, labour supply, borrowing limits |

| Financial Component | Illustrative Results | Source |
|---|---|---|
| Operating & investment credit from formal sources | Derived demand for credit showed increasing elasticity over time; small farms were relatively insensitive to interest rates | I. Singh & C.Y. Ahn, 'A Dynamic Multi-Commodity Model of the Agricultural Sector: A Regional Application in Brazil' *European Economic Review*, Vol. 11, 1978 |
| Initial savings; borrowing limits for credit for modern inputs & general expenses | Actual borrowing exceeded predicted for small farms, while large farms borrowed less than predicted | F.C. Peres, 'Derived Demand for Credit Under Conditions of Risk', Unpublished Ph.D. Thesis, The Ohio State University, 1976 |
| Savings & borrowings from money-lender & co-operative; borrowing limits for formal & informal credit | Credit was required for production of high-income crops; interest rate had little effect | M.G. Schluter, 'The Interaction of Credit and Uncertainty in Determining Resource Allocation & Incomes on Small Farms, Surat District, India' Occ. Paper 68, Dept. of Agric. Econ., Cornell University, 1974 |
| Cash constraints; formal credit | Fifty percent reduction in formal credit borrowing limit reduced sharecropping & farm income, while increasing income variance | A.C. de M. Soares, 'Resource Allocation and Choice of Enterprise Under Risk on Cotton Farms in Northeast Brazil' Unpublished Ph.D. Thesis, The Ohio State University, 1977 |

228

Another approach to treating risk exists with quadratic models used to generate EV frontiers relating expected income to income variance.  Farmer behaviour usually approximates some point along the frontier where income and capital requirements are less and enterprise combinations more diversified than obtained with profit maximisation.

Two types of analyses are frequently conducted in programming studies.  The first is similar to the before-after approach discussed earlier.  Solutions of models without loans or with only informal loans are compared with solutions specifying borrowing limits for formal loans.  This approach conforms with the resource allocation model discussed in the first section where loans are expected to influence input usage.  The second analysis involves parameterising the interest rate for formal loans to determine levels and elasticity of loan demand.

Several similar results emerge from these studies. Technological change, adoption of new varieties and cropping systems, mechanisation and farm income are frequently found to be constrained by current formal loan supplies.  Borrowing limits must be relaxed to obtain socially desired changes in these variables.  Likewise, evaluations of credit programmes conclude that formal loans have resulted in desirable farm changes.  Furthermore, productive alternatives exist so farmers could pay substantially higher interest rates with limited reduction in borrowings.  Small farms appear particularly insensitive to interest rates.

Methodological Problems

The similarity of research results would normally suggest conclusive evidence on these issues.  Several methodological issues, however, require caution in interpretation.

The actual or expected impact of borrowing or demand for
loans may be substantially under or over-estimated in
a particular study because of several reasons.  First,
few studies attempt to capture the full complexity of
farm household behaviour.  Model activities are largely
limited to the farm and only Alexander included the
allocation of household resources to off-farm business.
Since loan funds are fungible, the true impact of loans
for production purposes is hard to determine without an
integrated household model.  Furthermore, savings behaviour
should be tied to production possibilities so a fixed level
of savings should be inappropriate when technology changes.

Second, many studies focus on working capital.  In
many countries, little long term credit exists.  Therefore,
short term loans are borrowed in excess of working capital
needs to help finance investment.  Thus the impact of
short term loans must be considered in relation to investment, not just production as is normal.

Third, true costs and benefits of borrowing may not be
adequately captured by interest rates and borrowing limits.
Borrowing costs, especially for small farmers, may far
exceed interest rates.  Also, the reliability of the credit
source, expectations about the need to repay, and non-credit
services will influence the extent to which a borrower
will switch from an informal to a formal source or borrow
rather than use savings.

Fourth, in spite of subsistence constraints, valuation
of reserves, safety first constraints, quadratic programming,
etc, it is not clear that research has adequately dealt
with risk and uncertainty.  If credit were priced at equilibrium rates, repayment expected, and farmer attitudes
toward risk adequately captured, optimum borrowing might be
significantly less than estimated.

Fifth, compared to some other methodologies, mathematical
programming models offer fewer possibilities for statistical
tests of goodness of fit. In this review, only two studies
- Day and Singh, Singh and Ahn   - dealt with model valid-
ation in any detail. Some models may be so tightly constrained with (sometimes) arbitrary constraints that few
feasible solutions are possible. Thus it is not clear if
farmer behaviour has really been captured by the models.

Finally, there are questions and problems concerning
the applicability of programming models to many low income
countries. Few low income countries have sufficient data,
computer capability and staff to use these models.

*Summary and Directions for Future Research*

This paper has addressed methodological problems in
analysing the micro-level impact of loans. The first section
reviewed the farm resource allocation model explicitly or
implicitly underlying much research. The second section
reviewed selected examples of empirical research. Many
studies are largely descriptive and are more useful in
generating hypotheses than in rigorously assessing loan
impact. The more analytical econometric and mathematical
programming studies are relatively few, are confined to a
few countries, and also have methodological problems.

Three important methodological issues were identified.
First, most studies use the farm as the basic unit of
analysis. Little attention is given to the interdependence
of production and consumption activities typical in most
farm-households in low income countries. This shortcoming
is sometimes justified by the explicit goals of agricultural
credit programmes of increasing farm production, but also

may be due to inherent complexity of conceptualising a
broader framework and the traditional separation of
production and consumption theory in neo-classical economics.

Secondly, and related to the first, few studies
recognise the fungibility of money. Borrowed funds enter
the household's total cash resources and become indistinguish-
able from other funds. Funds ostensibly obtained for farm
production may result in additionality in consumption or
non-farm activities. A narrow focus on farm analysis will
tend to understate the credit impact on farm-household
welfare and fungibility creates difficulties in assessing
this bias.

Third, most studies have not adequately resolved the
attribution problem, that is, separated the effect of loans
from other factors simultaneously affecting farm production,
yields, income, etc. Differences in output and input
prices, production technology, and managerial constraints
may all contribute to differences found between borrowers
and non-borrowers or before and after borrowing. Especially
important is non-price rationing of credit resulting in
concentration of loans to larger, well-established, richer
farmers. Thus, differences between farmers may explain
credit allocation rather than the impact of borrowing.

Future research on rural finance requires greater
appreciation of such methodological issues. The input
demand and efficiency gap econometric models illustrate
potential analytical approaches for measuring loan impact
that minimise the attribution problem. Likewise, some of
the recent programming models attempt to capture more of
farm household complexity and interdependencies. But new
methodological approaches[11] using an integrated farm-
household framework of production and input demand and

232

supply analysis have not been explored extensively for
financial studies.

The immediate priority, however, is to develop a
data base sufficient for more detailed analysis of agricultural finance. Fungibility and farm-household decision-
making indicate the need for collecting comprehensive data
on sources and uses of farm household liquidity. All
sources of liquidity need to be quantified and related to
the various farm and household uses. Careful monitoring
of production expenses, investment, consumption and non-
farm activities is necessary to accurately describe when
and where additional liquidity is allocated. Once described, more rigorous analysis can be used to identify
factors explaining allocation and impact of loans. Massive
cross-section surveys currently undertaken in many countries
are not suitable for this purpose. Much more emphasis is
required in carefully collecting longitudinal data, particularly from panel households, even at the expense of
smaller sample size.

1  This issue is discussed in greater detail in C. C. David,
   "Conceptual Issues in Analyzing Impact and Demand for
   Agricultural Credit', ESO No. 610, Department of Agri-
   cultural Economics and Rural Sociology, The Ohio State
   University, May 1979.

2  C. B. Baker hypothesised that financial constraints may
   have an effect on relative input costs and, therefore,
   relative factor use, eg capital becomes relatively more
   expensive than labour. However, fungibility of money
   or credit reduces this effect. ("Credit in the Production

Organization of the Firm", *American Journal of Agricultural Economics,* Vol. 50, No. 3, August 1968.)

3   See E. P. Rice, "Problems and Results in Evaluating Agricultural Credit Projects", Paper presented at the Conference on Rural Finance Research, San Diego, California, 1977.

4   The Study by G. M. Scobie and D. L. Franklin represents one of the few systematic attempts to evaluate extension in supervised credit programmes ("The Impact of Supervised Credit Programs on Technological Change in Developing Agriculture", *Australian Journal of Agricultural Economics,* Vol. 21, No. 7, April 1977.

5   It is interesting to note, for example, the significantly different results obtained in the Colombian study between the borrower-non-borrower and before-after credit comparisons. Borrowers' input use and yield per hectare is 104% and 6% higher, respectively, than non-borrowers. But for borrowers, input use per hectare increased only by 56% and yield per hectare rose 35% after borrowing.

6   M. G. Schluter, "The Interaction of Credit and Uncertainty in Determining  Resource Allocation and Incomes on Small Farms, Surat District, India", Occasional Paper No. 68, Department of Agricultural Economics, Cornell University, February 1974.

7   See, for example, P. B. Rao, *The Economics of Agricultural Credit-Use in Southern Brazil,* Andhra University Press, Andhra Pradesh, India, 1973.

8   K. W. Chung and Mokhtar Tamin, "The Effect of Capital Availability and Credit on the Use of Resources in Padi Farming", *Kajian Ekonomi Malaysia,* Vol. VIII, No. 2, 1971.

9   A. M. Mandac and R. W. Herdt, "Economic Inefficiency as
    a Constraint to High Rice Yields in Nueva Eciya, Phil-
    ippines", Paper presented at International Rice Research
    Institute, Laguna, Philippines, 1978.

10  Inderjit Singh and Choong Yong Ahn, "A Dynamic Multi-
    Commodity Model of the Agricultural Sector: A Regional
    Application in Brazil", *European Economic Review*, Vol.
    11, 1978.

11  L. J. Lau, W. L. Lin and P. A. Yotopoulos, "The Linear
    Logarithmic Expenditure System: An Application to Con-
    sumption-Leisure Choice", *Econometrica*, Vol. 46, No. 4,
    July 1978.

RURAL CREDIT, FARM FINANCE AND
VILLAGE HOUSEHOLDS

*Michael Lipton*
*Institute of Development Studies*
*University of Sussex*

*The Family Enterprise*

A family enterprise is a way of pooling the requirements, availabilities, prospects and problems of the family with those of the enterprise. In particular, the work requirements and availabilities of the family can be timed to allow for seasonal farm needs: social activities and domestic work are often drastically curtailed during the seasonal work peak of farm activities, but expand in the slack season.[1] Similarly, families' decisions about when to send older children to school vary with work requirements on the farm.

Borrowing and repayment are ways of redistributing over time the cash requirements and disposals of a family, or an enterprise, or a pooled family enterprise. Most familiarly, deficit-farm families regularly borrow in the slack season, when rewarding activities are scarce both on their own farms and in paid employment; and repay at harvest time, when both on-farm output and off-farm earnings are more readily accessible.

This paper examines some of the ways in which the pooling activities of the family enterprise may complement, substitute for, or otherwise interact with, the time-redistributing activities of rural credit. It will be necessary to look at three sorts of change, over time, in income or output, which the family farm enterprise may seek to handle through credit or otherwise.

The first is largely predictable *seasonality*: for example, in family nutrition, or in farm work and output. The second is largely unpredictable *risk*: for the family, say, a health need; for the farm, say, expenditure on coping mechanisms to handle livestock during a drought year. The third is *trend* during the life under any particular management of a family farm. In the family context, this involves the period covering marriage, separation from the parents' household enterprise, formation of a new enterprise and its possible subsequent enlargement, and eventual abandonment (through death, bankruptcy, etc). In the farm context, this trend could involve increasing reliance on purchased inputs and marketed outputs.

To approach these three sorts of change in a rural community, and the actual and potential role of credit in them, we need to consider three "ideal types" of family enterprise. First come the deficit farmers and near-landless, hiring out labour, buying in crop,[2] and almost always net borrowers. Second are small and middle surplus farmers, hiring in some labour and selling some crop. These are normally substantial net borrowers only during periods of change which are due to 'risks' and 'trends' rather than 'seasonalities': for example, during natural disasters, such as droughts, or at the initial stages of adoption[3] of profitable farm innovations. Such periods would be handled by drawing down stocks, especially food-grains,[4] and/or by the sale or mortgage of assets.[5] Third,

most rural communities contain one or two better-off
family enterprises that comprise substantial net lending,
highly localised, with a surplus position from the entrepreneurial activity, usually farming, trading or transport.

Any useful model of rural credit must therefore
establish the links among three main components:

- types of *contingency* that may induce borrowing:
  these are seasonality, risk and trend (this is
  apart from the relatively small type of loan transaction to support purchases of fixed or working
  capital, or consumer durables, with repayment to
  follow as the benefits from the purchased item
  accrue);

- types of *response*, involving credit operations,
  intra-family enterprise adjustments, and perhaps
  asset disposals (or acquisitions, or restructurings)
  and changes in the levels of stocks;

- types of *family enterprise*: deficit (or near-
  landless) farms, small-to-middle surplus farms, and
  surplus-cum-lending enterprises.

*The Inadequacy of Existing Approaches*

Most discussions of credit behaviour in poor rural
environments concentrate on the extent to which farm
investment is affected by the price or availability of
production credit.  Such discussions, however tempting in
their simplicity, are like attempts to understand a
logically unified book by rigorous, but exclusive, attention
to a single parenthesis, inside a paragraph, inside a
chapter, within a book.

The parenthesis analyses the supply to (and, in a few of the better analyses, the demand from) an independent productive undertaking of extra credit for extra farm activities. But, presumably, it is the profit-risk characteristics of the *total* (not just the marginal) portfolio of production activities that the decision-taking unit seeks to optimise.

The paragraph, therefore, considers the selection of this portfolio from the set of available alternatives. If the purchase of a pumpset, financed by a loan, changes the profitability and risk of farming, then the decision to take or reject the loan cannot be explained without reference to the size, composition, profit-probability functions, and interasset covariance of expected profit (those with and without a pumpset-plus-loan) of the whole portfolio of farm assets.

But that paragraph is itself part of a chapter. The particular portfolio is chosen because of the farm's preference structure and information. The preference structure, and especially the profit-risk trade-off, is that of the family farm. Its risk-aversion increases with risk, decreases with liquid assets and expected income, varies according to past experience in risky situations, etc.[6] But all these relationships deal with the risks, experiences, assets, etc of the farm-household unit - comprising consumption as well as production activities. There are various factors which can make farm-households less averse to new risks involved in borrowing,[7] for example, reduced risks of harvest failure caused by ownership of a pesticide sprayer, or reduced risks of ill-health caused by ownership of a clean source of drinking water.

Why do some farm-households borrow more than others?
Even a static, partial-equilibrium answer requires us
(a) to set the parenthesis (decisions to borrow for investment) into the paragraph (decisions about the portfolio of
productive assets); and (b) to set the paragraph into the
chapter (the preferences, incomes and risks of the farm-
household as they affect not only production but also
consumption - including costs of illness, education,
dowries, etc).

To go beyond static explanations of family-farm credit
decisions, this chapter must be read as part of a book: the
particular rural economy-cum-society (eg a village of
residence). Within such a book, individual chapters would
need to analyse the preferences, incomes and risks of the
three main types of family enterprise mentioned above.

The final chapter would need to analyse the effects
on credit of the ways in which the types of household
interact:

- as demanders (or, for some households, as suppliers)
  of credit, sometimes restricted to particular uses,
  seasons or persons;

- as demanders or suppliers of cash, to the extent
  that such interaction is linked to credit in a
  major way, eg because savings by wealthier farmers
  find more profitable outlets as consumer loans (to
  support poorer farmers' dissaving) than as support
  for investment;

- as transactions in other markets in the village (eg
  as landlord and tenant, employer and employee,
  trader and grain buyer or seller);[8]

- as individuals who, separately or collectively, transact with outsiders in these respects - with urban banks, with traders in the next village, etc:

- as members of groups (eg extended family, caste, class, ethnic group, tribe) such that intra-group transactions - in credit or other services - differ from inter-group transactions in frequency, typical size, ease, or terms.

## A Model of Rural Credit Behaviour

How could such a 'book' be compiled? A promising approach would be to set up a simulation of a village and to observe credit behaviour and its effects over time. It would be necessary to assign values to the initial assets, debts, yearly farm inputs and outputs, and yearly family requirements of a representative member from each of the three types of family enterprise; to see what sorts of optimal response emerged to (likely) patterns of (simulated) contingencies; and to trace plausible time-paths of the asset and liability distribution, and of farm inputs and outputs, among the three interacting types of family enter- prise, in a model of a closed village economy. At a later stage other factors such as outside lenders, could be allowed for.

The village might comprise, say, 800 people in 160 households of a given structure realistically divided among the three types of enterprise. For each type, plausible parameters would be specified in equations determining own- farm production, wage-rates paid or received, and consumption functions; and hence savings, labour-market behaviour, and net credit requirements or supplies.

At this stage, smooth flows of labour, inputs, outputs, and consumption over time would be assumed. Circumstances under which this set-up would be at least potentially stable - in which 'steady-state' behaviour in land, labour and credit markets would preserve inter-household distribution of income and assets - would then be specified. (Of course many sets of parameters could never produce even a partially stable set-up, so that one would need to move to and fro - to iterate - between simulated potentially stable situations and simulated parameter sets, until a set that was both plausible and potentially stable was obtained.)

The next step would be to 'disturb' the steady-state outcome, allowing in turn for seasonality, risk and trend, in both family and enterprise, as it affects each group of households. Some disturbances must be assumed to affect all three groups. Drought, in particular, enforces sale of assets and increases indebtedness, thereby making assets cheap and borrowing dear. This would seem to imply progressively increasing inequality, without a lower asymptote for deficit farmers' income, especially since Jodha's evidence is that post-drought 'recovery' of asset positions is far from complete for the poorer households.[9]

Some 'shake-out' mechanism is needed to explain why this ever-growing, crisis-to-crisis inequality - which would eventually eliminate deficit farmers - is not in fact generally observed. Marxists would claim that the magnates and bigger surplus farmers do not allow the 'descending spiral' to push labourers (who in these environments are also usually sustained by some income as deficit farmers) below the point where they obtain the production and reproduction costs of labour. But this (a) assumes more accurate collusion among magnates than seems plausible, (b) does not take account of magnates' interests as *lenders*, and (c) seems

to imply that magnates, under conditions of growing excess
supply of labour, are motivated by obligation or charity to
keep alive more workers than they need.

The neo-classical answer - that the poorest vote with
their feet by emigrating if rewards get too low - seems at
least as implausible,[10] especially under conditions of
widespread drought. Perhaps the answer lies in counter-
vailing factors, mainly the dispersal of holdings to large
and clamorous extended families or to the next generation
of joint families under multi-inheritance. Other factors
might include default, random mismanagement or ill-fortune.

*Policy Questions: Redistribution and Efficiency*

The model focusses attention on a number of questions.
How might supply and demand for credit respond to seasonalities, risks and trends - for magnates, surplus farmers,
and deficit-cum-near-landless? What might be the likely
course and outcome of resulting interactions among the
three groups? What could be the policy implications of such
interactions?

To begin with the latter question: the objectives of
credit policy are, first, to improve rural equity (and rural
life as a whole) by removing the poor from the area of
power of local moneylenders; and, second, to improve the
dynamic efficiency of rural production, by diverting both
supply and demand for money to lend away from consumption
needs, towards high-yielding productive activities. It must
be stressed, in these policy contexts, that the two aims are
linked. Asset and income redistribution are dynamically
efficient for at least three reasons connected with the use
of credit by family enterprises as producer-consumer units.

First, in many villages, inequality diverts investible resources into the 'consumer credit cycle' of lending and dissaving. For the better-off, the privately highest-yielding use of extra cash (which often accrues to them via fungible loans from institutions), or of extra grain surpluses, is not investment, but extra lending to finance consumer borrowing by the poor; subsequently, the better-off can use their local knowledge (and power) to reduce the risk of default. For the poor, the highest-yielding use of extra cash is often not investment, but the repayment or replacement of moneylender, trader, or big farmer credit for consumption. Such credit earns rates of return of well over 20 per cent (often 'real' because loans and repayments are made in grains instead of cash), and further it gives lenders not only status and power, but also economic advantages in other markets. Therefore, both the gains to lenders and the economies to borrowers, if they direct extra resources towards consumer-credit uses (res-pectively, extra lending and either repayment or extra and creditless consumption), are likely to exceed gains from productive investment. If there is a redistribution of command over productive assets, however, this reduces both the supply and the demand for consumer credit - the supply as the magnates' assets and surpluses fall, the demand as the deficit farmers' assets, and prospects of subsistence with fewer loans, rise. This diverts the family enterprise's surpluses (as enhanced by institutional loans) towards productive investment. Big farmers invest more, because redistribution has reduced the demand for consumer loans from them; small farmers invest more, because redis-tribution has reduced their need to divert funds towards debt management.

The second way in which the family-enterprise structur-ing of the rural economy causes redistribution to induce

efficiency, is a version of the 'Sen effect'.[11] This is
the tendency of smaller (family) units - operating labour-
intensively, providing direct and literally paternalist
supervision, and offering family workers the *average* product of their labour - to produce at a given technology
more output, per unit of non-labour inputs, than do larger
units. Larger (commercial) units have higher land/labour
(and usually capital/labour) ratios, experience positive
and rising marginal supervision costs, offer workers
incentives that comprise only the *marginal* product of
labour, and, if the hire of workers is localised (and
especially at peak seasons), tend to pull up wage-rates
monopsonistically.

The 'Sen effect', as applied to rural credit for
family enterprises, suggests that (a) rates of return to
extra credit (where it does go alongside extra productive
investment) would be greater on smaller farms, and (b)
defaults would be a lower proportion of loans for smaller
borrowing units. There is mounting evidence for both
propositions, and it suggests that redistribution of loans
- and of assets - towards smaller family enterprises would
increase their contribution to total output.

The third link between redistribution and the
efficiency of credit for family enterprises concerns risk.
If assets and income, and especially security against
disaster, increase for the poorest, then their willingness
to include high-risk, high-expected-return investments in
their portfolio also increases. In particular, they
become readier to use credit for extra production activities
instead of using it to repay loans for, or to increase,
current consumption. However, it is only at low or near-
subsistence income levels that risk-aversion is likely to
fall substantially when the level of assets (or expected
income) rises. Hence a rise in the poorest farmers' assets,

consequent on redistribution, could be expected to raise
'risky' productive investment substantially. But the
corresponding reduction in the average assets of the better-
off - from, say, ten times the per-family village average
to five times - need not make these families substantially
reduce the proportion of their portfolio comprising high-
risk, high-productivity assets.

The average expected annual yield of the village's
net asset portfolio is therefore increased, through the
effects on credit in family enterprises, inasmuch as redistribution (a) cuts supply and demand of consumer credit,
diverting both to production; (b) pushes credit towards
households who combine it with more labour; and (c) reduces
risk-aversion (in poor households made somewhat less poor)
more than it increases risk-aversion (in rich households
made somewhat less rich).

*Redistribution over Time: Seasonality*

So far I have been examining the general framework
within which the distribution of credit (or assets generally)
from rich to poor villagers can be seen, in the context of
interacting family enterprises as a means to the increased
social efficiency of credit use. A partial substitute for
such redistribution among families is the capacity of the
individual family enterprise to redistribute its own
resources and requirements over time. Seasonally, this
could involve (eg) scheduling social and domestic obligations in the slack season; or carrying over grain stocks
against risk in bad years. In terms of trends, this could
involve (eg) shuttle migration, in the context of the 'share
family',[12] to deal with family maturation while exploiting
the rising urban share in work chances. Such adaptation
is severely limited, especially for deficit farmers in poor

and risk-prone environments, because resources scarcely
suffice to ensure short-run survival, let alone to permit
long-run planning based on deferred gratification. Deficit
farmers are therefore compelled, when a bad harvest disrupts
the normal seasonal cycle of borrowing and repayment, to
move more deeply into consumer debt, and/or sell productive
assets - in both ways reducing future prospects to build
up production and to reduce consumer debt.[13]

Can the seasonal fluctuations of the deficit-farm and
near-landless  family enterprise be reduced, rendered more
contravariant, or otherwise made more manageable, in ways
that will (a) directly permit reduction in dependence on
seasonal consumer credit, thus redirecting both supplies
of such credit and demands for it towards productive uses,
and (b) achieve such aims indirectly, by raising the lean-
season 'floor' that is from time to time pushed down by
natural disasters?

Seasonal fluctuations affect the deficit farmer's
credit needs in two ways: via food availability and via
food requirements. Food availability is lowest just before
harvest, when prices are high and on-farm stocks low, but
when off-farm work is probably available. Food requirements - for an entire family at work (on or off the deficit
farm), and for protection against disease - are also highest
late in the wet season.[14] It is not surprising that, at
this time, credit to deficit farmers and the near-landless
is in most demand. Yet credit supply is relatively short,
since seasonal costs are high, but incomes less so, for the
main lenders - traders and surplus farmers. Transactions
thus take place at seasonally high interest rates: advance
grain sales at bargain prices by deficit farmers to traders;
grain purchases, in return for large commitments of hired
labour through the harvesting and threshing seasons, by the

landless from big farmers.  Such credit might be diverted
towards productive uses, and the deficit farmer's readiness
for a high-yield but somewhat riskier portfolio enhanced,
in several ways.

Firstly, some of the flows could be smoothed out, eg
if irrigation permitted double-cropping, or if (in areas
where water-management or pest-control would not be severely
damaged) crops or varieties were introduced with different
time-schedules, permitting staggered cropping.

Secondly, residual levels from some sub-systems could
be altered, with the effect of smoothing.  To some extent
improved on-farm storage could reduce the demand for consumer
credit by increasing the edible foodgrains left in on-farm
consumption-orientated stores towards the end of the slack
season.

Thirdly, various factors presently correlated, which
tend to raise demand and lower supply for consumer credit,
could be uncoupled.  This possibility arises for risks and
trends, as well as for seasonality.  The localised portfolio
of lenders comprises ventures that tend to go sour together;
and I have proposed remedies for this, including elements
of equity lending and have suggested ways to render the
borrower's asset values covariant with his liability
values.[15]  The alternative approach to 'uncoupling' -
creation of contravariant *asset* values for (deficit-farm)
borrowers - may require implausibly sophisticated financial
markets (eg shares in food-stocking companies).

Fourthly, investments could be made in new, explicitly
counter-seasonal activities.  In one-season agricultures,
this is difficult without irrigation (animal husbandry
normally yields most, and requires most labour-time for both

draught and milk, at the same time as crops[16]). One
approach is to look for activities with very low capital/
labour ratios (preferably using non-perishable farm outputs, as with some crafts and textile or leatherwork).
Such activities avoid the problem of tying up a lot of
scarce capital to be used for only part of the year, but
can offer sufficient return to attract effort in the slack
seasons when its opportunity-cost is low. To achieve the
objective of significantly reducing the deficit and near-
landless units' dependence on credit for slack-season
consumption, such capital should be firmly steered to the
poorer and more seasonally workless groups. Further it
should not require too great caloric expenditure to operate;
and preferably it should be owned individually or jointly
by those who work it.

For all these four types of activity, the true social
rate of return on investment may well be substantially
above the apparent rate. This is because such activities
cause the supply and demand for credit to be diverted: from
consumption support to production support; from larger to
smaller (and more labour-intensive) units; and from safer
to higher yielding operations. Moreover, credit transactions
due to reduction of seasonal peaks and troughs, will take
place at lower unit administrative cost.

*Unpredictability and Risk*

If the date of onset, the volume, and the distribution
of seasonal rainfall were perfectly predictable, there
would still remain the need for expensive adjustments, as
compared to a situation where a similar volume of annual
crops could be taken at any time with the same production
cost. However, with perfect predictability, one would

expect that a number of competing merchants would hold
and dispose of stocks at normal rates of profit, and that
credit markets (subject to constraints imposed by local
knowledge and power) would adjust similarly. That this
does not happen is due to the superimposition, on seasonal
variations, of random yearly shocks.

These are of two types. Broadly, those affecting
the enterprise will benefit a very large number of borrowing
farmers at once. Bad rains will hit all deficit farmers,
and most surplus farmers too; although in a fairly big and
fairly closed economy the magnates can gain more by price
rises than they lose by output falls. Demand-induced
price rises will benefit magnates and surplus farmers, but
hurt deficit farmers who are net buyers of the affected
commodity, though they may be compensated, by increases
in the demand for their labour as surplus farmers seek to
raise output in response to higher prices. Random shocks
affecting the family tend - except for now rare events
such as sudden non-seasonal changes in disease incidence -
to hit a few borrowers and lenders each year, raising
demand for credit (and reducing both repayment and credit
supply) for the affected group, but not for the economy as
a whole.

It is the coincidence of random shocks with macro-
disturbances - of, say, serious illness with bad rainfall
- that characteristically destroys the creditworthiness of
a deficit farmer, and impels the family down the slope of
default, loss of assets, and eventual landlessness. Especially if slack season debts remain unpaid when (say)
drought and illness strike, a deficit-farm family has
little chance of survival. Hard-working, entrepreneurial
families can be innocently sentenced to many years of *de
facto* bond-slavery, during which their skills, enterprise,

and capacity to save are shifted out of the family farm, towards underpaid employment in discharge of debt (simply to declare bond-slavery illegal, without providing alternative sources of income and security, is *at best* useless).

Can this be avoided?  Asset redistribution would provide the deficit-cum-landless group with cushions against the debt spiral, but this requires considerable political skill and courage, for which fulmination against village usurers provides no substitute.  Usurers are paid for real local knowledge, incur substantial loan costs,[17] and at present discharge a role, in consumer lending, which institutions are unwilling or unable to fulfil. Restrictions on their interest charges, or legislation to forgive debts due to them, produce little result except to dry up future credit, especially for poorer or riskier borrowers.

There are other measures which offer more immediate promise.  First, public-sector and co-operative institutions - whether directly, via support to traditional lenders or by channelling funds on an agency basis via revolving credit and savings associations[18] - can make more (non-subsidised, repayable) consumer credit available to meet family contingencies, and can expand such support when times are bad overall.  Admittedly, the impact of expanding credit when output is low is inflationary.  However, the attempt by institutions to replace traditional moneylenders, and to provide more *production* credit for deficit farmers, is hopeless so long as such farmers must turn to moneylenders for *consumption* credit.  Far better for institutions to use a given volume of resources to deal with the total credit situation in a few places to increase financial self-sufficiency there - and then to 'revolve' their credit on

elsewhere - rather than to fail to handle producer credit
in isolation in many places.

The second possibility for ameliorating the credit
problems now caused by family contingency lies in social
security.  It is the conventional wisdom that very poor
countries cannot afford it, although the experience of not
only China and Cuba, but also Sri Lanka, cast doubt on this.
Even if direct cash compensation for (say) health contingencies poses insuperable administrative or financial
problems, it could well prove possible for real services to
be provided free of charge, for all who require them, over
a wide field in health and primary education at a much
lower level of GNP per person than is now usual.  If this
released many poor family enterprises, such as deficit
farmers, from the need to divert surpluses away from
investment and towards repayment of, or substitution for,
emergency credit; or if it forced wealthy lenders to look
for a 'vent for surplus' with higher social returns than
emergency lending; then basic security against social
welfare contingencies might have a substantial 'hidden'
return, apart from the effect in persuading family enterprises to accept high-risk, high-expected profit activities
in their *production* portfolio.

A word should be said about the role of the extended
family, or the larger kin group, in providing informal
mutual insurance against the need to borrow when emergency
strikes the nuclear family.  Sociologists no longer accept
simplistic accounts of the unilinear decline of extended
families, but nevertheless, as the successful nuclear
family finds more chances to turn effort and enterprise
into income, so it is bound to become increasingly reluctant
to share that income with the siblings of either spouse,
or to see it used as a reserve for the emergencies of remoter

kin.  For the really poor, extended families[19] and kin-
groups[20] have proved flexible sources of insurance; but, as
some succeed and leave poverty, motivations diverge,
insurance breaks down, and 'poor relations' of the newly
successful place increasing demands upon informal credit
in emergencies.  Social action, along lines already indicated, is needed if such demands are not to deplete the
pool of credit available for production, and (by encouraging
the successful to reduce their obligations) to cause the
successes of some to lead to the distress, in unfavourable
contingency, of others.

*Trends*

Apart from seasonality and risks, what of the third
sort of change - trends - that affects the family enterprise?
Greater commercialisation, higher yields, ageing, family
enlargement, separation, etc are more predictable than such
risks as drought, but less predictable than the pattern of
the seasons.  Until recently, family trends were much more
important than trends in the economic or technical environment
(or set of options) facing the farm enterprise.  It is still
probably the case that a couple, planning the family enterprise ten or twenty years ahead, would adapt decisions
(including credit decisions) much more to the expected
pattern of family formation and separation, than to the less
reliably predictable, and probably more slowly changing,
pattern of ecological and economic environments.

Chayanov, in his analysis of Russia, saw trends in
family size and structure as crucial (and trends in the
techno-economic environment, apparently, as negligible) in
determining the family's labour input.[21]  In Chayanov's
Russia, the area of land farmed expanded fairly smoothly

alongside extra labour inputs. However, even in contemporary
Kenyan cases where land is not so plentiful, the need for
food has to be offset against the 'drudgery' of labour. The
point of balance - at which (rising) marginal disutility
of effort (to farm more land) just equalled (falling) marginal
utility of (falling) food output from extra effort - would
clearly depend on the number of hands to work, and the
number of mouths to feed. A clear pattern of effort-acreage
decisions, corresponding to family trends (formation,
enlargement, separation), was thus predicted by Chayanov.

While a closely parallel, completely independent, and
justly celebrated 'life-cycle theory' of saving has been
developed for Western economies,[22] no account of credit or
capital-market decisions for the family enterprise in less-
developed villages has been attempted. Presumably, given
normal weather, many smallholdings that can generate a small
surplus while both spouses work and before children arrive,
will become substantially deficit holdings during late
pregnancy and lactation. At that time, debts will be
incurred and/or liquid elements in past surpluses run down.
Between school and marriage, children may well add more to
enterprise output than they take from family income,
especially as the mother is again freed for work. Marriage,
especially if costs to parents are involved, can force
further debts, as strong youngsters leave ageing parents
suddenly unable to work land without hiring in labour to
replace the missing children.

*Research Directions*

A good deal of speculation is possible along the various
lines suggested by this paper. What is needed, however, is:

- empirical work, showing how credit positions differ
  in a village as between different stages of family
  development, ideally over time, but as a second
  best across a cross-section;

- theoretical models of how family development affects
  credit positions (in deficit, surplus and magnate
  groups), where such development is (a) responded to
  only *ex post*, or (b) more or less anticipated;

- numerical simulations of credit positions of
  various families, and hence of magnate, surplus
  and deficit groups, over their periods of family
  development.

I suspect that the 'credit history' of a village, and
especially the supply - and demand - for producer credit,
could prove extremely sensitive to the family structure of
one or two magnate households - and to innovations, such
as malaria control, that affect the composition of deficit-
farm borrowing families. Little has been said here about
the inter-group transfers induced by credit, and by changes
in credit positions due to seasonality, risk and trend. I
have only given a hint of the complexities behind rural
credit markets; but this suffices to reveal the dangerous
absurdity of policy recommendations based on the market for
*extra* investment finance, as if that could be considered in
splendid, static isolation.

1  A dramatic, very thoroughly researched, and unpublished
   example is for Shoshong, S. E. Botswana, in 1971-72.
   L. Syson and A. Seager (UNDP, *Shoshung Activities Research,*

computer printouts) showed that, during the agriculturally
slackest seasons (17.8.71 - 8.11.71 and 19.7.72 - 15.8.72),
domestic work took up the largest part of a person's
activities for 152 person-half-days per four-week period
per household; in the busy season (1.3.72 - 10.6.72) the
average fell to 90 person-half-days. Families' decisions
about when to send older children to school also vary
with work chances on the farm.

2  The complication that even some deficit farmers sell a
cash-crop to buy cereals makes no basic difference to
the arguments below. It increases the vulnerability of
such farmers to unfavourable changes, but improves their
average access to (fungible) cash, so that the effects
on their requirements for credit, and the price they have
to pay for it, are indeterminate.

3  If the adoption is profitable, subsequent credit requirements should fall. Credit appears to be an important
determinant of adoption behaviour only in environments
with (a) severe initial inequality (IRRI, *Changes in
Rice Farming in Selected Areas in Asia*, Los Banos, 1978,
p. 95) or (b) substantial security of water supply (M.
Schluter, "The Interaction of Credit and Uncertainty in
. . . Surat District, India", *Occasional Paper* No. 68,
Employment and Income Distribution Project, Department
of Applied Economics, Cornell University, 1974).

4  Storage and depletion of food, and acquisition and sale
of assets (see M. D. Morris, "What is Famine?", *Economic
and Political Weekly* IX, 44, 1974), are alternatives to
adjustments between family and enterprise, and to credit,
as ways of dealing with the non-static nature of economic
life. Interactions with storage and assets are largely
neglected here, in the interests of simplicity; but the

256

planner has to choose the optimal balance between outlays
to improve storage, asset markets and credit, under
different conditions relating to the operation of the
family.

N. S. Jodha, "Role of Credit in Farmers' Adjustment
against Risk in Arid and Semi-Arid Tropical Areas of India",
*Occasional Paper* No. 20, ICRISAT Economics Programme,
Hyderabad, 1978, p. 11, compares (i) increases in indebtedness and (ii) net reduction in assets (excluding
land and buildings) as between a normal year and the
subsequent drought year (in 1972-73 prices). In two
areas in Rajasthan, asset values fell by Rs. 1300-1500
per household, while debts rose by only Rs. 350-400. In
the areas in Maharashtra and Gujarat, the figures were
Rs. 500-650 for asset reduction and Rs. 200-250 for debt
increase.

6 M. Lipton, "Agricultural Risk, Rural Credit and the
Inefficiency of Inequity", in J. Roumasset and J-M.
Boussard (eds), *Risk in Agriculture*, SEARCA, Philippines,
1979.

7 For evidence that farmers, even at high income levels,
as in the USA, curtail borrowing for production in order
to leave 'credit reserve' for consumption if things go
wrong see, P. J. Barry and C. B. Baker, "Reservation
Prices and Credit Uses: A Measure of Response to Uncertainty", *American Economic Review*, Vol. 53, No. 2, 1971.

8 For the impact of "multiple binds" on credit - of the
way in which lenders can use their monopsony (eg for
employees) or monopoly (eg of transport or land-to-rent)
in non-credit markets - see A. Bhaduri, "Agricultural
Backwardness under Semi-Feudalism", *Economic Journal*,

Vol. 83, No. 329, March 1973. A converse effect - credit dependence that weakens the tenant's bargaining power - is discussed in IRRI, *Changes in Rice Farming in Selected Areas in Asia*, Los Banos, 1978, p. 121.

9   Jodha, *op. cit.* For other discussions of the "descending spiral", in which productive assets are progressively lost (partly via foreclosures) by the poor to the rich from one bad year to the next, see F. Bailey, *Caste and the Economic Frontier*, Manchester, 1957, pp. 73-85; IRRI, *op. cit.*, p. 149, summarising T. K. Pal's work in Orissa; S. Epstein, *South India: Yesterday, Today and Tomorrow*, Manchester, 1973, pp. 165-67.

10   Because townward emigration is smaller, less permanent, and more concentrated upon less poor families, villages and countries than is usually believed. See M. Lipton, *Why Poor People Stay Poor*, Temple Smith, 1977.

11   See A. K. Sen's work and the ensuing discussions in *Economic Weekly*, (Bombay), 1963-64, and the useful summary in A. R. Khan, *The Economy of Bangladesh*, Macmillan, 1972, p. 133. For recent evidence see A. Berry and W. Cline, *Agrarian Structure and Productivity in Developing Countries*, Johns Hopkins University Press, Baltimore, 1979.

12   Epstein, *op. cit.*

13   Jodha, *loc. cit.*

14   S. Schofield, "Seasonal Factors Affecting Nutrition in Different Age Groups and Especially Pre-School Children", *Journal of Development Studies*, Vol. 11, No. 1, 1974; R. Chambers and R. Longhurst with D. Bradley and R. Feachem,

"Seasonal Dimensions to Rural Poverty", Discussion Paper No. 142, Institute of Development Studies, Sussex, 1979.

15  M. Lipton in *Risk in Agriculture, op. cit.*

16  UNDP, *loc. cit.*, Shoshong Survey.

17  A. Bottomley, "The Costs of Administering Private Loans in Underdeveloped Rural Areas", *Oxford Economic Papers,* Vol. 15, No. 2, 1963.

18  F. J. A. Bouman, "Indigenous Savings and Credit Societies in the Third World - Any Message,", Agricultural University of Wageningen, mimeo, 1978.

19  See Epstein, *op. cit.*, on the "share family".

20  For a fascinating example during the transition to an urban environment (Lagos) see P. Morris, *Loss and Change,* Routledge and Kegan Paul, London, 1974, pp. 46-50.

21  A. Chayanov, *Theory of Peasant Economy* (tr. D. Thorner, ed. B. Kerblay), Irwin, 1966.  See also D. Hunt, "Chayanov's Model of Peasant Household Resource Allocation and its Relevance to Mbere Division, Eastern Kenya", *Journal of Development Studies,* Vol. 15, No. 1, 1978.

22  F. Modigliani and R. Brumberg, "Utility Analysis and the Consumption Function", in K. Khara (ed), *Post-Keynesian Economics,* Rutgers, 1954.

# FARM LEVEL CREDIT USE AMONG CO-OPERATIVE
# FARMERS IN NIGERIA

*Adeniyi Osuntogun*
*Department of Agricultural Economics*
*University of Ife*
*Nigeria*

## *Background*

There is a growing recognition among Nigerian farmers
of the effect of improved inputs and new technology on
agricultural yield.  The use of these improved inputs and
the adoption of the yield-inducing techniques have given
rise to an increased demand for agricultural credit.
Accordingly, the Federal Government has established various
types of financial institutions and it has also encouraged
the development of credit schemes, including the co-operative
credit scheme which is the focus of this paper.

The paper is based upon a study of co-operative farmers
in Oyo, Ondo and Ogun states of Nigeria.  It identifies the
extent to which the co-operative farmers use credit, the
purposes for which it is used, the sources of credit, the
terms of the loan and the nature of co-operative credit
problems from the farmers' perspective.  The study has been
undertaken to bridge the gap in knowledge and also to lay
down a sound factual basis for formulating agricultural
co-operative credit policies.

Since this study focussed on co-operative farmers,
twelve primary societies were selected in the three states.

Five of the societies were located in Oyo state, four were
in Ondo state while the remaining three were in Ogun state:
220 farmer-members were randomly selected and interviewed
from the primary societies.  The distribution of the respondents consisted of 92 farmers from Oyo state, 73 farmers
from Ondo state and 55 farmers from Ogun state.  The selection of both the number of societies and the members was,
to a large extent, influenced by the stage of development
of co-operative activities in the three states.  Thus Oyo
state, which was         first according to available statistics, had the highest number of societies and members.
It was followed by Ondo state which was ranked second and
Ogun state which was ranked third.

*Use of Credit*

   The main crops raised by the respondents were cocoa,
kola, palm produce, rice, cassava, yam and maize.  The
average size of farm was about 1.5 hectares.  In the course
of the investigation, we discovered that credit played an
important role in the farming activities of our respondents.
All the farmers interviewed claimed that they used credit
during the 1977 production season.  The average account of
credit used per borrower varied from N92.4 in Ondo state
to N155.9 in Oyo state (Table 1).

   The co-operative farmers that were interviewed in the
course of this study used credit for farm and non-farm
purposes, (see Table 1).  Farm uses of credit accounted for
only 39.4% of the total funds borrowed by the respondents
in the three states.  The inter-state comparison indicates
that whereas the percentage of borrowed funds used for
farming purposes amounted to 52.1% in Ondo state, it varied
from 33.3% in Oyo state to 39.6% in Ogun state.

Table 1

Use of Credit by Some Co-operative Farmers in Oyo, Ondo and Ogun States, Nigeria

| Item/Use | Oyo State | | Ondo State | | Ogun State | | Total | |
|---|---|---|---|---|---|---|---|---|
| | % of Funds | No. of Replies | % of Funds | No. of Replies | % of Funds | No. of Replies | % of Funds | No. of Replies |
| Number of replies | – | 92 | – | 73 | – | 55 | – | 220 |
| Total amount borrowed (N) | 14,345 | – | 6,743 | – | 7,334 | – | 28,422 | – |
| Amount used for farming (N) | 4,738 | – | 3,513 | – | 2,905 | – | 11,201 | – |
| *Farm Use* | | | | | | | | |
| Land clearing | 53.0 | 22 | 56.5 | 25 | 40.6 | 25 | 50.0 | 72 |
| Ridging | 12.0 | 11 | 9.0 | 12 | 21.7 | 18 | 14.2 | 41 |
| Planting | 4.0 | 5 | 4.6 | 11 | 17.2 | 11 | 8.6 | 27 |
| Fertiliser/Chemicals | 9.0 | 13 | 19.8 | 16 | 5.6 | 5 | 11.5 | 34 |
| Weeding | 11.0 | 11 | 4.6 | 7 | 11.5 | 5 | 9.0 | 23 |
| Harvesting | 5.0 | 7 | 3.3 | 7 | 3.4 | 2 | 3.9 | 16 |
| Processing | 3.0 | 2 | 0.2 | 2 | – | – | 1.1 | 4 |
| Miscellaneous | 3.0 | 2 | 2.0 | 2 | – | – | 1.7 | 4 |
| *Non-Farm Use* | | | | | | | | |
| Payment of school fees | 57.9 | 46 | 55.7 | 21 | 13.8 | 9 | 42.5 | 76 |
| Payment of dowry | 1.6 | 2 | 4.6 | 2 | 8.7 | 5 | 5.0 | 9 |
| Payment of hospital bill | 5.4 | 18 | 4.6 | 5 | 2.6 | 4 | 4.2 | 27 |
| Payment for durable goods | 12.9 | 7 | 8.6 | 4 | 26.4 | 4 | 16.0 | 15 |
| Building/Repairing house | 15.0 | 11 | 3.3 | 4 | 0.9 | 2 | 6.4 | 18 |
| For religious ceremony | 3.6 | 11 | 2.2 | 2 | 3.5 | 2 | 3.1 | 15 |
| For child naming ceremony | 0.9 | 2 | 2.5 | 2 | 2.3 | 2 | 1.9 | 6 |
| For burial ceremony | 2.7 | 4 | 3.0 | 2 | 2.6 | 2 | 2.8 | 10 |
| Miscellaneous | – | – | 15.4 | 4 | 39.2 | 12 | 18.1 | 16 |

Table 1 also indicates that land clearing was the
most important farm level credit use of the respondents.
It constituted the largest single use both in terms of
the magnitude of credit use, as well as the number of borrowers using loans.  On average, 50% of the total funds
used for farming by the farmers interviewed was spent on land
clearing.  One of the main reasons that could account for
this is the rising cost of hired labour.  The past one and
a half decades has featured the rapid development of the
non-agricultural sector of the Nigerian economy, particularly
the construction and mining sub-sectors.  This has contributed to rapid rural-urban migration which has resulted in
the acute shortage of farm labourers.  The shortage has
contributed greatly to the rise in the cost of the services
of the few that remained as farm labourers.  Ridging ranked
the second most important agricultural use of credit.  About
14% of the total funds was spent on this item by 41 of the
respondents.

The amount of credit used for fertilizer and chemicals
was relatively small, with only 11.5% of the total funds
used for farm purposes being committed to this item.  Land
clearing, ridging, fertilizer and chemicals together accounted for 75.7% of all borrowed funds used for farm purposes.
Planting, weeding, harvesting and processing accounted for
only 22.6%: in most cases, these activities were carried
out by the farmers themselves and members of their families.
Hence, there was little need to borrow for the payment of
these services.

Non-farm uses constituted the bulk of the funds borrowed
by the respondents in 1977.  This category of uses accounted
for 60.6% of the total borrowed funds in the three states.
The most predominant non-farm use of credit was school fees.
On average, 42.5% of the total borrowed funds used for non-
farm purposes was spent on school fees in the three states.

In two of the states school fees accounted for over 50%
of the funds used on non-farm purposes.  The result of
this analysis, which emphasises the value that farmers
attach to their children's education  is similar to the findings of Adegboye[1].  In his study of loan procurement,
Adegboye discovered that children's education ranked first
among reasons for pledging cocoa farms for loans.

Contrary to the findings of others.[2] borrowing for
ceremonial purposes did not feature prominently among our
respondents .  When all farmers are considered as a group,
the three categories of religious, naming and burial cerem-
onies accounted for only 7.8% of the total funds used for
non-farm purposes.  This result confirms the result of a
similar study that was conducted by the author in two villages of South Western Nigeria.[3]

*Sources and Sizes of Loans*

The farmers interviewed in the course of this study
depended largely on their co-operative societies for the
credit they used in 1977 (see Table 2).  Co-operative societies accounted for almost 85% of the total amount borrowed.
Table 2 contains information on the size of loans received
by the respondents from co-operative societies.  Most of
the loans were of small size: 38.4% of the loans were for
₦200 or less.  About 26% of the loans were between ₦200.1
and ₦400.  Thus, a total of 64.7% of all loans made by the
co-operatives were for ₦400 and below.  Only 26.8% of the
loans exceeded ₦500.

The findings of the analysis of co-operative loans have
significant policy implications both for the co-operative
credit scheme and the development of peasant agriculture.
The magnitude of the loans made by the societies, in some
cases, seemed small relative to the needs of the farmer.

264

Table 2

Value of Loans Received by some Farmers from Co-operative Societies
in Oyo, Ondo and Ogun States, Nigeria

| Size of Loan | Oyo State | | Ondo State | | Ogun State | | Total | |
|---|---|---|---|---|---|---|---|---|
| | No. of Loans | Percent of Loans | No. of Loans | Percent of Loans | No. of Loans | Percent of Loans | No. of Loans | Percent of Loans |
| Less than ₦100 | 5 | 4.4 | 15 | 18.1 | 5 | 8.1 | 25 | 9.7 |
| ₦100.1 – ₦200 | 14 | 12.4 | 35 | 42.2 | 25 | 40.3 | 74 | 28.7 |
| ₦200.1 – ₦300 | 16 | 14.2 | 20 | 24.1 | 3 | 4.8 | 39 | 15.1 |
| ₦300.1 – ₦400 | 11 | 9.7 | 5 | 6.0 | 13 | 21.0 | 29 | 11.2 |
| ₦400.1 – ₦500 | 14 | 12.4 | 3 | 3.6 | 5 | 8.1 | 22 | 8.5 |
| Over ₦500 | 53 | 46.9 | 5 | 6.0 | 11 | 17.7 | 69 | 26.8 |

This resulted in some borrowers supplementing co-operative
credit with loans from other sources, especially the informal
non-institutional sources of credit.  Previous studies
have shown the adverse effects of borrowing from such
sources on the development of small-scale agriculture.[4]
Practices of borrowing from some informal sources might also
have implications for the repayment of co-operative loans.

The co-operative farmers included in this study did not
depend much on informal sources for the credit they used in
1977.  Only 10.2% of the total loans borrowed were from
this category of lenders, (Table 3).  An inter-state comparison shows that the most predominant informal source of
credit varies among the three states.  Thus while "friends"
were the leading informal credit source in Oyo and Ogun
states, money lenders constituted the principal informal
source of credit in Ondo state.  It is important to emphasise that it was only in Ondo state that money lenders
were active.

Another interesting development in the financing
of  Nigerian agriculture is the role of the commercial
banks.  In general, commercial banks are reluctant to lend
to small-scale farmers.  This is due to a number of factors
some of which include the high risk associated with agricultural production, the high cost of administering such
loans, the absence of acceptable collateral security and
the shortage of personnel able to administer agricultural
loans.  Our investigation showed that only one loan was
received in Oyo state from the commercial bank.  Its value
was ₦1,500, which constituted 10.5% of the total borrowed
funds by the respondents in Oyo state.

*Loan Terms*

The terms and conditions of lending are part of the

Table 3

Non Co-operative Society Sources of Borrowed Funds
Used by Some Co-operative Farmers in Oyo, Ondo
and Ogun States, Nigeria

| Source of Credit | Oyo State | Ondo State | Ogun State | Total |
|---|---|---|---|---|
| Number of farmers interviewed | 92 | 73 | 55 | 220 |
| Total amount borrowed (₦) | 14,345 | 6,743 | 7,334 | 28,422 |
| *Relatives* | | | | |
| Number of loans | 2 | 6 | – | 8 |
| Percent of total amount borrowed | 1.3 | 8.1 | – | 2.6 |
| Average size of loan (₦) | 90.0 | 91.4 | – | 91.1 |
| *Friends* | | | | |
| Number of loans | 7 | 5 | 1 | 13 |
| Percent of total amount borrowed | 2.6 | 3.0 | 0.7 | 2.2 |
| Average size of loan (₦) | 52.8 | 40.0 | 50.0 | 47.7 |
| *Esusu Group*[5] | | | | |
| Number of loans | 1 | 13 | 2 | 16 |
| Percent of total amount borrowed | 0.3 | 7.4 | 0.1 | 2.2 |
| Average size of loan (₦) | 40.0 | 38.3 | 45.0 | 39.3 |
| *Money lenders* | | | | |
| Number of loans | – | 2 | – | 2 |
| Percent of total amount borrowed | – | 13.3 | – | 3.2 |
| Average size of loan (₦) | – | 449.0 | – | 449.0 |
| *Commercial Banks* | | | | |
| Number of loans | 1 | – | – | 1 |
| Percent of total amount borrowed | 10.5 | – | – | 5.3 |
| Average size of loan (₦) | 1500.0 | – | – | 1500.0 |

items which should be taken into account in evaluating the
performance and effectiveness of a credit system.  In our
survey area, loan terms differed for different types of
lenders.  The co-operatives, which provided the bulk of
the loans used by our respondents, had a relatively more
liberal lending policy compared to the other sources of
credit.  The extension of co-operative credit was usually
based on the borrower's personal integrity and financial
ability to repay the loan.  His past record and the extent
of his involvement and active participation in the society's
affairs were also very important.  The cost of a co-operative
loan was relatively small: on average, it amounted to about
14%.

Unlike the co-operatives, the informal sources of
credit, with the exception of relatives, required some
form of additional security for loan besides the borrower's
personal integrity and financial ability to repay the loan
when due.  Such securities include land, crops and the
borrower's personal belongings such as a farm-house.  The
rate of interest charged by most informal lenders, especially the money lenders, ranged from 40% to 85%.

*Opinions of Farmers*

Since the co-operative societies were the major sources
of loans for the members, the respondents were asked for
their impressions of the loan activities of their societies.
In Table 4 the responses are summarized.  It is important
to emphasise that the most mentioned response was "No
complaint", which portrays a good impression of the societies' loan activities.

Inadequacy of co-operative loans was the most mentioned
problem.  Over 41% of all the respondents gave this complaint.
It was due to this problem that co-operative farmers resorted

Table 4

## Complaints of Some Farmers on the Loan Activities
### of their Co-operative Societies

| Nature of Complaint | Oyo State | Ondo State | Ogun State | Total |
|---|---|---|---|---|
| | Percentage of Respondents | | | |
| Society's loans are inadequate | 36.9 | 38.2 | 53.5 | 41.4 |
| Society should extend time of repayment of loans | 10.3 | 5.5 | – | 6.4 |
| Non timeliness of the disbursement of loans | – | 5.4 | – | 1.8 |
| Society should assist in giving capital equipment | – | 3.6 | – | 1.2 |
| No complaint - I am satisfied with the society | 52.8 | 47.3 | 46.5 | 49.2 |

to borrowing from the other credit agencies, mostly
the informal lenders, to supplement the amounts that they
had borrowed from their societies. The other problem
mentioned was the extension of time of repayment of loans.
This problem was common in Oyo and Ondo states.

Problems of non-timeliness of the disbursement of loans
occurred only in Ondo state, but only 5% of the farmers interviewed in the state mentioned this problem. Also, it
was in Ondo state that a small number of the members expressed the desire for their societies to assist in giving
capital equipment.

*Policy Implications*

Credit played an important role in the farming activities of the respondents, with all the farmers having
borrowed money for this purpose in 1977. The average amount
borrowed per respondent was ₦129.2, but only 39.4% of the
total funds borrowed was used on farming. This situation
is serious given the fact that the future development of
Nigerian agriculture depends to a large extent, on the small
farmers. This study shows that, contrary to a widely held
opinion, a very small proportion of the borrowed funds is
spent on ceremonial purposes. Hence, one of the principal
reasons that could be responsible for spending a small
proportion of borrowed funds on actual farming purposes is
the inadequate supply of essential welfare services in the
rural areas. Services like modern housing, health and
educational relief rarely exist in the Nigerian rural sector. Most farmers borrow to provide these services themselves.

In order to encourage farmers to invest more in agriculture, the government should step up its welfare services in the rural areas. This should include

improved housing schemes and health services. The
government should also take over a larger share of the
cost of the nation's education.

Co-operatives can be useful means of channelling
farm credit to small-holders. Our analysis suggests the
need for increasing the supply of loanable funds to the
societies. This can be achieved through policies which
will encourage rural savings in the co-operatives. In
addition, funds could be mobilised through the Agricultural Credit Guarantee Scheme which is currently
organised by the Central Bank of Nigeria and the commercial
banks. Such funds could be channelled for investment in
agriculture through the primary co-operative societies.

1   R. O. Adegboye, "Procuring Loans through Pledging of
    Cocoa Trees", *Journal of Geographical Association of
    Nigeria*, Vol. 12, Nos. 1 and 2, 1969.

2   For example, R. Galleti, K. D. S. Baldwin and I. O.
    Dina, *Nigerian Cocoa Farmers: An Economic Survey of
    Yoruba Cocoa Farming Families*, Oxford University Press,
    1956; and, C. O. Ilori, *Agricultural Credit Problems in
    Nigeria: A Case Study*, F.A.O. Agricultural Credit Case
    Studies, Working Paper No. 3, 1974.

3   Adeniyi Osuntogun, "Agricultural Credit Strategies for
    Nigerian Farmers", *AID Spring Review of Small Farmer
    Credit*, Vol. VI, 1972; and  Adeniyi Osuntogun, "Credit
    as an Input in Agricultural Production: A Study of the
    Nature and Use of Credit by a Sample of Cocoa Producers
    in Some Villages of Western Nigeria", *Proceedings of the
    Fifth International Cocoa Research Conference*, Cocoa
    Research Institute of Nigeria, Ibadan, 1977.

4   See, for example, M. S. Igben, "Agricultural Credit
    Practices of Major Lenders in the Western State of
    Nigeria", M.Sc. Thesis, University of Ibadan, 1973.

5   'Esusu' groups are thrift and credit groups.

## LOAN REPAYMENT DELINQUENCY IN UPPER VOLTA

*Thomas Stickley and Edouard Tapsoba\**
*Department of Agricultural Economics*
*Michigan State University, USA*

*Introduction*

Upper Volta is one of the Sahelian countries most severely affected by the 1970-73 drought. It has made a strong commitment to increasing agricultural production and improving the quality of life in rural areas where most of its population lives.

Since 1965 the Voltaic Government has pursued a regional approach to rural economic and social development through the creation of Organisme Regional de Developpement (ORD). As one of its first recovery projects in the Sahel, the US Agency for International Development (USAID) has agreed to provide substantial material and technical assistance to the ORD in the eastern region of Upper Volta through an Integrated Rural Development Programme. This programme began in January 1975 and is being complemented by various UN and EEC projects plus bilateral projects from France and Switzerland to provide additional technical and material assistance.

The major responsibilities of ORD are to provide
extension services for farmers and artisans, to motivate
and organise the population in the planning and execution
of development programmes, to assist in agricultural
research, to provide farm credit, to improve the marketing of farm products, and to participate in the extension
of infrastructural programmes.

The purpose of USAID's Integrated Rural Development
Programme in the Eastern ORD is to increase the Eastern
ORD's capacity to assist small farmers to increase
agricultural production and incomes; and to achieve a
measurable impact on farmer productivity in four
"intensive" zones. This is to be achieved through
three types of activity. Firstly, it involves the
expansion of the capacity of the ORD for administration
and outreach through the construction and equipment
of improved central and field facilities and the
provision of logistical support for field staff; the
training of ORD personnel; and a programme of technical
assistance. Secondly, it involves the generation of
basic data through applied research related to traditional and improved farming systems; to credit requirements and alternative credit systems; to technical
possibilities and economies of animal traction and
animal production; and to marketed surpluses, marketing
systems, and price fluctuations. Thirdly, it involves
the testing of production and marketing interventions
primarily in the intensive zones with AID providing
support mostly in the form of medium term credit for
animal traction and a revolving fund for the purchase
of cash crops by the ORD.

As a part of its growing involvement in rural development
work in the Sahel, the Agricultural Economics Department at
Michigan State University engaged in an AID contract to fill
five technical assistance positions in AID's Integrated Rural
Development Programme in the Eastern ORD.  This contract
began in May 1977 and is expected to continue for a total of
four years.  The technical assistance provided by MSU to the
Eastern ORD is a combination of programme implementation and
applied research to improve programme design and execution.
The five technicians provided by MSU are: Production Economist,
Marketing Economist, Credit and Co-operative Economist, Live-
stock/Range Management Specialist and Audio-Visual Specialist.

Already the Integrated Rural Development Programme has
accomplished much in terms of expanding the administrative
capacity of the Eastern ORD through extensive logistical and
technical support.  Through MSU's applied research programme,
production of the basic economic data has been completed.
And through the medium term credit programme, 1365 sets of
animal traction packages have been placed in the hands of small
farmers throughout the Eastern ORD.

*The Medium-Term Credit Programme*

The applied research programme relating to the animal
traction medium term credit programme has three components:
the organisation of existing data to establish an accounting
system for the animal traction credit programme; special studies to bring together the data needed on special problems
relating to the credit programme (e.g. insurance of traction
animals, payment of incentive premiums to loan collection
agents, special lending activities such as cereal banks and
village stores); and an inventory of all 869 current borrowers
with medium term animal traction loans outstanding.

It was in the inventory of 869 current borrowers of

medium term credit conducted in October 1978, that data for
the current paper was collected. The objectives of this inventory of credit were firstly, to discover and correct on
the spot any incorrectly completed medium term animal traction
credit contracts; secondly, to discover problems with the
medium term animal traction credit programme and propose
solutions; thirdly, to monitor effectiveness of the programme
of vaccination of traction animals; fourthly, to find the reasons for delinquency in loan repayment; fifthly, to monitor
the insurance programme of traction animals; and sixthly,
to develop complete statistics on number of borrowers, amount
of credit disbursed, and repayment.

*The Rate of Delinquency*

Data from the inventory of credit showed delinquency
rates on the medium-term animal traction credit programme both
in terms of the number of borrowers delinquent and the amount
of loans delinquent.

The number of borrowers delinquent was calculated two
ways: (a) as a percentage of all borrowers and (b) as a percentage of those borrowers who had loans due during the
accounting year. The number of borrowers delinquent as a
percentage of *all* borrowers of medium term animal traction
credit on June 30, 1978 was 71. This is a delinquency rate
of only 8%.

The number of borrowers delinquent as a percentage of
those borrowers who had loans due during the accounting year
(July 1, 1977 through to June 30, 1978) was 149, 71 of which
failed to repay any part of the instalment that was due. This
is a delinquency rate of 48%.

The amount of loans delinquent was also calculated in two
ways: (a) as a percentage of all loans outstanding and (b) as

a percentage of the loans due for collection during the accounting year.  The amount of loans delinquent as a percentage
of all loans outstanding, on June 30, 1978 was between 1 and
2%: 51,905,405 FCFA[1] was outstanding in medium term animal
traction loans of which 706,987 FCFA was delinquent.

However, the amount of loans delinquent as a percentage
of the amount of loans that should have been collected during
the accounting period was substantially higher.  2,315,205
FCFA should have been repaid, but of this amount, 706,987 FCFA
was delinquent on June 30, 1978.  This is a delinquency rate
of 31%.

The practical uses of these varied definitions of delinquency are many.  For example, the administrator who wants
to show a low rate of delinquency can choose the definition
that produces the lowest figure.  We suggest that the most
meaningful definitions of delinquency are based on the number
of borrowers who failed to repay all or part of their loan
instalment as a percentage of all borrowers with loan instal-
ments due, and on the amount of loans not repaid as a percentage of all loans due for repayment.  In the Eastern ORD of
Upper Volta these rates were 48% and 31% respectively for
the accounting year of July 1, 1977 through to June 30, 1978
for the medium term animal traction credit programme.

*Causes of Delinquency*

Regardless of the definition of delinquency preferred, an
understanding of the causes for this delinquency is essential
if the delinquency rate is to be reduced.  The inventory of
credit offered evidence which could show that 37% of the
cases of delinquency were the fault of the borrowers, 37%
were the fault of the lending institution (the ORD),

and 26% were the fault of nature.

The 37% of the delinquency cases which could be attributed to borrowers were broken down into borrowers who had an attitude of indifference and of feeling no obligation to repay their loans (19%) and borrowers who were able but unwilling to liquidate chattels to meet their loan repayment obligation (18%).

Of the 869 borrowers included in the inventory, 328 responded to an additional question asked to determine their attitudes toward repaying loans to a private money lender as compared to repaying loans to the ORD. They were asked for a particular reason for repaying their loans to the private money lender before they would repay to the ORD. The results were as follows:

- It is necessary to repay loans from a private money lender in order to qualify for a new loan next year: 51% (of respondents).
- Private money lenders are more severe in their loan collection procedures than the ORD: 12%
- Delinquency of a loan from a private money lender brings disgrace to the family: 11%
- There is no possibility of not repaying - one is obliged to repay the private money lender: 9%
- Repayment to the ORD can be delayed until the borrower has the means to repay: 7%
- Loans are received from private money lenders in secret and repaid on time to prevent the money lender from telling the secret: 4%
- Repayment must be the result of the investment made with the loan. If it is not, one is justified in delaying repayment of ORD animal traction credit: 3%
- The private money lender is located nearer and therefore gets repaid before ORD: 1%

- The private money lender is present at harvest time
  and takes part of the harvest as repayment of the
  loan: 1%
- Repayment of ORD credit is not necessary because: (1)
  the ORD is linked to the Government to whom the borrower pays taxes regularly and (2) the borrower gave
  gifts to the ORD agent to get approval of his loan: 1%

Evident from these responses is the need for the ORD to
change its image to one in which the borrower feels that it
is as important to repay the ORD as it is to repay private
money lenders.

The ORD itself could be considered as the cause of 37% of
the cases of delinquency in repayment of medium term loans.
This was either through mistakes or through neglect (omissions
in service).  The 37% of the delinquencies caused by the ORD
were due to the following mistakes made by the personnel of
the ORD:

- Part of the animal traction package arrived too late
  for use during the first season of the loan: 29% (of
  delinquencies).
- Traction animals purchased were too small: 3%
- ORD agents arriving without prior warning to collect
  loan repayments: 3%
- The ORD agent who was sent to collect the loan was
  different from the person who made the loan: 2%

Besides these mistakes, the credit inventory also brought
attention to other omissions in ORD services linked to the
medium term animal traction credit programme.  Firstly, the
practice of doing an economic analysis of a potential borrower's expected costs and returns to determine his debt-carrying
capacity was not adopted as a standard procedure to be followed
by ORD agents before giving medium term animal traction loans.

Secondly, the terms and conditions of the animal traction loans were not made clear to borrowers at the time they accepted the loan. Thirdly, often ORD personnel offered no help in training the traction animals. Fourthly, at times no one from the ORD came to ask for repayment of the loan. Fifthly, often no one from the ORD was on hand when borrowers were selling their products to claim loan repayment.

The 26% of the cases of delinquency caused by nature can be divided into causes associated with weather and low crop yields and causes associated with the health and family problems of the borrowers. Causes of delinquency related to weather and low crop yields were death or illness of the traction animals (10%) and low crop yields caused by inadequate rainfall (7%). Causes of delinquency related to the health and family problems of the borrowers were illness during the growing season (5%), death of the borrower (2%), and financial problems in the family (2%).

*Reducing Delinquency*

Delinquency caused by borrowers can be reduced through both prevention and cure. It can be prevented through a more careful screening of loan applicants to avoid giving loans to farmers with bad attitudes about their responsibility to repay ORD credit. The motivation for this more careful screening can be through a system in which commissions are paid to field-level credit agents as a percentage of loans collected. Field-level credit agents motivated to have high collection rates will be thinking of this at the time loan applicants are being screened and they would be more careful about approving loans.

In the Eastern ORD of Upper Volta such a system of payment of commissions to field-level credit agents has been installed. Each field-level credit agent and his immediate

supervisor are paid commissions on loan collections as
follows:

| | Percentage of Loan Collections for: | |
| --- | --- | --- |
| | Field-Level Credit Agent | Supervisor of Field-Level Credit Agent |
| Basic commission on all loans collected | 0.8 | 0.2 |
| Additional commission if more than 100 persons benefited from the credit programme | 0.4 | 0.1 |
| Additional commission for 100% repayment | 0.4 | 0.1 |
| Additional commission on delinquent loans collected | 0.4 | 0.1 |
| Additional commission on loans collected before the year in which the loan is due | 0.4 | 0.1 |

The effects of delinquency caused by borrowers can also
be reduced through loan guarantee requirements. In the
Eastern ORD, loan guarantee requirements are not all strictly
enforced, but more favourable consideration is given to
loan applicants who can offer most forms of loan guarantee.
These include payment of a registration fee on each loan
received (deposited in a loan guarantee fund), insurance of
traction animals, unlimited liability of a village group for
repayment of loans for any group member, purchase of stocks
in the ORD by the village group of which the borrower is a
member, and sale of harvested crops through the ORD.

Delinquency caused by borrowers can be reduced by putting
pressure on those capable of but unwilling to repay their loans.
This pressure should come from the other members of the village

group.  The system of unlimited liability for repayment of
loans is needed for pressure from this source to be most
effective.  Pressure can also come from the field-level credit
agents of the ORD.  This includes the implementation of a
strong, and well-publicised loan foreclosure policy.  From
such a policy, farmers will learn that their animal traction
package will be confiscated if they do not repay their loans.
Such a policy is currently in effect in the Eastern ORD of
Upper Volta.

Reducing delinquency caused by the lender involves
stronger support to field-level credit agents, stronger village
groups and estimation of a potential borrower's debt-carrying
capacity.

In the Eastern ORD support to field-level credit agents,
has taken several forms: a technical manual on the credit
system has been distributed to each field-level credit agent
and his supervisors; adequate blank forms and other office
supplies necessary for administering the credit programme are
in the hands of the field-level credit agents; transportation
by motorbikes is available to all field-level credit agents;
a system of commission payments based on loan repayments
(described above) is in effect; and annual short courses are
administered for training all field-level credit agents to
inform them of changes in the system and to concentrate on
solving their problems.

There are also measures to strengthen village groups
before distributing credit through them to their members.  In
the Eastern ORD, credit is administered to individual borrowers through their village groups (pre-co-operatives).
Standards have been recently set for these village groups.
These standards are to be met before credit can be distributed through them to their members.  It must be at least
two years since the group was organised; there must be a

stable number of members (not necessarily a large number but
a minimum of 10 members); and cohesion, understanding and confidence among the members.  ORD must have confidence in the
officers of the group and the procedures by which all decisions affecting the group are made.  The groups must have
a reputation for repaying loans on time and have successfully
completed at least one activity.  Upholding these standards
before lending money through village groups to their members
will strengthen the village groups and improve repayment
rates of loans to their members.

The importance of estimating potential borrower's debt-
carrying capacity has been stressed in the Eastern ORD.  A
system is currently in use whereby each field-level credit
agent together with each potential borrower estimate the
potential borrower's debt-carrying capacity.  From estimated
annual income is subtracted his estimated annual expenses.
The resulting net annual revenue is the maximum that he can
use for making annual repayments on a loan.  With these annual
repayment possibilities a total debt ceiling for a medium-
term animal traction loan is determined.  The likelihood of
repayment problems later is greatly reduced after making this
estimate of his debt-carrying capacity.

Random incidence of natural hazards also affects loan
repayment.  There are, however, certain protective precautions
that can be taken to reduce the rate of delinquency caused
by nature.  Several precautions have been taken in the Eastern
ORD for this purpose.  Firstly, as a precaution against the
high incidence of low crop yields resulting from frequent
drought conditions in the Sahel, the policy of exercising
extreme conservatism has been adopted in doing the economic
analysis for estimating the debt-carrying capacity of a potential borrower.  Secondly, borrowers of credit for the purchase of traction animals are required to insure those animals.
The cost of this insurance for the full term of the credit is

added to the loan amount when the loan is made. Thirdly,
surviving family members of borrowers who die are expected
to repay their loans. In certain cases, the village groups
of which these borrowers had been members may repay these
loans. Normally, however, it is the deceased borrowers'
families who bear this responsibility. Fourthly, a loan
renewal policy is in effect in the Eastern ORD in which borrowers who have suffered from natural catastrophes can have
loans renewed. In this way loans that would become delinquent
because of natural causes are saved from the "delinquency"
classification. Excuses acceptable for renewing loans are
crop failure resulting from drought, death or serious illness
of the borrower and deficiencies in ORD services vital to the
successful use of the animal traction package (e.g. traction
animals that were not trained in time for use in the growing
season and failure to deliver a vital piece of the animal
traction package). The loan renewal policy requires payment -
at the time of renewal of interest on the loan for the time
period the loan is extended. Finally, if all the above
mentioned precautions fail to prevent delinquency and the
loans have to be written off, the loan fund is protected from
erosion with the loan guarantee or "bad debt" fund. The
source of this fund is a registration fee collected on each
new loan given.

*Conclusion*

Contrary to the popular belief that institutions should
not expect high rates of repayment of loans in drought-prone
areas such as the Sahel, it is argued here that there is
a great deal that lending institutions themselves can do to
get higher rates of loan repayment. The excuses of bad weather
and recalcitrant farmers have been too willingly accepted as
the reasons for loan delinquencies to hide a major reason for
this delinquency - namely, shortcomings in the performance of
the lending institutions themselves. Lending institutions

can reduce delinquency caused by their own inadequacies
through improvements in the services they offer to the
borrowers.  But the responsibility of the lending institution
does not stop there.  Delinquency caused by the borrower and
by nature can also be reduced through certain measures taken
by the lending institution.

\* The authors are on assignment to the USAID Integrated
Rural Development Program in the Eastern ORD, Fada
N'Gourma, Upper Volta.

1  214 FCFA = $1 US (1979).

INDEX

high-yielding varieties 16, 92,
115; - Programme (India) 41, 116
household, farm 4, 10-12, 16, 18,
Part Three *passim*
housing 269-70
Howell, John 1-14, 141-66

IMF 60
incomes, distribution of 12, 17, 22,
30, 147, 242
India 4, 6, 35-58, 102, 107, 133,
136, 156, 158, 169, 171, 179-80,
184, 185; All-India Rural Credit
Survey 45; Reserve Bank 39-40, 42,
46, 48, 49, 51-3, 55; State Bank
37, 43-4
Indonesia 133
inflation 2, 20, 60-1, 64, 67, 69,
79, 96, 250
information, lender 8, 88, 90-1,
111, 125, 145, 146, 149, 168-9,
170-2
infrastructure, financial 5, 33,
274
inputs 5, 6, 8, 16, 37, 44, 50-4,
86, 93, 94, 108, 115-17, 149,
180, 191, 197, 205, 211, 236,
240, 241, 259; demand function
215-17, 231; subsidies 1, 78, 197,
205
insurance 23, 28, 251-2, 275, 276,
281, 283; loan 101, 189
Inter-American Development Bank 66
interest-rates 6, 16-22, 31, 32, 60,
69, 77, 79, 86-9, 101, 102, 110-
15, 118, 123, 132, 144, 148, 150,
159-60, 168, 188, 195-6, 228, 229,
243, 250, 267; concessionary 4, 5,
7, 12, 16-17, 19, 25, 29, 31-2,
42, 119-22, 126, 143, 183, 187,
195-6, 205, 246; differential 4,
23, 29-30, 40; negative 2, 22, 25,
60-1, 69, 79

Jamaica 4, 5, 59-80
Jodha, N.S. 158, 241

Kenya 131, 191, 253
kinship 107, 112, 251-2
Korea 79, 206

Ladman, J.R. 161
Lagrange multiplier 202
land 194, 262; settlement 141, 144,
148; tenure 107, reform 1, 27, 33,
82, 157; - development banks 36,
46, 120, 185; — Improvements Act
(India 1883) 179
lending, costs of 2, 6, 10, 19, 21,
22, 25, 26, 28, 29-30, 38, 44,

55-6, 75-8, 87-8, 96-7, 99, 100-
1, 110-11, 118, 139, 140, 150,
151, 152, 170, 186, 187, 193, 248,
250, 265
Lenin 124
Lesotho 189, 190
liability, joint 8-9, limited 193,
unlimited 281-2
Lipton, Michael 11, 30, 235-58
loans, costs of 8, 18, 21, 32, 89, 96,
122, 143, 148, 203, 217, 229, 237;
discipline 96-9, 193; distribution of
9, 22, 25-9, 38-42, 46-7, 64-6, 69,
93, 96, 144, 243-5; group 8, 44, 135,
138, 170, 171; impact of 201-34; in
kind 18, 92, 143, 145; quotas 7, 23,
27-8, 138, 139; risk 28, 96, 110, 111;
size limits 7, 23, 26-7, 42, 93, 95,
96, 110, 114, 122, 263; *see also*
fungibility; guarantees

Malaysia, Bank Pertanian 177
management, borrower 94, 96, 135, 137,
138, 205, 218, 231; co-operative 9, 38,
157, 187; lender 5, 8, 19, 26, 74, 90,
91, 97, 152, 174
Mandac, A.M. 218
Manley, Michael 60
marketing 5, 6, 37, 44, 51, 53, 54, 55,
78, 88, 145, 150, 152, 274; co-operative
158-9, 191, 192; Boards 143, 172, 183
markets, commodity 6, 54, 108, 123-8;
financial Parts One and Two *passim*,
fragmentation of 2, 17, 21, 90,
informal 2, 5, 6, 7, 10, 18, 21, 32,
47-8, 52, 54, 86, 102, 109-15, 123-7,
132, 265, 267, 269 *see also* kinship;
moneylenders; pawnbrokers; traders
Marxism 30, 241
Mexico 28, 210
Meyer, Richard L. 11, 201-34
Michigan State University 275
migration, rural-urban 242, 262, shuttle
245
Miracle, M.P. 83
moneylenders 2, 18, 52, 110, 114, 115,
122, 132, 144, 145, 176, 186, 195,
242, 243, 250, 265, 267, 278-9
Morocco 210
mortgages 44, 185, 194

National Commercial Bank (Jamaica) 62, 73
nationalisation 4, 22-3, 26, 61, 125
Near East 172, 174
Nigeria 11, 259-71; Central Bank of 270
Nova Scotia, Bank of 62

OECD 82
Osuntogun, Adeniyi 11, 259-71
overdues 48-9, 51, 52, 186, 193-4, 196